Rediscovering the Social Group

For Henri Tajfel

Rediscovering
the Social Group
A Self-Categorization Theory

John C. Turner

with
Michael A. Hogg,
Penelope J. Oakes,
Stephen D. Reicher
and
Margaret S. Wetherell

Basil Blackwell

First published 1987
First published in paperback 1988

Basil Blackwell Ltd
108 Cowley Road, Oxford OX4 1JF, UK

Basil Blackwell Inc.
432 Park Avenue South, Suite 1503
New York, NY 10016, USA

British Library Cataloguing in Publication Data

Turner, John C.
Rediscovering the social group.
1. Social groups
I. Title
302.3   HM131
ISBN 0–631–14806–X
ISBN 0–631–16586–X (Pbk)

Library of Congress Cataloging in Publication Data

Turner, John C. 1947
Rediscovering the social group.
Bibliography: p.
Includes index.
1. Social groups.   2. Social interaction.
3. Group identity   4. Self-perception.   I. Title.
HM131.T794   1987   302.3   86-13704
ISBN 0–631–14806–X
ISBN 0–631–16586–X (pbk.)

Typeset in 10½ on 12 point Sabon
by OPUS, Oxford
Printed in Great Britain by Billing & Sons Ltd, Worcester

Contents

Preface

This book presents a theory of the social group (and derivative sub-theories of social attraction, co-operation, influence and group polarization). Since it is a psychological theory, a theory of the social psychological processes underlying group behaviour, it is also a theory of the relationship of the individual to the group. In this respect it touches, too, on problems of the metatheory of social psychology: the extent to which the psychology of the individual can contribute, without reduction, to the explanation of social phenomena. In the early part of the book an attempt is made to show what it is about group behaviour that needs to be explained social psychologically and why a new theory is necessary. The middle of the book outlines the theory and tries to show how it can provide new and interesting insights into the main group phenomena studied by social psychologists. The later chapters discuss specific research areas from the perspective of the theory and where possible present relevant data.

The book is about rediscovering the group in at least three ways. Theoretically, it is argued that the group is not just a particular realm of social behaviour, which may or may not be of interest to particular researchers, but is a basic process of social interaction. Psychologically, the group process embodies a shift in the level of abstraction at which the individual self operates, a shift from personal to social identity, which is not a deviation from but a part of the normal state of affairs of self-perception and social interaction. The group is seen as having a psychologically and not merely socially causal role in everyday behaviour. Empirically, data are reviewed and reinterpreted to demonstrate the distinctive role of the group and show the insufficiency of current theorizing which treats the group as an epiphenomenon. And, metatheoretically, the self-categorization theory, although based on a critique of what has been termed the interdependence theory, can nevertheless be seen as a return to the founding ideas of the latter – that interdependent individuals form a social-psychological system which transforms qualitatively their character as individuals and gives rise to 'supra-individual' properties.

Inevitably, a new theory in seeking to justify itself and distinguish its ideas from the contemporary orthodoxy must criticize aspects of the latter. This is particularly important in the present case because it can be argued that the current theoretical neglect of group processes is not an aberration of a specific generation of researchers, but follows from the theory of the group that is actually dominant. Nevertheless, it would be quite wrong to understand that criticism as a recrimination against or a wholesale rejection of what has gone before. The interdependence theory (by which I mean the implicit consensus about the general character of group processes that has developed in the subject over the last 30 or 40 years in the wake especially of the founding ideas and work of Sherif, Asch and Lewin) represented a major scientific advance, and the self-categorization theory is an attempt to build theoretically on that advance and the empirical generalizations it has produced. A good theory is amongst other things one that stimulates enough interesting research to reveal (as it must) its own inadequacies – this is just as true of the self-categorization theory as it is of the interdependence theory. If there remain researchers who feel that their perspective has been criticized unfairly, I can only assert that this is far from my intention and is more probably an expression of the difficulty of dealing with such a large subject matter than anything else.

The self-categorization theory is also the product of a distinct European tradition of research on social categorization processes and social identity initiated by the late Henri Tajfel. In many respects the theory is an attempt to spell out in explicit fashion the assumptions we need to make about psychological group formation to understand the results of the social categorization studies on intergroup behaviour that Henri began (with Tajfel, 1970, and Tajfel, Flament, Billig and Bundy, 1971). In doing this it makes use of and develops two concepts taken from an earlier theory of intergroup behaviour developed by Tajfel and myself (Tajfel, 1972a, 1978; Tajfel and Turner, 1979, 1986; Turner, 1975): the concept of social identity itself and the assumption of an 'interpersonal-intergroup continuum' of social behaviour. In the earlier work on intergroup behaviour it was not social identity but the idea that intergroup comparisons were focused on the achievement of positive ingroup distinctiveness that was the major explanatory notion. Further, the interpersonal-intergroup continuum was conceptualized as varying from 'acting in terms of self' to 'acting in terms of group' (Tajfel, 1978; Turner, 1978) – as if the latter were not an expression of the former. The self-categorization theory makes social identity the social-cognitive basis of group behaviour, the mechanism that makes it possible (and not just the aspects of the self derived from group memberships), and by asserting that self-categorizations function at different levels of abstraction makes both group and individual behaviour 'acting in terms of self'.

Because the self-categorization theory developed out of this earlier work and the central role of the social identity concept in it, it is also referred to in the book as the social identity theory of the group, and this is a perfectly acceptable alternative name. Unfortunately, our earlier analysis of intergroup behaviour is already known as (the) social identity theory (of intergroup behaviour) and this plus the close links between the theories has led to a tendency to lump them together as one. This does not matter too much and in fact on occasion is useful in describing the whole tradition of work − providing, that is, that the 'lumping' is a terminological convenience and it is understood that they are substantively different theories, in terms of the problems they address and the hypotheses they propose. The intergroup theory is outlined in the references cited above. The self-categorization theory is presented in this book.

The form of authorship of this book perhaps needs some explanation. Although I have acted as editor where the chapters were not written by me (chapters 5-8 were written respectively by Michael Hogg, Penelope Oakes, Margaret Wetherell and Stephen Reicher), this is not an 'edited' book. It is written as a unified theoretical monograph. Also, we worked together more or less as a collaborative research team for several years in the Department of Psychology at the University of Bristol (from 1978, when the research on the present ideas began, to approximately 1981), and have maintained close links thereafter. People have made distinctive contributions, reflected in their individual chapters, but at the same time ideas and data have been freely exchanged and everybody's work has in some degree both stimulated and been influenced in turn by everybody else's. The several names on the title page, therefore, indicate not only that each has written some part of the book but also that the book as a whole reflects our collaborative association. I have tried hard to minimize repetition of material and points across chapters, but occasionally I have thought some small repetition useful − to remind the reader of earlier points or where I thought the expression of a difficult or abstract idea from different angles likely to aid comprehension. Margaret Wetherell and I, for example, have worked together closely in developing our approach to group polarization, but, nevertheless, polarization is discussed in both chapters 4 and 7 – in the former case as a theoretical derivation from self-categorization theory and in the latter as an instance of the research application of the theory. I think the reader will find the difference in emphasis in the chapters valuable and any minor repetition fully justified given the novelty of the analysis.

The book is dedicated to Henri Tajfel. His influence on the book extends further than the direct use we have made of his theoretical and empirical work. There is also the approach to social psychology which he taught, characterized by a commitment to the importance of developing theory in empirical research and a rejection of what is often known as 'piecemeal empiricism', a commitment to methodological rigour and the value of laboratory and other experiments (sensitively interpreted in terms of the interaction between general processes and the social context – see Turner, 1981a, for a statement of the experimental approach espoused by this book), a rejection of individualism, and a belief in scholarship and science. There is also a personal influence. We all spent happy years being taught by and/or working with Henri at the University of Bristol and I think will always look back on that period as one of great human as well as intellectual pleasure. Over the 11 years that I spent at Bristol, beginning as Henri's research student and leaving in effect just a few months after his death, he became a close and irreplaceable friend and a person for whom I developed the deepest respect. This book is dedicated to him in part in recognition of our intellectual debt, in part in memory of the human being.

Finally, I should like to acknowledge the financial support of the Social Science Research Council (as was), London, the Australian Research Grants Scheme, Canberra, and the Institute For Advanced Study, Princeton – who have all helped to make the book possible through their funding of relevant research. The Institute For Advanced Study deserves special thanks, since, very generously, they paid me to spend a year (1982/3) as a member of the School of Social Sciences working on the ideas that eventually became the self-categorization theory. Amongst the individuals who have contributed in some way, directly or indirectly, to the book, I should like to thank in particular Howard Giles, Philip Smith, John Colvin, Craig McGarty and Sharon Stephens for her excellent typing of various earlier drafts of parts of the book.

John Turner
March 1986

Authors

John C. Turner is Associate Professor in Psychology in the School of Behavioural Sciences, Macquarie University, Sydney, Australia.

Michael A. Hogg is Lecturer in the Department of Psychology, University of Melbourne, Australia.

Penelope J. Oakes is Lecturer in the School of Behavioural Sciences, Macquarie University, Sydney, Australia.

Stephen D. Reicher is Lecturer in the Department of Psychology, University of Exeter, England.

Margaret S. Wetherell is Lecturer in the Psychological Laboratory, University of St Andrews, Scotland.

1

Introducing the Problem:
Individual and Group

Introduction

How does a collection of individuals become a social and psychological group? How do they come to perceive and define themselves and act as a single unit, feeling, thinking and self-aware as a collective entity? What effects does shared group membership have on their social relations and behaviour? Is there such a thing, in fact, as a psychological group as distinct from a merely social arrangement?

These issues can be conceptualized as the related problems of psychological group formation and the psychological reality of group phenomena. More generally, they have to do with the relationship of the individual to the group (and society) and between psychological and social processes. Put most simply, the issue is whether there exists as a distinct phenomenon and the nature of the *psychological* (or, strictly speaking, *social psychological)* group.

The present book proposes a new theory of the psychological group – of antecedents, processes and consequences – and outlines the main applications of the theory to group phenomena and relevant empirical research. The book also argues more widely for the importance of the group as a distinctive, explanatory process in social psychology, and in this respect seeks the reinstatement or more correctly the rediscovery of the social group in the subject, as being essential for its theoretical progress.

Descriptively speaking, a psychological group is defined as one that is psychologically significant for the members, to which they relate themselves subjectively for social comparison and the acquisition of norms and values (i.e., with which they compare to evaluate themselves, their abilities, performances, opinions, etc., and from which they take their rules, standards and beliefs about appropriate conduct and attitudes), that they privately accept membership in, and which influences their attitudes and behaviour. In the usual terminology, it is a (positive) *reference* group and not merely a *membership* group as defined by outsiders, i.e., it is not simply a group which one is objectively *in*, but one which is subjectively important in determining one's actions.

This definition is not intended to restrict our awareness of the full reality of the human group – of the fact that collective life is biological, sociological, political, ideological, historical, and so on, not just social psychological – but it does indicate a deliberate limitation in subject matter and purpose. The aim is not to provide a complete scientific account of the social group, but to contribute to the construction of one of the necessary building blocks of such an account, by developing a theory of the social psychological aspects of the group, of the psychological processes underlying and making possible the transformation of human individuals into a social group.

In chapter 1 the problem of psychological group formation will be put into historical context. In chapter 2 the contemporary orthodoxy on the question will be summarized and then evaluated with regard to developments in the three major areas of group process: group formation (and cohesion), social co-operation and social influence. We shall conclude that the theoretical orthodoxy and the widely noted neglect of the group concept (and indeed the 'social dimension' *in toto*, Tajfel, 1984) which has accompanied it both need to be rejected. It will be argued that the empirical data themselves demonstrate beyond much reasonable doubt (until some more persuasive 'individualistic' account comes along) that group membership has a pervasive *psychologically and not merely socially causal* role in social interaction. Chapter 3 will present the new theory of group membership and behaviour, the *self-categorization theory*, as a solution to the problems raised in the preceding chapters and in particular as an explanation of the psychological reality of the group process that in no way contradicts the assumption of modern experimental social psychology that psychological or mental processes reside only in individual minds. The fundamental idea is that group behaviour is the behaviour of individuals acting on the basis of a categorization of self and others at a social, more 'inclusive' or 'higher order' level of abstraction than that involved in the categorization of people as distinct, individual persons.

The remaining chapters elucidate, amplify, illustrate and seek to concretize these notions by applying the theory respectively to understanding social influence (chapter 4), group cohesiveness/social attraction (chapter 5), the 'salience' of social categories, i.e., the conditions under which different ingroup-outgroup memberships or self-categorizations in terms of, for example, race, sex, class, nationality, religion, age, or just 'us' and 'them' divisions become effective situational determinants of social perception and behaviour (chapter 6), the polarization of ingroup norms (i.e., 'group polarization', Moscovici and Zavalloni, 1969, chapter 7), and, finally, crowd behaviour (chapter 8). The last topic brings us full historical circle, back to the issue and arena within which the first controversies about the group in social psychology were fought out and the classic ideas forged (see this chapter). Chapter 9 will provide a brief conclusion.

Individual and group

The problem of the book is not a new one. On the contrary, it was the subject of the major controversy present at the birth of modern social psychology in the early part of this century. It was expressed at that time as the issue of the reality and distinctiveness of group phenomena: does group behaviour imply social or psychological processes irreducible to or different from the properties of individuals, does the group possess a mental unity or reality *sui generis*?

To illustrate: if one thinks of some instance of real-life collective action, an army in battle, a rioting crowd, a political party in conference, or even a nation on the brink of some great historical event, the participants will often seem to act and feel in a spontaneously unitary fashion. Their behaviours may seem co-ordinated and concerted almost as if there were some single, directing consciousness (or unconsciousness). They may behave with 'one mind', as if in fact they were not a collection of separate individual beings but one supra-organism (this may be symbolized explicitly by one or more leaders, who personify the shared attitudes, values and goals). Of course this is not always so and varies in degree but we know that it can be so.

Furthermore, the fact of the apparent higher order unity of many collective phenomena is not something we have to think about, but something we 'see' directly; it is registered in 'naïve' perception and speech. When we see a crowd, a team, an army, we do not see Dick, Jane, Henry, Mary, Howard, and so on as separate personal entities, and then summarize cognitively. In a real sense we see the group as one whole entity. Similarly, we say 'the army is in a defeatist mood', 'the party reacted to the leader's speech with euphoria','the mob turned ugly', 'the nation is apprehensive but prepared'. We attribute behavioural, social and *psychological* or *mental* (to do with thinking, perceiving, feeling, personality, etc.) characteristics directly to social groups as if they were real and unitary psychological beings in the same way that we assume that individuals are. We do this as readily with large groups such as nations and races as with small. Part of this point, that we perceive individuals directly as group members, is confirmed by research on social stereotyping (the assignment of characteristics to individuals on the basis of their membership in some group), but the larger part is different, that we perceive groups directly as 'individuals' (i.e., as unitary individual entities).

The question arises: is this fact of naïve perception and speech, reflecting an apparent reality, valid? Are groups real in the same vivid, tangible way that we tend to assume individual persons are real? Do they have superordinate mental properties above and beyond or at least different from those of their individual members? Is there a distinctive group psychology, do groups have their own kind of mind?

There is a basic issue here which has to do with the definition of the science of social psychology, and which explains why the problem of the group became (and arguably still is – at least covertly) the central controversy of the new field. The issue can be stated in the form of a paradox.

The apparent reality of the group and the notion of a distinctive group psychology imply at the very least the superordinate social properties of human action. Human social behaviour may be analysed in terms of structures, processes and laws that operate at the level of social relationships without reference to individual psychology. It exists *sui generis*, at its own level of reality, with its own distinctive, emergent forms (as studied, for example, in sociology, economics or anthropology). Nevertheless, it is a basic assumption of modern psychology that psychological processes reside only in individuals – in the most literal sense, at least, there is no such thing as a 'group mind'.

The paradox, then, is that if we reject the concept of the group mind and seek individual psychological explanations of group behaviour, do we not inevitably deny the very properties (higher order, emergent) of social behaviour that gave rise to that concept, and reduce the group in kind to the level of the part, the individual? Moreover, if we reject all psychological explanations of social behaviour (as many sociologists, anthropologists and others advocate) as tending to reductionism (i.e., the denial of the distinctive character of the phenomenon supposedly to be explained), are we not equally condemned to an indefensible stand? For how could it possibly be true that the individual mind did not play a determining, indispensable role in the working out of social processes? We are caught, it seems, in a limbo between a psychology which can only be individualistic and a sociology which for precisely that reason can never be psychological, and all the time knowing or 'seeing' that in some sense the group is as psychological as the individual.

The issue is how scientifically to retain the psychological reality of the group whilst rejecting both the fallacy of the group mind and the reduction of group life. If one substitutes 'society' or 'social interaction' for 'group', one has for all practical purposes defined the distinctive scientific problem of social psychology. Thus Floyd Allport, one of the founders of modern social psychology, stated in a late paper: 'we must try to discover some more satisfactory paradigm for "the group and the individual". Some way must be found to describe in general terms that layout of conditions surrounding and involving individuals which we have called "the group", and to formulate, in the precise yet *universal* manner of science, what actually goes on in the situation we call "collective" action. In this broader sense the problem of the individual and the group is really the "master problem" of social psychology' (1962, p. 7). Similarly, from an opposed theoretical perspective, another major figure, Solomon Asch, agreed that 'both the individualistic and group-centered doctrines introduce an external relation between individual and group; both neglect the essential problem of social psychology – how individuals create the reality of groups and how the latter control their further actions' (1952, p. 256).

The early protagonists, in arguing about the reality of the group and so the relationship of the individual to the group, knew well that they were debating the general issue of the interaction between psychological and social processes and hence the key problem of the subject. Their views are still highly relevant today, although in some cases forgotten, since they delineate the main positions that can be taken and formulate the pertinent arguments, and their influence, whether acknowledged or not, is still very much with us. More importantly, it is argued that at the level of metatheory their debate ultimately produced a solution to the problem of individual and group and this solution is one basis of the present theorizing. Before proceeding, therefore, it is worth summarizing the most germane of their ideas as historical background and metatheoretical context for the present work.

The early theorists: the group mind thesis, individualism and interactionism

It is useful to classify the early theorists into three camps (which, it is worth pointing out, are related to but not perfectly correlated with the three doctrines above): (1) the pre-experimentalists, LeBon, McDougall and Freud, who took for granted some kind of distinctive group psychology, (2) the individualistic researchers represented by

Floyd Allport, and (3) the cognitive social psychologists, Sherif, Asch and Lewin.

The group psychology of LeBon, McDougall and Freud

LeBon (1896), discussing the group in the form of the crowd, argued that people in a crowd gave rise to a collective or group mind. He referred to this idea as the law of mental unity of crowds (p. 26) and stated that mental unity and not physical proximity was what defined a psychological crowd. The psychology of the crowd was qualitatively different from that of the individuals who composed it. The collective mind reflects the fundamental, shared, unconscious qualities of the 'race'; the conscious individual personality is lost. Whereas the individual acts consciously from reason, the crowd acts unconsciously from instinct. Crowds are intellectually inferior, driven by emotion and instinctual urges, and free of the restraints of civilized life and reason.

These special features are explained by three processes: (1) the 'de-individuation' process – the anonymity of crowd members and the sense of invincible power produced by being in a crowd lead to a diffusion of their feelings of personal responsibility, a loss of personal identity, which removes the controls and restraints on the anti-social impulses which exist in the individual; (2) 'contagion' – actions and emotions spread through the crowd through a form of mutual imitation, leading to uniformity and homogeneity in which personal differences disappear and the shared, collective interests of members become primary; (3) 'suggestion' or 'suggestibility' – this is the basis of contagion; it is the acceptance of influence on irrational grounds because of some kind of emotional tie to and submissive attitude to a person or group (suggestion implied a 'mesmeric', 'hypnotic' form of influence in which the rational individual will is lost).

A crowd is a return to primitivism and barbarism, to intellectual inferiority, reasoning by images instead of logic, leadership on the basis of prestige, contagion and the repetition and affirmation of messages, not reasoned explanation. It is motivated by instinct, the racial unconscious and other hereditary influences and acts amorally with the ferocity, spontaneity, enthusiasm, violence and heroism of primitive beings. By and large, therefore, LeBon blackened the group/crowd as a vicious mob, but yet he also stated that crowds could be better or worse than individuals since they were not moral or immoral but impulsive. They could be violently antisocial but in a crowd people could also become heroic and altruistic (towards other members), sacrificing their personal interests for the collective interest. Further, he also believed that the greatness of a particular society (nation, race, civilization) was bound up with its collective mind, its collective 'genius'.

McDougall (1921) stated the point that crowds could be better or worse than their individual members as a paradox of social life (p. 20): the group feels and thinks on a lower plane than the average member, it degrades the individual in a sense, 'assimilating his mental processes to those of the crowd, whose brutality, inconstancy, and unreasoning impulsiveness have been the theme of many writers', and yet human beings realize their higher potentialities only by participation in society, 'only by participation in group life does man become fully man, only so does he rise above the level of the savage'. Art, literature, science, language, morality, etc., are, after all, expressions of mankind in society. His book, *The Group Mind* (originally published in 1920), is an attempt to resolve this supposed paradox.

He argued that every organized human society has a 'collective mind', but he rejected the idea of a collective consciousness or unconsciousness. There was mental unity in society in the sense that any mind was 'an organized system of mental or purposive forces' (p. 9), and the minds of the members of society formed such a system, but this group mind did not exist as a supra-personal being outside of the individual minds. It was not an individual mind but existed within or rather was comprised of individual minds – it was the system of relations between the 'social' or 'socialized' minds of group members.

As McDougall put it: 'the collective actions which constitute the history of any such society are conditioned by an organization which can only be described in terms of mind, and which yet is not comprised within the mind of any individual; the society is rather constituted by the system of relations obtaining between the individual minds which are its units of composition (p. 9) . . . the individual minds which enter into the structure of the group mind . . . do not construct it; rather, as they come to reflective self-consciousness, they find themselves already members of the system, moulded by it, sharing in its activities, influenced by it at every moment in every thought and feeling and action . . . this system . . . does not consist of relations that exist external to and independently of the things related, namely the minds of individuals; it consists of the same stuff as the individual minds, its threads and parts lie within these minds; but the parts in the several individual minds reciprocally imply and complement one another and together make up the system which consists wholly of them . . .' (p. 11). It is tempting to quote further from McDougall, since he is making a fundamental, difficult and much misunderstood point in his definition of collective psychology, but enough has been said to illustrate that his basic concept is much more sophisticated than LeBon's, and in fact has much in common with that of the cognitive social psychologists.

McDougall further believed that the more organized the group, the more complex its psychology and the more developed its collective mind. An unorganized crowd might have some minimal collective mental life but not a developed 'mind' in the proper sense. A psychological group was defined by some degree of collective mental activity. The minimal conditions were: (1) some common object of mental activity – that members attended to the same thing(s) at the same time, (2) that all should experience the same emotion or reaction to the object of attention, (3) that the state of mind of each person should be affected to some degree by the mental processes of the others – a degree of reciprocal influence or interdependence should exist between their mental activity, i.e., how one person reacts to some event, for example, should partly determine how the others react, and (4), additionally but not necessarily, an awareness of the group as a whole should develop in the mind of each member. Since people had to be capable of reacting similarly to the same object, there had to be some degree of mental homogeneity – some similarity of mental constitution – among the individual group members. The greater the mental similarity, the more easily will psychological group formation take place.

The effect of the formation of a minimal psychological group (or crowd) is seen by McDougall in much the same terms as by LeBon – an exaltation and intensification of emotions, a loss of the sense of isolation and of the limitations of individuality, de-individuation, diffusion of responsibility, the spread of average, simpler, coarser ideas and emotions, and so intellectual inferiority – but the suggested mechanisms are different. Contagion was explained not by suggestion but 'primitive sympathy', a process whereby instincts are aroused by the expression of the appropriately corresponding emotion in others, e.g., the sight of anger in others might tend to elicit an aggressive instinct in oneself, leading to a corresponding and similar experience and expression of anger. Only the simplest ideas and feelings are capable of being shared by all and so spread through primitive sympathy and provide a basis for group formation. In addition, the idea of de-individuation, loss of one's personal self, is supplemented by a more positive concept of 'depersonalization', defining oneself in terms of or identifying with the group as a whole, but also leading to a lowering of personal restraints on antisocial actions. He fell back too on an instinct of submission to the power of the crowd, which made members suggestible to its influences in LeBon's sense.

McDougall asserts that it is the development of a collective mind which overcomes the excesses of primitive crowds. The preconditions of such a development are: (1) continuity of existence of the group, (2) some idea of the group as a whole and all that defines it in the minds of the members – the diffusion of this idea in their minds represents the *self-consciousness of the group mind*, (3) intergroup relations, which promote a sense of identity, of 'we-ness' and self-consciousness, (4) a body of traditions, customs and habits, and (5) the development of organization and social structure, a co-operative division of labour in the group, which raises the level of group performance.

Basically, the organized group develops the faculties of the individual – self-consciousness, volition, purposive action, the capacity for co-ordinated, reasoned behaviour – through the emergence of collective volition, experience and the division of labour, all based on group self-consciousness, the 'group spirit', the shared idea of the group as a whole in the minds of the members.

Freud's (1921) ideas may be summarized more briefly since much of his characterization of the psychological group is taken from LeBon and McDougall. He attempts to explain their special features, primarily their increased emotionality and intellectual inferiority, in terms of (his) psycho-analytic theory. For example, instead of group psychology representing a regression to LeBon's racial unconscious, Freud talks of the group being led by the 'id' and 'repressed' impulses (the unconscious biological drives and anti social components of personality).

His main points are that people behave qualitatively differently in groups, because instinctual impulses come to the surface; that group formation is based on 'erotic' (sexual-emotional) ties between members; that 'suggestion' is influence mediated by erotic ties and hence its prevalence within the group; and that these emotional bonds derive from two interrelated forms of identification on the part of members, a primary identification with the leader such that the leader becomes a part of one's ideal self (the 'ego-ideal'), leading to a mutual identification between members based on their perception of the similarity of their ego-ideals.

For Freud, the psychological group represented a form of mass hypnosis of the members by the leader (based on their inhibited sexual feelings towards and their substitute introjection of the loved leader into their self-concepts) plus a mutual identification and suggestibility between members because of their shared relationship to the leader.

LeBon, McDougall and Freud all assume and seek to analyse the distinctive psychology of the group. LeBon explains it in terms of the submergence of the conscious individual personality and self into the shared racial unconscious and mutual influence based on an irrational process of suggestion. McDougall postulates a much more complex process of development of collective mental life from minimal common and interactive experience to group self-consciousness based on cognitive and motivational similarity, primitive sympathy, depersonalization and, very importantly, the emergence of social continuity and organization. Freud derives the psychological unity of the group from identification, emotional ties and suggestion, and the behavioural content from the id, the instinctual reservoir of personality. All emphasize the role of instincts and emotions, consciousness or unconsciousness, self and identity.

F. H. Allport's individualism

Floyd Allport (1924), at least on the surface, stood for a totally different approach. His orientation is that of a behaviourist applying learning theory or 'stimulus-response' psychology to social psychology and advocating the experimental method. He was an uncompromising individualist in metatheory: he rejected not only the idea of a group mind but also the reality of group concepts *in toto*.

His position is that the group is a nominal fallacy, a convenient fiction for summarizing the actions of individuals – the individual is the sole psychological reality and there is nothing in the group not already present in the individual member. Strictly speaking, in fact, groups do not exist – there are only individuals. Of course, people may behave differently in groups than when alone, just as they behave differently in other situations: people learn to respond appropriately (and therefore differently) to different situation-specific stimuli and other people are simply another class of stimulus situation (the social environment as opposed to the physical environment). There is no distinctive group psychology. Social interaction is a matter of conditioned stimulus-response sequences in which one person's response functions as another's stimulus, eliciting a further response, and so on. Social psychology is only general (i.e., individual) psychology applied to the more complex stimulus conditions of the social environment. For Allport, then, the group is nothing but the sum of its parts, an aggregation of individual realities. 'If we take care of the individuals, psychologically speaking, the groups will be found to take care of themselves' (p. 9).

He stated his position well in the following passage: 'There is no psychology of groups which is not essentially and entirely a psychology of individuals; it is a part of the psychology of the individual, whose behaviour it studies in relation to that sector of his environment comprised by his fellows. His biological needs are the ends toward which his social behaviour is a developed means. Within his organism are provided all the mechanisms by which social behaviour is explained. There is likewise no consciousness except that belonging to individuals. Psychology in all its branches is a science of the individual. To extend its principles to larger units is to destroy their meanings' (1924, p. 4). Allport is nothing if not definite, consistent and clear.

Allport also introduced two important ideas about social influence or 'contagion' as we have called it so far. His theory of 'social facilitation' was the translation of suggestion into the language of conditioned responses and learning theory. It was hypothesized that the sight and sound of others doing the same thing as oneself functioned as conditioned social stimuli to release and augment learned reaction tendencies previously existing in individuals. In other words, behaviour was 'facilitated' in the crowd: the mere presence of others tended to accentuate and make more likely the expression of certain kinds of behaviour. Importantly, however, social facilitation did not represent the emergence of new group properties; individual behaviour did not change qualitatively in groups, it was merely 'enhanced' so to speak (see chapter 8). The concept served to summarize experimental data on the effects of being in a co-acting group (being in face-to-face contact with others performing similar tasks to oneself) – there was apparently an increase in the quantity but a decrease in the quality of performance, an intensification of activity but a lowering of its intellectual value. The concepts of social facilitation, contagion, suggestion and primitive sympathy are evidently similar, and it transpires, too, that so are their effects, namely, the homogenization, intensification and intellectual inferiorization of action (and emotion) in the crowd.

Other studies demonstrated that group members tended in their judgements to converge on their average opinions across various tasks. He interpreted this as a tendency to avoid extremes, reflecting a process of *conformity*, based on an attitude of submission to the group. This hypothesis that intragroup conformity leads to convergence on the average opinion is still widely accepted today (see chapters 4 and 7).

A final related idea that should be noted is his distinction between the *nonsocial/physical* and *social* environment, leading to the apparently commonsensical but in fact questionable notion that there is 'nonsocial' (reacting to things) and 'social' behaviour (reacting to people) and, more currently, the faculty of 'perception/cognition' (the perception of things) and, as a subclass, 'social perception/cognition' (the perception of people). It can be and has been argued persuasively that all human behaviour and perception is social from the point of view of the actor/perceiver – in the sense of being based upon, influenced, or mediated by society and its products (such as language, cultural values, or scientific knowledge) – whether or not it is directed at physical objects or other people (e.g., Farr and Moscovici, 1984; Moscovici, 1976; Tajfel, 1969a, 1972a).

The interactionism of Sherif, Asch and Lewin

Sherif, Asch and Lewin were cognitive social psychologists. They employed the experimental method like Allport but saw behaviour as a reaction to the psychological meaning of the situation, mediated by the individual's perception and cognition, not an expression of instinctual urges or blind conditioning. They also rejected any concept of a group mind – taking for granted that psychological processes belong only to individuals – but not the idea of a distinctive group psychology.

They argued each in their own way, like McDougall, that there was a genuine interaction in group functioning between individual psychological and social processes: the notion that groups were composed of 'nothing but' individuals was, they asserted, a platitude, which missed the point that people were changed psychologically in group settings. Through social interaction, group members created collective products such as norms, slogans, stereotypes, values, etc., which were internalized by and transformed the psychology of individuals. In other words, they argued that Allport's claim that there were only individuals failed to understand that the group concept was needed precisely to explain the nature of individuals.

Muzafer Sherif (1936; see too his critique of individualism in the study of intergroup relations, e.g., Sherif, 1967) explicitly rejected Allport's views about the sufficiency of purely individual analyses. Being in a group has psychological consequences which change the nature of the individual. He illustrated this thesis by applying the 'Gestalt' law of the 'interdependence of parts' to the perception of other people. Gestalt psychology was a major influence on Sherif (and an even more important one on Asch and Lewin). It held that to explain behaviour it was necessary to understand that we did not experience stimuli as isolated, elementary units, but as organized 'wholes' ('fields', 'configurations', or, in German, *Gestalten*). We reacted to the total perceptual field, and the character of the parts in that field were determined by their membership in the whole. Gestalt psychology took it for granted that the whole was different from the sum of its parts: that the perceptual organization of stimuli into an interdependent, 'dynamic' system produced new, higher order properties which were different from the properties of the individual stimuli and changed their character. An example of the point that we perceive in terms of patterns and that the patterning process takes precedence over the units is provided by the fact that a melody will be perceived as the same thing whether the individual notes are in the musical key of C or G, even though these two sets of notes are quite different (Schellenberg, 1978, p. 64).

The law of the interdependence of parts, therefore, was that 'when the organism is stimulated by different parts of a stimulus field, the parts fall into a functional relationship and each part influences the other parts. The result is . . . that the properties of any part are determined by its membership in the total functional system' (Sherif, 1936, p. 84). It was this principle extended to the social field that produced a new psychology of groups according to Sherif: when we interact with other people 'in some form of closed system' (p. 84), we and they become a total functional system, perceptually and behaviourally, producing new whole-properties such as slogans, values, standardized emotional experiences, etc., that take precedence over and change our individual responses. Thus the group most certainly could not be reduced to a mere aggregation of individual actions. He then developed this general principle with a careful theoretical and empirical analysis of the formation of social norms.

First, he argued that perception, evaluation and judgement are relative: they depend on 'stable anchorages' or 'frames of reference', i.e., standards or contexts against which one compares things. The essential idea is that how one sees or feels about some stimulus varies with and depends on the context against which one judges it, the 'frame' to which one 'refers' it. For example, the same climate may be experienced as hot or cold depending on whether one compares it to the weather of the Arctic or Australia. Secondly, society and culture provide us with internal frames of reference in the form of 'social norms', 'customs, traditions, standards, rules, values, fashions, and all other criteria of conduct which are standardized as a consequence of the contact of individuals' (p. 3). (A social norm is usually defined as any shared standard or rule that specifies appropriate, 'correct', desirable, expected, etc., attitudes and conduct.) This is why there is cultural relativism in the perception of the physical world and the evaluation of conduct: a 'cold' day in Australia may be regarded as excessively 'hot' in an English summer, and 'sexual decadence' in China may be seen as healthy 'high spirits' among the young members of a Californian commune. Thirdly, social norms and values are bound up with our self-identity, our sense of who and what we are, and so even the 'ego', the 'I', the conscious self at the core of individuality, is, in fact, socially constructed – 'Values are the chief constituents of the ego . . . These values are the social in man. In this sense, one may say, the ego is the social in him' (pp. 185–6).

Fourthly, he illustrated experimentally the formation of a social norm as a *socially produced but psychologically internalized* frame of reference. In these deservedly influential and famous experiments people are placed in an objectively ambiguous situation, where no external standards or frames of reference are available. They must estimate the apparent movement of a point of light in a completely darkened room. Unknown to the participants the light is in fact stationary, but, under these conditions, will appear to move (an optical illusion known as the 'autokinetic effect'), varying erratically from person to person and trial to trial. Initially, they confront the situation on their own and make a series of judgements as the light is turned on and off. Over time the individual's judgements will stabilize to fall within a particular range and around a particular reference point or norm within that range. These ranges differ from person to person. When two or three people with already established individual ranges and norms are brought together to make successive judgements in a group setting, their responses gradually converge until a shared or common range and norm is established. As Sherif points out, these common norms are peculiar to each group, they are a social product of interaction between the individuals and hence they illustrate that 'new and supra-individual qualities arise in the group situations' (p. 105). At the same time they are psychological structures, internalized by the members, since, when returned to isolation, members continue to act in terms of their group norms (later research has shown that such 'autokinetic' norms are extremely long-lasting).

Asch (1952) developed a sophisticated and extensive critique of both individualism and the group mind thesis, of which only a few points can be noted here. Allport's rejection of the reality of group concepts, for example, was based upon, he argued, a fallacious distinction between concrete 'things' (such as real individuals) and abstract 'relations' (such as groups or systems of things), the latter not being granted full reality. Asch points out that relations are just as real as things, and in fact that all things are only 'groups' or systems of relations between lower level elements (e.g., a molecule is a system of atoms, an atom is a system of neutrons, protons, etc., the latter dissolve into groups of even more elementary particles, and so on) just as groups/systems of relations appear as unitary things when looked at from a more macroscopic perspective.

Further, the stimulus-response concept of social interaction was fundamentally wrong: it missed the two essential points about human interaction and group formation in particular – that they embody 'psychological interaction' and take place in and are made possible by a 'mutually shared psychological field'. The paramount fact about human interactions, he asserted, is 'that they are happenings that are *psychologically represented* in *each* of the participants. In our relation to an object, perceiving, thinking, and feeling take place on one side, whereas in relations between persons these processes take place on both sides and in dependence upon one another . . . We interact . . . via emotions and thoughts that are capable of taking into account the emotions and thoughts of others' (1952, p. 142). We refer our own actions to the other and the other's acts to ourselves – we act in a shared field of mutual reference, on the 'common ground' of shared mutual awareness of ourselves and our objective environment.

The mutual psychological field is the first requirement of group formation: '. . . group actions . . . are possible only when each participant has a representation that includes the actions of others and their relations. The respective actions converge relevantly, assist and supplement each other only when the joint situation is represented in each and when the representations are structurally similar. Only when these conditions are given can individuals subordinate themselves to the requirements of joint action. These representations and the actions that they initiate bring group facts into existence and produce the phenomenal solidity of group processes. These are also the conditions necessary for the idea of a goal that can be achieved jointly' (pp. 251–2). Thus for Asch group facts become real because individuals are capable subjectively of mutual reference, of grasping their interrelations, of seeing themselves as joint members of a shared social field that exists independently of them as individuals, and of regulating their behaviour in terms of these shared understandings. Group facts have their foundation in individuals but they cease to be 'merely' individual facts by virtue of their reference to others.

Individualism fails to understand that there is a 'socially structured field within the individual' (p. 253) – that shared social facts are represented in and hence transform the mind of the individual – and that the individual-group relationship is a 'part-whole relation unprecedented in nature', since it is 'the only part-whole relation that depends on the recapitulation of the structure of the whole in the part' (p. 257) – that the group is made possible by the capacity of the member to perceive and act in terms of the collective (as well as to distance him- or herself from it).

Finally, it is worth noting that Asch recognized and criticized the reification of social determinism as a modern form of the group mind fallacy. He had no time for the view that the individual plays no role in macro-social processes, that the latter follow their own laws independently of individual thought and purpose, and that individuals are merely the passive vehicles of sociological forces. (In his famous empirical work on social conformity – see Asch, 1956 – he set out to demonstrate the autonomy of the individual in relation to the group, to refute the idea of group influence as an irrational, passive, slavish process of suggestion).

Asch is a difficult writer to do justice to; his thinking is powerful, subtle and rich and remains a fundamental contribution to the problem of the psychological group, perhaps unsurpassed since.

Lewin's (see Marrow, 1969, for a bibliography) influence and contribution have been in many ways more diffuse and pervasive than either of the other cognitive social psychologists. As a 'field theorist' influenced by Gestalt ideas he assumed that groups were, if not more than, then at least different from the sum of their parts. He too defined the psychological group in terms of the interdependence of the members: '. . . it is typical of well-organized groups with a high degree of unity to include a variety of members who are different or who have different functions within the whole. Not similarity, but a certain interdependence of members constitutes a group' (1939).

He analysed intragroup relations as a social field of forces in the individual's 'life-space' (the totality of the psychological experience of the individual at any given time, always including both the person and the environment in interaction), and saw individual and group as forming an interdependent system. He employed and introduced into the field concepts of whole-properties of groups such as their degree of 'cohesiveness' (the resultant of the forces which keep members together, forces of mutual attraction and mutual repulsion between members), group standards (social norms), social atmospheres, leadership styles (democratic, authoritarian or 'laissez-faire') and group decisions.

He emphasized that to understand and change the behaviour of the individual, one had to see them as members of a social system and their behaviour as determined or regulated by the dynamic properties of that system. Groups were more or less cohesive, with more or less power over their members and, depending on that power, exercised more or less pressure on members to ensure conformity to group standards and decisions. Groups were not only real, not only had different properties from individuals, they had power, and it was often easier to change the whole group than to change the individual in isolation from the group.

The behaviour of the person was a function of the interplay between the person and the environment as represented psychologically in the life-space; the life-space/the psychological environment included the various social systems of which the person was a member and associated group forces; therefore, 'individual' behaviour was inevitably socially and psychologically transformed and determined by group membership.

Lewin's impact was all the greater because he demonstrated with his colleagues that it was possible to manipulate complex social/group relationships experimentally and change behaviour by taking the group into account. His contribution to the problem of the individual-group relationship was contained in his programme of research and working assumptions as much as in any direct theoretical discussion of the issue, and much of the current orthodoxy about group processes can be traced to the body of work which he and his colleagues initiated.

Conclusion

This is not the place for a detailed assessment of the current status of the ideas of the early theorists. There are many empirical and theoretical insights which have stood the test of time and been incorporated into modern thinking, just as other ideas are almost certainly wrong, or implausible, or too abstract or general to be very useful. For our purposes, the important point is that we see that in the idea of an interaction between social and psychological processes which transforms individual psychology there is a relatively developed metatheory for the conceptualization of the psychological group, a metatheory which rejects both the notion of a group mind (in the simple literal sense) and the individualism that denies the distinctive psychological properties of the group. It is this 'interactionist' perspective that we shall seek to develop theoretically and empirically in the remainder of the book.

Under the influence of Sherif, Asch, Lewin and others group processes became a central topic of social psychology during the 1940s and 1950s. The theoretical momentum of the interactionist perspective, however, has not been sustained up to the present day. By the late 1960s it was evident that the group was a topic of declining interest (although there are many reservations to be made to this statement) and that a new individualism was abroad (which is not to imply that it was ever fully absent). It is not the intention to explain, except very partially, the re-emergence of individualism nor to review research on group processes since the early debate. Instead in the next chapter the current consensus on the nature of the psychological group will be presented and evaluated.

2

Rediscovering the Social Group

The contemporary conceptualization of the psychological group

What is a psychological group from the viewpoint of contemporary social psychology? How is the relationship of the individual to the group conceptualized at present?

There is in fact good agreement about the major features of group formation (e.g., Cartwright and Zander, 1968; Shaw, 1976, pp. 6–12; Turner and Giles, 1981a, pp. 3–7). These can be summarized by the concepts of 'identity', 'interdependence' and 'social structure'. The identity (or perceptual/cognitive) criterion is that individuals should have some collective awareness of themselves as a distinct social entity; they should tend to perceive and define themselves as a group, to share some common identity (e.g., Tajfel and Turner, 1986).

The criterion of social structure (e.g., Sherif, 1967) is that over time the relations between members should tend to become stabilized, organized and regulated by the development of a system of role and status differentiations and shared social norms and values that prescribe beliefs, attitudes and conduct in matters relevant to the group.

The interdependence criterion is that members should be positively interdependent in some way. There is also reasonable agreement in the field that interdependence is the theoretically important – i.e., underlying and causal – process in group formation. Cartwright and Zander (1968), for example, review theoretical definitions of the group in their authoritative textbook and conclude that some form of interdependence is the common element. They define a group as 'any collection of interdependent people' (p. 48). Influential theorists who regard interdependence of some kind as a primary criterion of group formation include Asch (1952), Davis, Laughlin and Komorita (1976), Deutsch (1949a, 1949b, 1973), Festinger (1950, 1954), Homans (1961), Lewin (1948), Lott and Lott (1965), Pruitt and Kimmel (1977), Horwitz and Rabbie (1982), Shaw (1976), Sherif (1936, 1967), Thibaut and Kelley (1959) and Zander (1979).

Several different kinds of interdependence have been suggested. For example, in the last chapter we saw that Sherif, Lewin and Asch stressed that group members were interdependent in the sense that they formed a 'functional unity' or 'dynamic system' or shared a 'mutual psychological field', whereas McDougall refers to the importance of reciprocal influence or interaction between the mental processes of individuals, and all theorists take for granted the central role of mutual influence between members in forming collective emotions, attitudes and actions.

In recent years the emphasis has been on forms of interdependence related to or assumed to be related to the satisfaction of individuals' needs or, which is much the same thing theoretically, the achievement of rewarding outcomes, i.e., *motivational* interdependence. By motivational interdependence is meant the idea that actions and characteristics of others relevant to the satisfaction of one's needs are functionally related by the structure of the situation to actions and characteristics of one's own relevant to their needs. Thus, at one extreme, people may co-operate to achieve some otherwise unattainable goal; at the other, they may associate simply because they find each other's company mutually rewarding.

The most important forms of interdependence studied since the early theorists have come to represent an implicit theory of group membership that can be summarized as follows. It is assumed that motivational (functional, objective) interdependence between people for the mutual satisfaction of their needs (achievement of co-operative goals, validation of beliefs, values and attitudes, attainment of rewards, successful performance of tasks, etc.) gives rise more or less directly (in the positive case) to social and psychological interdependence in the forms of co-operative and/or affiliative social interaction, mutual interpersonal influence and mutual attraction or 'group cohesiveness'.

Putting this in other words, it is assumed that people have individual needs (motives, goals, drives, desires, etc.), that at least some of and probably most of these needs are satisfied directly or indirectly by other people (e.g., people with a need for dominance will find the company of others with a submissive personality rewarding, or people seeking social change will associate in political organizations because only organized mass action, they may believe, can produce such an outcome), that where people perceive, believe, or expect to achieve mutual satisfaction from their association, they will tend to associate in a solidary fashion, to develop positive interpersonal attitudes and to influence each other's attitudes and behaviour on the basis of their power to satisfy needs for information and reward each other in other ways. To the degree that they do so, we have a group.

The concept of group cohesiveness is closely related to the inter-dependence theory. It has been defined in several ways with varying connotations: as that group property which decribes the psychological forces maintaining people's membership in a group (Cartwright, 1968; Zander,1979), the index of the degree of interdependence between members (Lewin, 1948), the psychological cement or glue that makes people 'stick together' in a group (Golembiewski, 1962, p. 149), or, most popularly, simply as the degree of attraction to the group or between group members (e.g., Festinger, 1950; Festinger, Schachter and Back, 1950). Lately, it has been equated with interpersonal attrac-tion (Lott and Lott, 1965). It tends to be assumed that attraction to others is based upon the operation of a 'need-satisfaction' or 'reinforce-ment' principle (a reinforcement, reward, or other positive outcome is, in effect, simply any stimulus event which satisfies a need or reduces some motivating drive-state): mutual liking between people is hypothe-sized to reflect the extent to which positive, gratifying, or rewarding outcomes are associated directly or indirectly with being in each other's company. It is hypothesized too that group cohesion increases the degree of social interaction, co-operation and influence between mem-bers (Shaw, 1976). The concept, therefore, embodies the essential property of group belongingness from the interdependence perspective – the degree to which the mutual satisfaction of individuals' needs has led to their transformation into a psychological group.

Sherif and his colleagues' well-known field studies on intergroup conflict (Sherif, 1967) show how it is possible to see a shared identity and intragroup organization as aspects of group membership which evolve as derivative phenomena from social interdependence between members and provide excellent illustrations of the hypothesized transi-tion from the goal relations between people to their formation into a cohesive group.

These studies comprised three field experiments in 1949, 1953 and 1954 lasting approximately three weeks each and conducted in diffe-rent locations in the USA. The participants were 11 to 12-year-old white, middle class boys who believed they were attending a normal summer camp. In fact, the camp authorities were the researchers and camp activities were organized as experimental manipulations to test hypo-theses about group formation and intergroup conflict. The studies fol-lowed four basic stages (but only the last study included the final stage).

In the first phase, camp activities and living arrangements were organized on a camp-wide basis and normal interpersonal friendships developed spontaneously between the boys. In the second phase, the boys were divided into two groups who bunked in different dormitories and engaged in separate activities (e.g., camping, cooking, games, finding places to swim, etc.). The boys in each group faced joint problems, played and worked together, pooled their efforts, divided up the work and organized different duties. They were put in a series of situations which were attractive to them and which required co-operative interaction. Despite the fact that the groups had been formed so as to separate members from the friends they had formed in the first stage, the result was the development of strong intragroup bonds and organization with boys now picking the great majority of their friends (approximately 90 per cent) from their own groups. Sherif concluded that when a number of individuals without previously established relationships interact in conditions that embody goals with common appeal to the individuals and that require interdependent activities for their attainment, a definite group structure consisting of differentiated status positions and roles will be produced (p. 76).

In the third phase the two groups were brought into contact in a series of competitive games and activities where there was a definite conflict of interests between them, since the winners would receive prizes. Relatively rapidly the competition between the groups changed from friendly rivalry into overt hostility. The hostility was accompanied by negative outgroup attitudes and stereotypes and heightened solidarity and pride within the groups. Finally in the last phase the conflicting groups were provided with a series of 'superordinate goals', 'conditions embodying goals *that are compelling for the groups involved, but cannot be achieved by a single group through its own efforts and resources*' (p. 88) and that therefore require collaboration for their successful achievement (e.g., pooling finances to hire a movie that both groups wanted to see). The superordinate goals led to intergroup co-operation and gradually the breaking down of hostility between the groups and emergence of positive bonds across group boundaries. It can in fact be argued that intergroup co-operation actually led to the formation of one superordinate group (Doise, 1971a). Thus in line with Sherif's hypotheses that the structure of the relations between people's goals leads to positive or negative social relationships, negative inter-dependence between the groups in the form of a conflict of interests created a strong psychological division between the groups, and posi-tive interdependence in the form of collaborative and later superordin-ate interests produced group belongingness and intragroup organiza-tion in the second stage, the reduction of intergroup conflict in the final stage, and co-operative, cohesive interaction in both.

There was clear evidence too that group belongingness was expressed in and accompanied by the creation of distinctive symbols of a collective identity: 'As the group became an organization, the boys coined nicknames . . . Each group developed its own jargon, special jokes, secrets, special ways of performing tasks, and preferred places' (p. 80) and of course they invented names for themselves (the 'Red Devils', 'Bull Dogs', etc.) and for places of special significance to them, and even made their own flags.

It is important to distinguish here between Sherif's own theoretical and especially metatheoretical understanding of his research results and the implicit contemporary theory of the group to which they have contributed. It is also important to note that there are numerous empirical determinants of group cohesiveness (e.g., interaction and physical proximity, similarity in attitudes and values, common fate, mutually attractive personality traits, shared threat/a common enemy), which are nevertheless all assumed to be explicable in terms of the process of mutual need satisfaction (Lott and Lott, 1965).

For instance, another good example of group formation on the basis of mutual need satisfaction, but this time stressing implicit rather than explicit interdependence, is provided by Festinger's related theories of social influence and social comparison (1950, 1954). He hypothesizes that people are attracted to and form groups with similar others because we need to compare ourselves with similar others both to evaluate our opinions and abilities and gain consensual validation for our beliefs and attitudes. Thus although for Festinger the major empirical determinant of group formation is similarity (for which there is much evidence), the essential process is still that of mutual need satisfaction, since similarity is assumed to be attractive because it is rewarding and it is rewarding because it gratifies informational needs for self-evaluation and 'subjective validity' (i.e., the need to be confident that one's attitudes are correct, appropriate, valid).

We have seen that the concept of interdependence did not arise in a historical vacuum and that it was originally proposed as a contribution and solution to the problem of the reality of the group and the distinctiveness of group psychology. As initially employed by Sherif, Lewin and Asch, the idea of functional interdependence had an important Gestalt or 'field-theoretical' content. It implied that members formed a 'dynamic whole' (a system, field, Gestalt) which was more than or at least different from the sum of its parts – the character of the parts (the individual members) was transformed by their interdependence (membership in the group). There was thus a psychological discontinuity between individuals in isolation or aggregate and interdependent people (in a group). The relationship between individuals in a group was mediated by their membership in the whole.

In this respect the concept was extremely successful. It served to legitimize the group as an object of scientific enquiry by conferring on it a degree of reality, and to bring the problem of the individual-group relationship out of the philosophical arena and into the laboratory. One result was that during the 1940s and 1950s group processes became a central area of research in social psychology. By and large, the reality of the group is now accepted, at least at the *social* level of analysis. Even Allport (1962) in a thoughtful if reluctant article eventually conceded the social reality of the group as a collective structure formed by the relations between particular segments of individual behaviour.

The story, however, has been different at the level of the *psychological* reality of the group. As soon as researchers began in the 1940s and 1950s to investigate in detail the exact processes underlying interdependence between people there was an almost universal return to a form of implicit individualism. That is to say, the idea that the relations between group members might be mediated *psychologically* by their membership in a joint unit seems to have been lost or perhaps more accurately simply not found necessary. Instead, interdependence within a group has been studied as a relationship between (as if) isolated persons, and intragroup relations have been assumed to be no different in kind from *interpersonal* relations, i.e., no theoretical distinction tends to be made between social relations conditioned by the unique individual characteristics of the interactors (which are what is meant here by 'interpersonal') and those based on their shared group memberships.

This process of 'individualizing' the interdependence concept seems to be associated with the revision of its meaning from the idea of 'functional unity' between members to that of mutual dependence for need satisfaction as researchers sought a more systematic causal analysis of group belongingness and group process. In many respects, therefore, it can be seen as part of the normal ebb and flow of scientific progress, a by-product of what in itself was an important advance. The revision of meaning is apparent even in Sherif's work, for example, despite his firm adherence to his interactionist metatheory that individuals are changed psychologically in groups: in his 1936 book, 'functional relations' between group members clearly implied emergent 'whole-properties', the interrelatedness of members of a dynamic field; in his theory of intergroup conflict, however, the explanatory burden is carried by the notion of functional relations as conflicts of interests or superordinate goals, the idea that intergroup attitudes follow intergroup relations (Ehrlich, 1973; Turner, 1981b), and the former meaning plays no direct theoretical role. Why should the mutual need satisfaction perspective be 'individualizing'? Perhaps because it begins with the needs of people as 'givens' and therefore implies that they are individual properties and construes them as the instigators of social action, prior to and having precedence over collective life, whereas in the earlier formulations individual and group were an indissoluble unity.

Examples of the analysis of group processes as interpersonal relations are numerous. For instance, the interpersonal relationship *par excellence*, the dyad or couple, has been regarded as a perfectly adequate theoretical analogue of the group (Thibaut and Kelley, 1959). The group property of cohesiveness was reduced in practice and then theory to interpersonal attraction (Lott and Lott, 1965), and in fact has virtually ceased to exist as an independent field, being displaced by the latter. Lott and Lott (1965) argued seriously that attraction to the group is nothing more than (the 'nothing but' argument of Allport again) liking for the specific individuals who compose it and that the idea of attraction to the group *as a whole* is meaningless. Intergroup co-operation and conflict have been investigated since the studies of Sherif and his colleagues primarily as interpersonal or dyadic relationships (Billig, 1976; Stephenson, 1981) in experimental games such as the 'Prisoner's Dilemma' (see table 2.1) – not to speak of explanations of racism, ethnocentrism and fascism in terms of individual psychopathology and prejudices (see Turner and Giles, 1981a) – and the major theoretical model has been in terms of personal self-interest (Eiser, 1978). That theories of social influence have been characterized by individualism is evidenced by numerous facts (see Moscovici, 1976; Reicher, 1982; Turner and Oakes, 1986; Wetherell, 1983; Wetherell, Turner and Hogg, 1985) – many of which will be discussed later – but is illustrated perhaps most simply by an implicit assumption that social norms form through the averaging of individual positions as members exchange their separate and private stocks of information. The group whole, the social norm, is assumed to be exactly the sum of its parts, the members' individual opinions – there is no gain or loss in collective wisdom, no conception that conformity to the group norm need not be a process of purely interpersonal convergence. It is for this reason that the phenomenon of group polarization (see chapters 4 and 7) has been assumed by definition to be inexplicable in terms of normal intragroup influence.

The result of this trend is that at least in practice modern social psychology has largely come to agree with Allport that the group is a *superfluous* concept. It may be useful at the descriptive level for summarizing certain kinds of relationships and as a unit of social analysis, but, *theoretically*, in terms of determining psychological processes, so the dominant consensus runs, the concept *adds nothing* to the explanation of behaviour. A 'group' is merely the product of interpersonal relations and processes or, more precisely, the same thing as relatively stable relations of interpersonal co-operation, attraction and influence between people. It is not surprising, then, to discover that there has been a gradual decline of interest in group processes in the mainstream of social psychology over the last 20 years or more and an accompanying growth of individualism (see the excellent survey and discussion by Pepitone, 1981; also Cartwright, 1979; Sampson, 1977, 1981; Steiner, 1974; Tajfel, 1981a, 1981b). Such a decline is both a natural and inevitable development of the dominant theory of the group.

The psychological reality of the group

Is the above conclusion empirically valid? Can social behaviour be explained satisfactorily in terms of individual and interpersonal processes? Do the research data support the idea that the group is a theoretically superfluous concept, merely an expression of positive interpersonal relationships based on interdependence between individuals for the satisfaction of their needs? A full answer would amount almost to a review of the whole of social psychology. Instead we shall focus on some recent developments in research directly relevant to group processes, namely, group formation and cohesion, social co-operation and social influence.

Social categorization and group formation

Lott and Lott (1965) equate cohesiveness and implicitly therefore the formation of a group with the development of mutual interpersonal attraction. The evidence for this idea has never been very compelling (e.g., Cartwright, 1968, p. 95; Sherif, 1967, pp. 74–5; Turner, 1984) and most of the data cited by Lott and Lott are equivocal in this respect, being only assumed on theoretical and metatheoretical grounds to indicate purely interpersonal attraction. A body of research has now appeared which seems to refute the hypothesis more or less directly.

In the original studies, Tajfel, Flament, Billig and Bundy (1971; Tajfel, 1970) were not directly interested in group formation but in the minimal conditions for intergroup discrimination. They designed an experimental situation embodying an ingroup-outgroup relationship which was so 'stripped down' and (apparently) empty of psychological significance that no discrimination was expected. The intention was to add variables cumulatively to see at what point ingroup favouritism would occur (Tajfel, 1978, pp. 10–11).

The baseline setting was defined by the manipulation of social categorization (ingroup-outgroup membership) *per se*, the division or classification of subjects into two distinct groups unconfounded by all the variables that normally determine intragroup cohesion or intergroup attitudes. The subjects (schoolboys) were divided into groups ostensibly on the basis of a trivial, *ad hoc* criterion but in fact randomly (and in later studies explicitly randomly, e.g., Billig and Tajfel, 1973; Locksley, Ortiz and Hepburn, 1980; Turner, Sachdev and Hogg, 1983); there was no social interaction or contact between or within groups, no conflicts of interest, previous hostility, or link between members' self-interest and group membership, nor any other form of functional interdependence within or between groups, and group membership was anonymous, i.e., individuals knew which group they belonged to personally but not the affiliations of others. The subjects believed they had been assigned to groups simply for administrative convenience. Their task was to make decisions (privately) about awarding money to pairs of anonymous others identified only by group membership and a personal code number.

These so-called 'groupings', therefore, were purely perceptual or cognitive (a social categorization may be defined as a cognitive representation of a social division into groups) and hence are referred to as *minimal* groups. The unexpected result was that even in this highly controlled setting the subjects discriminated in favour of ingroup members and against outgroup members (and did so in a way that was gratuitously competitive). It was found that not only did they give more money to ingroup than outgroup members, when this was unrelated to their personal gain, but they were willing to give less in absolute amounts to ingroup members in order to give them relatively more than outgroup members. They were also less concerned to maximize the joint profit of pairs of outgroup members than of pairs of ingroup members, when on some of the choices they made decisions relating to two recipients from the same group.

This finding of ingroup favouritism has been replicated in similar and related experimental situations and generalizes across subject samples, operationalizations of independent and dependent variables, modes of response and so far even different cultures (reviews are provided by Brewer, 1979; Turner, 1975, 1980, 1981b, 1983a; see Wetherell, 1982). It appears that imposing social categorizations upon people even on an explicitly random basis (e.g., Billig and Tajfel, 1973; Locksley et al., 1980; Turner et al., 1983) produces discriminatory intergroup behaviour, intragroup cohesion in the form of more positive attitudes towards and more reported liking of ingroup than outgroup members, ethnocentric biases in perception, evaluation and memory (e.g., Howard and Rothbart, 1978) and an altruistic orientation towards ingroup members (Turner, 1978). Notwithstanding issues of alternative explanation and methodology (which have been thoroughly discussed, e.g., Bornstein et al., 1983a, 1983b; Branthwaite, Doyle and Lightbown, 1979; St Claire and Turner, 1982; Turner, 1978, 1980, 1983a, 1983b), these data seem well established as reliable, robust and valid (in the sense of being an effect of perceived ingroup-outgroup membership).

It is difficult to avoid the conclusion that social categorization leads to psychological group formation – the subjects demonstrate collective behaviour in the form of shared responses systematically related to their own and others' group memberships, mutual attraction between ingroup members, ethnocentric attitudes and biases, and so on (see too Moreland, 1985). Also the data imply that some genuine process of identification with group membership takes place (Turner, 1975, 1978). If so, then it follows that interpersonal interdependence and attraction are not necessary conditions for group formation, since the very conditions of these experiments are designed to eliminate such factors as alternative explanations of the results. Although social categorization leads to intragroup cohesion (as well as intergroup discrimination), this is plainly an effect rather than a cause of group formation. Also it is not clear that such cohesion represents 'interpersonal' attraction, since the subjects have no idea of the specific persons in their group and have no reason to suppose that, individually, they are any more likeable than outgroup members. They seem to like the people in their group just because they are ingroup members rather than like the ingroup because of the specific individuals who are members.

The tradition of research in the social categorization or 'minimal group' paradigm, therefore, seems to demonstrate both that attraction and interdependence between specific individuals are not necessary conditions for group formation and that simply imposing a shared group membership upon people can be sufficient to generate attraction between them.

Some further issues remain. Is it possible that the 'external designation' of subjects as group members imposes a common fate upon them which somehow creates an implicit or indirect form of interdependence between ingroup members? Cartwright and Zander (1968, pp. 56–7), for example, recognize that psychological groups are sometimes formed because people are categorized from the outside, but assume that the process is still one of interdependence. It is possible that some such sequence could be operating, but on present evidence implausible. The concept of 'common fate' is an elastic term which in this context seems to do no more than redescribe the phenomenon to be explained. The empirical data are consistent that members' responses do not seem to be motivated by self-interest (e.g., Turner, 1978; Turner, Brown and Tajfel, 1979) or any assumed or perceived link between ingroup favouritism and the satisfaction of some individual need (other, that is, than some individual need tautologically defined only in terms of how the subjects behave, e.g., a need to act as group members, to be competitive, etc.).

Also, if not necessary, is interpersonal attraction at least sufficient for group formation? This is a complex issue to be dealt with in presenting the self-categorization theory.

Finally, there is the question that was and still is of immediate interest to Tajfel et al. (1971) and others primarily preoccupied with the implications of the data for intergroup conflict – of why group formation should result in discriminatory rather than some other kind of intergroup behaviour, of why in acting as group members do subjects display, apparently spontaneously, ingroup bias? A great deal of theoretical and empirical effort has been expended on this issue over the last decade and a half. Several hypotheses have been advanced and tested in one way or another, e.g., 'demand characteristics' or the 'experimenter effect' (i.e., that the data are in fact artifactual), a 'generic' (universal) norm of ingroup-outgroup bias which guides behaviour in appropriate settings, a tendency to 'cognitive balance' such that one favours social units to which one belongs, de-individuation, a categorization process which leads to the cognitive differentiation of ingroup and outgroup members and a tendency to seek 'positive distinctiveness' for groups which define one's social identity.

There is no need to duplicate here the arguments and material covered in the extensive literature and detailed reviews available. Suffice to say that the hypothesis favoured here, and the analysis that ultimately led to the theory of this book, is the *social identity theory* of Tajfel and Turner (1979, 1986). The theory defines 'social identity' as those aspects of an individual's self-concept based upon their social group or category memberships together with their emotional, evaluative and other psychological correlates, e.g., the self defined as male, European, a Londoner, etc. It assumes that people are motivated to evaluate themselves positively and that in so far as they define themselves in terms of some group membership they will be motivated to evaluate that group positively, i.e., people seek a positive social identity. Further, since groups are evaluated in comparison with other groups, a positive social identity requires that one's own group be favourably different or *positively distinctive* from relevant comparison groups. The basic hypotheses, then, are (1) that people are motivated to establish positively valued distinctiveness for groups with which they identify from relevant outgroups, and (2) that when social identity in terms of some group membership is unsatisfactory, members will attempt to leave that group (psychologically or in reality) to join some more positively distinct group and/or to make their existing group more positively distinct. Other hypotheses specify the different ways in which individuals can achieve positive ingroup distinctiveness and the conditions under which they may be pursued.

An important derivation from the theory is that competition (for mutual distinctiveness) can develop between groups in the absence of conflicts of interest. Applied to the minimal group paradigm, the theory interprets intergroup discrimination as just such a case of 'social competition' (Turner, 1975): subjects define and evaluate themselves in terms of the imposed social categories, compare ingroup with outgroup in terms of the only available value dimensions (money, 'points', evaluative scales) and seek positive distinctiveness for their own group by awarding it more money or favouring it in other ways. There is suggestive evidence along these lines that the intergroup discrimination does raise group members' self-esteem (Lemyre and Smith, 1985; Oakes and Turner, 1980; cf. Wagner, Lampen and Syllwasschy, 1986).

It is worth noting because of a certain amount of confusion on these points that the theory does *not* suggest that people always have a positive social identity – this is patently untrue (see Turner, 1980) – but that, under particular conditions, negative social identity is psychologically aversive and motivating (a simple analogy is that lack of food is highly motivating but obviously does not imply that people do not go hungry or indeed do not sometimes starve). Also, it does not state that people always discriminate in favour of ingroups over outgroups or that there will be a simple positive correlation between positive social identity and ingroup favouritism – this is to confuse an analysis of basic processes with a set of descriptive empirical generalizations (see Schlenker, 1974, and Turner, 1981a, on this distinction), but in any case discrimination against the outgroup is only one way of achieving positive social identity and is only predicted under certain specific conditions.

Social co-operation and the pursuit of individual self-interest

Research on 'mixed-motive' games and, in particular, the 'Prisoner's Dilemma Game' (PDG) is most relevant to this issue. The research directly tests the hypothesis that positive interdependence for the maximization of self-interest leads to co-operation. Reviews are provided by Colman (1982), Davis et al. (1976), Dawes (1980), Eiser (1978, 1980) and Pruitt and Kimmel (1977).

On each trial in the PDG (see table 2.1) the two players each make a 'co-operative' or 'competitive' choice (this terminology is used for simplicity; the behavioural choices may sometimes have other psychological meanings, see Pruitt and Kimmel, 1977) and receive rewards or payoffs according to the resultant pattern of choices. The reward or payoff matrix relates specific outcomes to specific patterns of choice, i.e., it defines the objective interdependence of the players in terms of the reward structure of the situation. The fascination of the PDG is that it embodies the conflict between individual competition and joint co-operation. The reward structure is such that from the perspective of each individual player (acting independently, as if in isolation) the competitive choice is always to be preferred to the co-operative choice (in terms of maximizing self-interest), but that from the perspective of both players joint co-operation is to be preferred to joint competition. To put it another way: if both players seek to maximize their self-interest independently of the other by competing, they will do less well than if they had both co-operated. The objective reward structure of the situation, in fact, is such that the players are positively interdependent: joint co-operation is the collectively rational strategy both in principle and practice (the research demonstrates that joint co-operation is the strategy that does actually in spontaneous play optimize the players' individual gains, see Oskamp, 1971; Wilson, 1971).

For this reason game theorists originally predicted that joint cooperation would be relatively rapidly achieved in the game (Coleman, 1982). Eiser points out (1978, p. 151) that the basic assumption underlying this whole body of research was that individuals would tend to co-operate when it was in their interests to do so. In fact, this prediction was quickly disconfirmed. The single most striking finding to emerge from the PDG has been the marked failure of people to co-operate (Eiser, 1980, p. 201); it has been estimated that on average only about 30 per cent of responses tend to be co-operative. Rapoport and Chammah (1965) found that co-operative choices increased to about 60 per cent of the total after 300 trials. Even the latter increase may only be found in circumstances where the players do not belong to

Table 2.1:   The prisoner's dilemma

		Player 2 choices	
		Co-operation	Competition
Player 1 choices	Co-operation	3, 3	1, 4
	Competition	4, 1	2, 2

Note: Each player makes a co-operative or competitive choice. The rewards on the left of each column are for player 1, and those on the right for player 2. The structure of the matrix is such that the outcome for individual competition when the other player co-operates is greater than the outcome for joint co-operation which is greater than the outcome for joint competition which in turn is greater than the outcome for individual co-operation when the other player competes. The absolute amounts specified are purely illustrative.

different groups (Wilson, 1971), but, in any case, 60 per cent co-operation after 300 trials of such a simple game, where the reward structure is well defined, would not seem an especially impressive achievement. The researchers themselves have certainly not thought so, for, since the early findings over 20 years ago, they have been preoccupied with the discovery of factors that would increase the level of co-operation. A closely related field of research on 'social dilemmas' (Dawes, 1980) has even emerged whose basic assumption or *raison d'être* is the apparent failure of people to co-operate when it is in their common interests to do so.

Several factors have been found to increase the level of co-operation in mixed-motive settings. The dominant solution has been to manipulate more or less directly the social and psychological relationship between the players to produce a mutually co-operative orientation. Some of the major variables that come under this heading are:

1 explicit instructions to adopt a co-operative rather than a competitive or individualistic orientation (e.g., instructions to act as 'partners', 'have regard to the common welfare', etc., as opposed to instructions to gain more than the other or as much for oneself as possible without regard to the other);
2 the degree of communication, face-to-face contact, or anticipated social interaction between players;

3 the degree of social closeness (eg., intimacy, friendship, etc.) between the players;
4 the degree of perceived similarity between players or the extent to which they share group membership(s);
5 the experience of sharing a common fate (as in a period of joint loss from mutual competition) or of shared threat (a common enemy, intergroup competition); the 'tit-for-tat' strategy in which each player duplicates the preceding choice of the other may be important here (and in producing perceived similarity), since it teaches amongst other things that players will sink or swim together (Pruitt and Kimmel, 1977);
6 the extent to which choices are made in a shared public setting (a mutually shared psychological field as Asch might express it) as opposed to anonymously and in private;
7 presentation of the reward matrix in 'decomposed' forms which make salient the mutual dependence of the players on each others' willingness to co-operate; and
8 conditions which facilitate and encourage the development of mutual trust and empathy, the attribution of the other's responses to their co-operative intentions and expectations that the other will co-operate.

Pruitt and Kimmel (1977) summarize these and other data by means of a 'goal/expectation' theory. They suggest that mutual co-operation in mixed-motive settings depends upon the development of a 'goal of establishing and/or maintaining continued mutual cooperation' and an 'expectation that the other will cooperate' . . . 'sometimes called "trust"' (p. 375).

In reviewing research on 'social dilemmas' (sometimes referred to as N-person, i.e., multi-person, PDGs) Dawes (1980) also finds that co-operation is increased by:

1 the extent of communication and contact between players;
2 the smallness of the group (which can probably be interpreted as social closeness, cohesiveness, intimacy, etc.) – co-operation decreases with increasing group size (i.e., as social distance between the members increases);
3 making choices in public rather than private;
4 expectations that the other will co-operate ('trust'); and
5 appealing to shared norms of acting for the common good, i.e., moralizing to the subjects about 'group benefit, exploitation, ethics, etc.' (p. 185).

He concludes that 'it is precisely the payoff utilities that lead the players to defect' . . . (i.e., compete) . . . 'while those connected with altruism, norms and conscience . . . lead the players to cooperate . . .' (p. 190) and stresses the importance of 'knowledge' (of social payoffs), 'morality' and 'trust' (p.191).

The authors of both these reviews, therefore, have explicitly abandoned the hypothesis that joint co-operation arises more or less directly from the objective structure of positive interdependence between interactors for the satisfaction of their individual needs (that people co-operate when it is in their interests to do so). What seems to matter for co-operation, the decisive condition, is the intervention of social psychological variables that produce a mutually co-operative relationship. If one looks carefully at the relevant variables – a shared self-definition as partners, being oriented to the common interest, shared goals and experiences, similarity, reduced social distance and increased social contact, empathy and trust, mutual attraction, the salience of shared norms and values, acting in 'public' (a shared social field) as opposed to as an isolated private individual, etc. – there is a strong implication that the general process underlying mutually co-operative intentions and expectations is the extent to which players come to see themselves as a collective or joint unit, to feel a sense of 'we-ness', of being together in the same situation facing the same problems. In other words, it appears that the fundamental process is one of becoming a psychological group.

The interdependence theory proposes that positive interdependence leads to co-operation, which in turn leads to the formation of a psychological group. The evidence, however, implies that psychological group formation may be the necessary intervening process before objective interdependence leads to co-operative activity. Instead of social co-operation producing the group, it may well be that, psychologically, the group is the basis of co-operation.

This conclusion is not changed by the fact that there are other kinds of experimental games in which the same choice maximizes self-interest from the perspectives of both individual and collective rationality (sometimes called games of 'pure co-operation'). Naturally in such settings, where the 'co-operative' choice is the only sensible one from the point of view of each player separately and both players jointly, co-operation will probably develop rapidly and directly. This is of little comfort to the interdependence theory, however, since, by definition, personal self-interest provides an alternative to positive interdependence as an explanation of the behaviour and, by the same token, it seems dubious that overtly 'co-operative' responses motivated by personal self-interest can properly be called co-operation in any genuine social or psychological sense. Even in such settings, therefore, the transformation of overt into genuine 'psychological' co-operation is likely to depend upon group formation.

Some data relevant to the general point are provided by Wilson and his colleagues (e.g., Wilson, Chun and Kayatani, 1965; Wilson and Kayatani, 1968). In a series of studies they compared the PD choices of members of the same team playing each other with the responses of the same teams playing other teams. The teams were shortlived, based on assignment by the experimenters and had little significance for their members (there was some social interaction between team members in deciding their joint choices on inter-team trials) and the structure of the reward matrix was identical across the two types of trial. Nevertheless, intragroup choices were approximately twice as co-operative (about 60 per cent) as intergroup choices. This difference illustrates that being in the same group can induce co-operation relatively independently of the objective reward structure of the situation (just as being in different groups appears to make people more competitive, e.g., McCallum, Harring, Gilmore, Drenan, Chase, Insko and Thibaut, 1985).

Another important line of evidence for this conclusion are data from research on intergroup conflict (Brewer, 1979; Dion, 1973, 1979; Doise, 1971a; Turner, 1981b; Worchel, 1979, 1985) which seem to demonstrate that the formation of ingroup-outgroup or superordinate social identifications may be more important in the development of intergroup competition or co-operation respectively than the simple fact of conflicting or collaborative interests as hypothesized by Sherif.

It can be concluded that social co-operation does not arise in a straightforward way directly from the pursuit of individual self-interest. It seems to depend upon the development of individuals into something we can call a joint or collective psychological unit.

Social influence and informational dependence

Social psychologists distinguish between two types of influence. Employing the terminology of Deutsch and Gerard (1955) — see Jones and Gerard (1967) for a summary of related ideas — there is *informational influence* which represents acceptance of others' responses (beliefs, opinions, attitudes, etc.) as evidence about reality and which leads to private attitude change, and *normative influence* defined as conformity to the positive expectations of others based on the desire for social approval and to avoid rejection. The former process reflects dependence on others for the reduction of uncertainty and the latter dependence on others for extrinsic rewards and to avoid costs. Only informational influence is regarded as 'true' influence (i.e., leading to private acceptance and genuine change in attitudes and opinions in order to be correct as opposed to merely 'going along' with the group without conviction to avoid ridicule or other sanctions). Normative influence represents public compliance, i.e., 'strategic' or 'tactical' conformity in overt behaviour or words, but which is not necessarily accompanied by any real belief in the rightness of what is done or said.

The theory of true or informational influence (derived from the core ideas and work of Sherif, 1936, Festinger, 1950, 1954, Deutsch and Gerard, 1955, Thibaut and Strickland, 1956, Jones and Gerard, 1967, and others) may be summarized in terms of three stages:

1 it is assumed that subjective uncertainty (lack of confidence in the objective validity of one's beliefs, opinions, attitudes, etc.) is produced by an asocial interaction between the perceptual apparatus of the perceiver and the objective characteristics of the stimulus world: the more objectively ambiguous, complex, problematic, unstructured the stimulus field, the greater the individual's uncertainty and their need for information to reduce uncertainty;
2 the need to reduce uncertainty in a given situation leads to informational dependence on others (social dependence); and
3 informational dependence leads to the acceptance of influence from others (and so movement towards the others or conformity) to the degree that others' responses are perceived to provide evidence/information about objective reality.

The experiments of Sherif (1936) on norm formation utilizing the autokinetic effect (see chapter 1) may be regarded as the classic demonstration of this theory. It will be recalled that the subjects are placed in an objectively ambiguous situation (they must estimate the illusory movement of a point of light in a completely darkened room) and that their judgements gradually converge on a modal range of estimates (at approximately the average of their initial personal ranges). It appears as if the subjects employ their own and others' responses as sources of information about the movement of the light and hence shift towards closer agreement as they implicitly exchange information. The shared 'frame of reference' that results is interpreted as the emergence of an internalized social norm and the beginning of the formation of a psychological group. This at least is how these and related studies are usually understood. But is this interpretation valid?

Moscovici (1976) has recently strongly criticized the dependence doctrine of influence in its various forms. He points out that the idea that influence results from dependence on others (whether to reduce uncertainty or gain approval) equates it with the exercise of power, in which those that 'have' unilaterally change those that 'have not'. He denies that conformity is always submission to the majority (the powerful, authority, the experts) and in his research, for instance, demonstrates that a consistent minority can influence and change a majority of group members. Since, by definition, a minority 'depends' more on a majority than vice versa (in terms of extent of available information and power to reward and punish), he argues that minority influence and innovation (and more broadly social change) are evidence against the dominant theory. His general critique is compelling and has done much to demolish the credibility of the informational dependence theory (which is not necessarily to endorse his own theory of minority influence). We shall not attempt to summarize the whole of Moscovici's critique, but will relate some of his insights to the theoretical problem at issue here.

To evaluate the conventional theory, it is useful to consider the two best-known and influential paradigms in research on social conformity, those of Sherif and Asch. The Asch conformity study (1952, 1956) may be seen as a direct test of Festinger's (1950, 1954) hypothesis of a physical reality continuum underlying 'subjective validity' (subjective confidence in the objective validity, correctness, appropriateness, etc., of one's responses). According to Festinger, dependence on social reality testing to evaluate one's responses (i.e., on social comparison and 'consensual validation': comparing with others and seeking their agreement as corroboration for the rightness of one's views) comes into play and increases only in so far as physical, non-social means of testing are unavailable, in so far in other words as the stimulus situation becomes more objectively ambiguous, unstructured, or problematic. Thus, where the stimulus to be judged is unambiguous such that direct perceptual tests provide unequivocal results, there should be no dependence on social reality testing and no need for consensual validation. This is exactly the situation in the Asch experiment.

In this paradigm subjects make judgements about simple physical stimuli: they are shown lines of differing length displayed on cards and must indicate on each trial which of three stimulus lines matches a target line. The stimuli are selected such that in the control situation, where individuals make judgements on their own, the task is so easy that errors virtually never occur and subjects experience no uncertainty as to the correctness of their responses. It follows that in the experimental condition, where the naïve subject is confronted on critical trials by the 'obviously incorrect' responses of a unanimous majority of (supposedly) his or her fellow subjects (but in fact confederates of the experimenter), that, whatever else the impact of this disagreement, it should not initiate any true process of informational influence. This is why conformity in the Asch paradigm is usually interpreted as public compliance, with the 'yielders' thought to be motivated by a fear of ridicule, a reluctance to stand out as different from the group. What the data actually show, however, is more complex.

It is commonly known that approximately 33 per cent of responses on the critical trials tend to be conformist. What is less acknowledged is the overwhelming evidence that, even if some component of the behavioural conformity represents compliance, informational influence processes are also at work in that subjects seem to *become uncertain* in face of the disagreement of their peers. Asch reports from post-experimental interviews that subjects quickly become worried by the question of whether they or the group are correct, that the great majority (even if independent in behaviour) experience uncertainty and doubt at some stage about whether they are right (some 70 per cent state this explicitly), look for ways in which the group could be right, and begin to think that there must be something wrong with them (40 per cent explicitly wonder about the soundness of their vision). Moreover, this uncertainty is related to conformity. The 'yielding' subjects report themselves as experiencing more doubt about their correctness and the soundness of their vision than 'independent' subjects. The fact that for the most part people do not conform behaviourally, therefore, does *not* indicate that the incorrect group does not have persuasive, informational power, but simply that the naïve subjects are not *finally* persuaded, that try as hard as they might to see things from the group's point of view, to be persuaded, they cannot in fact change what they see and so are unable honestly to agree.

Conformity in the Asch paradigm, therefore, is related to feelings of being right or wrong. It is not the case that, knowing that the majority is 'obviously' wrong, people conform simply to gain approval and avoid rejection. Even the fear of ridicule, of standing out, is related to situationally aroused self-doubt: it is because people begin to doubt their capacities, to wonder if the group is not right and if there is not something wrong with them, that they also begin to fear that the group will denigrate their incompetence and attribute personal defects to them. More importantly, in a setting where reality is as highly structured and unambiguous as it would ever seem to be, the disagreement of the group creates subjective uncertainty. As Moscovici points out, the uncertainty does not reflect the absence of physical tests or the nature of objective reality, it is a *social product of disagreement*.

That this should be so is a mystery with a very plausible solution —

that was provided by Asch (1952) at the outset. Subjects become uncertain because they disagree with people with whom they expect to agree. The disagreement is cognitively inconsistent, a puzzling problem that has to be explained in some way, including as one possibility that they personally may be wrong. They expect to agree because they have categorized the others as similar or identical to themselves (inter-changeable, equivalent) in terms of the attributes perceived as relevant to making a sound judgement (such as normal eyesight) and believe they are judging an identical stimulus situation. If similar perceivers confront the same stimulus, then they *ought* to agree. This is a natural and rational expectation.

This interpretation is fully consistent with the results of the Sherif experiment. Once again, the subjects are, from their own point of view, identical or similar perceivers judging an identical stimulus. It is impor-tant to realize that they do not know that the stimulus is objectively ambiguous (in the sense that it represents a scientifically established optical illusion). On the contrary, they assume that the light is really moving and that they are looking at the same thing. Hence the implicit feeling (in their self-reports) that they ought to agree, and, indeed, perceptually speaking, probably already do. The mutual convergence in their verbal reports seems to be experienced largely as a mutual co-ordination or standardization of their judgemental scales in the absence of external frames of reference (Sherif, 1936). This social influence, therefore, just as in the Asch paradigm, seems to depend upon a mutual recognition of identity between the perceivers, of being an appropriate reference group for each other, and a perception of the stimulus as a shared feature of the public world and not as objectively variable.

Supportive evidence for the importance of a shared identity is that one common reaction of Asch's subjects to the disagreement is to search for some relevant difference between themselves and the majority which could explain it. The gradual growth of self-doubt, of the fear of being different, of having some personal defect, is one aspect of this reaction. Also, we need not doubt (see Allen, 1975, p. 30) that had the majority been presented as, for example, visually abnormal or handi-capped in some way, then both uncertainty and conformity would have been markedly less.

Sperling (cited in Asch, 1952, pp. 487–91) tested the latter point that mutual influence depends upon a shared presumption of an identical stimulus. He explicitly informed subjects in the autokinetic situation that the movement of the light was objectively ambiguous, that it was in fact an optical illusion. The result was that amongst those subjects who believed Sperling mutual influence and convergence did not take place. (Some subjects did converge, but interestingly it was found afterwards that all of these had continued to assume that the light was really moving.) After all, if people are uncertain because of objective ambiguity, because the problem is 'out there' and not in their eyesight, then why should they trust anyone else's eyes? If the stimulus is *objectively* variable, then what is the point of reaching what must be an arbitrary agreement?

To summarize: the accepted theory is that stimulus ambiguity produces uncertainty, which leads to dependence on others for information, mutual influence and the formation of shared norms; social influence and the emergence of norms represent embryonic group formation (e.g., Shaw, 1976, p. 11). The classic data of Asch and Sherif, however, imply that uncertainty is a social product of disagreement with people categorized as identical to self. The perception of others as an appropriate reference group creates the shared expectations of agreement necessary for the arousal of uncertainty and mutual influence (see too Alexander, Zucker and Brody, 1970). The psychological group seems to be at the beginning and not the end of the influence process; its precondition, not its product.

Conclusion

This brief review of social categorization and group formation, social co-operation and social influence leads to some converging conclusions from the three areas. First, neither theoretically nor empirically is the group a superfluous concept; on the contrary, the very social relationships that are supposed to explain group formation seem at least in part to be based upon it. Secondly, the relationships of cohesion, co-operation and influence may not be interpersonal in the theoretical sense at all, since, under certain conditions, the perception of others as group members rather than as unique, different persons seems to be a precondition for such relations. Thirdly, instead, therefore, of the group as the product of interpersonal relations, it may be more appropriate to reconceptualize group formation as an adaptive social psychological process that makes social cohesion, co-operation and influence possible.

The functional or adaptive significance of such a mechanism is not difficult to grasp. For example, rather than cohesive group formation following from the successful achievement of group goals (the conventional theory), it would make as much if not more sense if group formation directly produced solidarity, co-operation and unity of action and values so as to make the successful attainment of shared goals more likely. There is in fact evidence, as we shall see presently, that there is not a simple relationship between a group's success in reaching its goals and rewarding its members and its cohesiveness. Failure, defeat, deprivation, etc., these too will sometimes increase the cohesiveness of a group, presumably then acting as the basis for future collective action.

These conclusions lead inevitably to two related questions. By what process does or could group formation produce these effects? And how does psychological group formation take place if not on the basis of interpersonal interdependence? The self-categorization or social identity theory of the group was developed in an attempt to provide the answers and is described in the next chapter.

3

A Self-Categorization Theory

Introduction

The self-categorization theory is a set of related assumptions and hypotheses about the functioning of the social self-concept (the concept of self based on comparison with other people and relevant to social interaction). It grew out of the research on social categorization and the related concept of social identity described in the previous chapter. An alternative name for the theory we shall sometimes use is the social identity theory of the group.

To begin with, therefore, it will be useful to avoid confusion by pointing out that the theory to be presented is related to but not the same as the social identity theory of *intergroup* behaviour referred to earlier. The earlier analysis was specifically directed at the explanation of intergroup discrimination (in the absence of conflicts of interest) and its central psychological hypothesis is motivational (or cognitive-motivational) – that individuals seek to differentiate their own groups positively from others to achieve a positive social identity. The current theory, developed later, is focused on the explanation not of a specific kind of group behaviour but of how individuals are able to act as a group at all. The basic hypothesis is a cognitive (or social-cognitive) elaboration of the nature of social identity as a higher order level of abstraction in the perception of self and others. Logically speaking, the current theory is more general and can be seen to include the former as a derivation. In practice, the former provided much of the stimulus for the latter in the form of working assumptions that needed exploration

Parts of this chapter closely follow an earlier statement of the theory in J. C. Turner (1985) Social categorization and the self-concept: A social cognitive theory of group behaviour. In E. J. Lawler (ed.), *Advances in Group Processes*. Greenwich, Conn.: JAI Press, vol. 2.

and the then as yet relatively unexamined concept of social identity. (In the intergroup theory the concept is only one of several important ideas that function as building blocks for the causal hypotheses – originally, for example, the central insight was that intergroup comparisons led to mutual differentiation and not convergence as in intragroup comparisons.) It is unfortunate in some ways that two such closely related theories should have similar names but also useful and understandable in terms of their origin, and now in any case the labels seem irretrievably to have stuck.

The self-categorization theory takes the form of a series of assumptions leading to hypotheses as to the basic process underlying the psychological group and elaborative hypotheses as to the antecedents and consequences of that process. The general theory of the group process forms a basis for the derivation of 'intermediate' sub-theories of the main group phenomena such as attraction, co-operation and influence (these are the phenomena discussed here, but additional sub-theories are possible, e.g., of altruism, emotional contagion, etc.). These sub-theories are the more detailed analyses of the particular consequences of group formation. In turn, they can be applied to even more specific problems in their field, yielding a third level of theorizing.

It is important to produce not only a unifying, general theory of the group, but also to show that it is non-vacuous, that it can generate distinctive, predictive and testable solutions to existing problems as well as new insights. For this reason, the development of the general theory went hand in hand with its detailed application to one concrete area, that of social influence, and as a criterion of its practical research usefulness in this area a commitment was made to determine whether the derived sub-theory could successfully explain the phenomenon of group polarization. The latter issue was chosen because reviewers in the area themselves admit that it has proved extremely difficult to explain elegantly and heuristically with current concepts, and perhaps because of this the topic is a good illustration of the theoretical divisions in social influence research. Thus an explanation of group polarization would show the power of the sub-theory in solving a long-standing conundrum (and a non-obvious finding) and unifying two branches of research, and this in turn would testify to the usefulness and plausibility of the general theory. In this chapter we shall present the general analysis of the group and its applications to social attraction and co-operation, and in the next the intermediate theory of social influence and its explanation of group polarization.

General assumptions and hypotheses of the self-categorization theory

Assumptions

The most basic assumptions are widely shared in social psychology. These are:

A.1 That the self-concept is the cognitive component of the psychological system or process referred to as the self. The self may be understood at least in part as a cognitive structure, a cognitive element in the information-processing system. The self-concept may be defined as the set of cognitive representations of self available to a person.

A.2 That the self-concept comprises many different components. Any individual possesses multiple concepts of self. If there is unity at all, it is only in so far as the different cognitive representations form a cognitive system, but the parts are highly differentiated and can function relatively independently.

A.3 That the functioning of the social self-concept is situation-specific: particular self-concepts tend to be activated ('switched on') in specific situations producing specific self-images. Any particular self-concept (of those belonging to any given individual) tends to become salient (activated, cognitively prepotent, operative) as a function of an interaction between the characteristics of the perceiver and the situation (Bruner, 1957; Oakes, 1983). (It is useful to distinguish between the 'self-concept', the hypothetical cognitive structure which cannot be observed directly, and the 'self-image', the perceptual output, i.e., the subjective experience of self produced by the functioning of some part of that structure.)

The more distinctive assumptions of the theory are:

A.4 That cognitive representations of the self take the form, amongst others, of *self-categorizations*, i.e., cognitive groupings of oneself and some class of stimuli as the same (identical, similar, equivalent, interchangeable, and so on) in contrast to some other class of stimuli. (Self-concepts are categories and like all categories are based on the perception of intra-class similarities and inter-class differences between stimuli: see Bruner, 1957; Campbell, 1958; Rosch, 1978; Tajfel, 1969b, 1972a; Tversky and Gati, 1978).

A.5 That self-categorizations exist as part of a hierarchical system of classification. They form at different levels of abstraction related by means of class inclusion (in Rosch's, 1978, sense), i.e., the more inclusive the self-category, the higher the level of abstraction, and each category is entirely included within one other category (unless it is the highest or superordinate level category) but is not exhaustive of that more inclusive category. The level of abstraction of a self-categorization, therefore, refers to the degree of inclusiveness of the categories at that level.

Thus, for example, 'wooden chairs' and 'leather chairs' are members of and entirely included within the category of 'chair', but they are not exhaustive of it, since there are other kinds of chairs which are also members. 'Chairs' and 'tables' are categories at an intermediate level of inclusiveness, which are themselves members of the higher order category of 'furniture'. Rosch herself (1978, p. 32) provides the examples of 'white oak' and 'red oak', 'oak', and 'tree' as categories at the subordinate, intermediate and superordinate levels of abstraction respectively in the classification of trees.

A.6 That there are least three levels of abstraction of self-categorization important in the social self-concept: (a) the superordinate level of the self as human being, self-categorizations based on one's identity as a human being, the common features shared with other members of the human species in contrast to other forms of life, (b) the intermediate level of ingroup-outgroup categorizations based on social similarities and differences between human beings that define one as a member of certain social groups and not others (e.g., 'American', 'female', 'black', 'student', 'working class'), and (c) the subordinate level of per-. sonal self-categorizations based on differentiations between oneself as a unique individual and other ingroup members that define one as a specific individual person (e.g., in terms of one's personality or other kinds of individual differences). These levels can be said to define one's 'human', 'social' and 'personal' identity respectively, based on inter-species, intergroup (i.e., intra-species) and interpersonal (i.e., intragroup) comparisons between oneself and others.

Ingroup-outgroup categorizations are what have been referred to in chapter 2 as social categorizations, but from the perspective of an identifying member of one of the categories. They can also be described as ingroup or social identifications. Although this level of identity is referred to as 'social' because it reflects socially shared similarities and differences between people, there is no implication that the human and personal levels are not also social in terms of their content, origin and function.

More importantly, personal self-categorizations are not regarded here as having any privileged status in defining the self. They do not represent the 'true' individual self which in some way invests the other levels with their significance. The self-concept in social psychology is usually equated with the personal self, but it is fundamental to our assumption that this is incorrect and that the personal self reflects only one level of abstraction of self-categorization, of which more inclusive levels are just as valid and in some conditions more important.

There will tend to be numerous specific self-categorizations at each level of abstraction across and within both cultures and individuals. People have different ideas of what it means to be 'human', belong to a variety of social groups and focus on different dimensions of interpersonal comparison according to the context. Which self-category becomes salient at which level of abstraction is a function of an interaction between the characteristics of the person and the characteristics of the situation (assumption 3). And, of course, there can be finer gradations of self-categorization within the broad levels of inclusiveness distinguished above (e.g., at the social level there are national and supra-national ingroups and outgroups such as 'NATO', 'Europe', the 'West').

A.7 That self-categorizations at any level tend to form and become salient through comparisons of stimuli defined as members of the next more inclusive (higher level) self-category.

The assumption here is that categorization and comparison depend upon each other and neither can exist without the other: the division of stimuli into classes depends upon perceived similarities and differences (comparative relations), but stimuli can only be compared in so far as they have already been categorized as identical, alike, or equivalent at some higher level of abstraction, which in turn presupposes a prior process of comparison, and so on *ad infinitum* (at least logically if not psychologically). The assumption can be broken down into several parts:

A.7.1 That category formation (categorization) depends upon the comparison of stimuli and follows the *principle of meta-contrast*: that is, within any given frame of reference (in any situation comprising some definite pool of psychologically significant stimuli), any collection of stimuli is more likely to be categorized as an entity (i.e., grouped as identical) to the degree that the differences between those stimuli on relevant dimensions of comparison (intra-class differences) are perceived as less than the differences between that collection and other stimuli (inter-class differences). The *meta-contrast ratio* (following Campbell, 1958, in particular) is defined as the ratio of the average difference perceived between members of the category and the other stimuli (the mean inter-category difference) over the average difference perceived between members within the category (the mean intra-category difference) and provides a simple quantitative measure of the degree to which any subset of stimuli will tend to be cognized as a single unit, entity, or group (i.e., perceptually categorized). Correspondingly, the *prototypicality* of a category member (Rosch, 1978), the extent to which a stimulus is perceived as exemplary or representative of the category as a whole, is defined by means of the meta-contrast ratio of the mean perceived difference between the target stimulus and outgroup (different category) members over the mean perceived difference between the stimulus and other ingroup (same category) members (the higher the ratio, the more prototypical the ingroup member).

This assumption summarizes the basic ideas on category formation of Bruner (1957), Campbell (1958), Tajfel (1969b, 1972a), Rosch (1978) and Tversky and Gati (1978). They all stress the determining role of intra-class similarities and inter-class differences. However, the present assumption goes further in making clear that such similarities and differences are not independent and additive, but aspects of the same meta-contrast, a perceived difference between (intra- and inter-class) differences. The members of some group, it is assumed, are perceived as similar rather than different, although they are separable stimuli, only in relation to the meta-contrast which groups them as less different from or more similar to each other than they are to yet other people. The meta-contrast principle is explicit that category formation is relative to the frame of reference (the pool of psychologically relevant stimuli) and hence the available contrasts provided by the salient stimulus field, and depends not just on 'similarities' between stimuli, as is usually assumed, but on *relative* similarities, on *more* similarity (or less difference) between certain stimuli than between those and others. Strictly speaking, the perception of any degree of similarity between stimuli, it is argued, implies a meta-contrast, an implicit comparison with one or more other stimuli which function as an external standard for classifying the initial stimuli as similar.

A.7.2 That the comparison of different stimuli depends upon their categorization as identical (the same, similar) at a higher level of abstraction, and takes place on dimensions which define their higher level identity. A related point is that stimuli probably tend to be compared in terms of the least abstract category which includes them all.

Thus 'like' can only be compared with 'like' and in terms of common features and, paradoxically, the very perception of 'difference' (a comparative relation) implies a higher level identity in terms of which the comparison took place (see Festinger, 1954; Goethals and Darley, 1977; Suls and Miller, 1977). 'Apples' and 'oranges' can be compared as 'fruit' in terms of being more or less 'sweet', 'nutritious', 'hard to grow', and so on (dimensions applicable to all 'fruit'), but less usefully as 'forms of life' (too abstract) and not at all as 'lemons', 'animals', or 'types of citrus fruit' (things which they are all not), and the very fact that we perceive them as 'different' types of fruit implies their higher level similarity as 'fruit'.

Together assumptions 7.1 and 7.2 imply that the comparison of stimuli perceived as identical at some level yields perceived differences and meta-contrasts resulting in their division into classes at the next lower level of abstraction, and so on. They also imply that all social comparison with others depends upon the categorization of others as part of a self-category at some level of abstraction.

A.7.3 That personal self-categorizations are based upon comparisons between self and ingroup members (that interpersonal are intragroup comparisons), ingroup-outgroup categorizations upon comparisons with other human beings (that intergroup are intra-human comparisons) and human self-categorizations are based upon comparisons with other species in terms of some higher level identity.

A.7.4 That the salience of any level of self-categorization varies with the frame of reference. Self-categories tend to become salient at one level less abstract than the self-category in terms of which they are being compared (i.e., the personal self becomes salient where comparisons are restricted to ingroup members, ingroup membership(s) becomes salient where comparisons include both ingroup and outgroup members of the human self-category, and so on).

A.8 That the salience of a self-categorization leads to the perceptual accentuation of intra-class similarities and inter-class differences between people as their characteristics are inferred from the defining identity of their class membership (Tajfel, 1969b; Tajfel and Wilkes, 1963; see, too, Doise, 1978; Eiser and Stroebe, 1972; Wilder, 1984, provides some recent illustrative data). As the nature of the stimulus is deduced from its classification at a given level, there is a perceptual 'discounting' of the similarities between classes that exist at higher levels and the differences within classes that exist at lower levels, and the corresponding similarities and differences that exist in terms of alternative self-categorizations at the same level. Thus the salience of a self-categorization enhances the perceptual identity within and contrast between self- and nonself-categories at that level.

A.9 That there is, therefore, a *functional antagonism* between the salience of one level of self-categorization and other levels: the salience of one level produces the intra-class similarities and inter-class differences which reduce or inhibit the perception of the intra-class differences and inter-class similarities upon which lower and higher levels respectively are based.

Hypotheses

Three general hypotheses follow from the above assumptions:

H.1 That, therefore, all things being equal (and ignoring for simplicity the human level of self-categorization) *there tends to be an inverse relationship between the salience of the personal and social levels of self-categorization.* Social self-perception tends to vary along a continuum from the perception of self as a unique person (maximum intra-personal identity and maximum difference perceived between self and ingroup members) to the perception of the self as an ingroup category (maximum similarity to ingroup members and difference from outgroup members).

At the midpoint of this continuum (where self-perception is likely to be located much of the time) the individual will tend to define him- or herself as moderately different from ingroup members, who in turn will be perceived as moderately different from outgroup members. Personal self- and ingroup-outgroup categorizations, then, are not mutually exclusive. On the contrary, they will tend to operate simultaneously most of the time, but their perceptual effects are inversely related. The 'basic level' of social self-perception in Rosch's (1978) sense, therefore, the level of abstraction that tends to maximize similarities within and differences between categories, is not constant but is a variable defined by the inverse relationship between personal self-ingroup differences and ingroup-outgroup differences. At any given moment the similar-ities and differences between the person, ingroup and outgroup will vary and hence the appropriate level of abstraction (the one that maximizes cognitive simplicity, stability and consistency) will also vary, but what will remain constant is the cognitive tendency of intra-personal similarities and interpersonal differences to reduce the percep-tion of intragroup similarities and intergroup differences, and vice versa.

H.2 That factors which enhance the salience of ingroup-outgroup categorizations tend to increase the perceived identity (similarity, equivalence, interchangeability) between self and ingroup mem-bers (and difference from outgroup members) and so *depersonal-ize individual self-perception* on the stereotypical dimensions which define the relevant ingroup membership. *Depersonaliz-ation* refers to the process of 'self-stereotyping' whereby people come to perceive themselves more as the interchangeable exemp-lars of a social category than as unique personalities defined by their individual differences from others. And,

H.3 That the depersonalization of self-perception is the basic process underlying group phenomena (social stereotyping, group cohe-siveness, ethnocentrism, co-operation and altruism, emotional contagion and empathy, collective action, shared norms and social influence processes, etc.).

This last hypothesis summarizes the point of the whole theoretical argument: group behaviour is assumed to express a change in the level of abstraction of self-categorization in the direction which represents a depersonalization of self-perception, a shift towards the perception of self as an interchangeable exemplar of some social category and away from the perception of self as a unique person defined by individual differences from others. Depersonalization, however, is not a loss of individual identity, nor a loss or submergence of the self in the group (as in the concept of de-individuation), and nor any kind of regression to a more primitive or unconscious form of identity. It is the *change* from the personal to the social level of identity, a change in the nature and content of the self-concept corresponding to the functioning of self-perception at a more inclusive level of abstraction. In many respects depersonalization may be seen as a *gain* in identity, since it represents a mechanism whereby individuals may act in terms of the social similarities and differences produced by the historical development of human society and culture. The next sections discuss briefly the antecedents and some of the consequences of depersonalization in explanation of hypothesis 3.

Antecedent conditions of depersonalization

The formation of ingroup categories

The antecedents of depersonalization are the determinants of the formation and salience of ingroup-outgroup categorizations. The formation of ingroup membership has two aspects: (1) the problem of the *spontaneous* or *emergent* social categorization of people on the basis of similarities and differences perceived in the immediate situation, i.e., the problem of the 'on-the-spot' perceptual formation of social categories from individual stimuli (as when, for example, simple proximity turns people into a group), and (2) the *internalization* of some *preformed*, culturally available classification such as in terms of sex, nationality, class, occupation, religion, or race.

The hypothesis in respect of both aspects is:

H.4 That psychological group formation takes place to the degree that two or more people come to perceive and define themselves in terms of some shared ingroup-outgroup categorization.

Emergent group formation is hypothesized to follow the meta-contrast principle:

H.5 That any collection of individuals in a given setting is more likely to categorize themselves as a group (become a psychological group) to the degree that the subjectively perceived differences between them are less than the differences perceived between them and other people (psychologically) present in the setting (i.e.,

as the ratio of intergroup to intragroup differences increases).
(These comparisons will be made on relevant dimensions selected
from the common features of the self-category that includes all
those being compared.)

The most distinctive feature of the hypothesis is the assertion of the
importance of the perceptual identity of people in the sense of their
forming a cognitive unit or perceptual category and the rejection of
interpersonal interdependence for need satisfaction as the basis of
group formation (and attraction). There is a mass of supportive data.
For example, there is evidence that 'cognitive unit-forming' relations
such as the perceived similarity of others to self in attitudes and values,
proximity and social contact, sharing a common fate or being in the
same boat, shared outcomes (success or failure on a joint task), shared
threat, a common enemy, and so on (e.g., Dion, 1979; Heider, 1958;
Hornstein, 1972; Lott and Lott, 1965; Sole, Marton and Hornstein,
1975; Turner, 1981b, 1982; Worchel, 1985) are fundamental determinants of group cohesion. Ingroup-outgroup differences, intergroup
conflict and competition (variables likely to produce a strong meta-
contrast between ingroup and outgroup) are known to have a powerful
positive impact on intragroup solidarity, morale and mutual acceptance between members (e.g., Blake and Mouton, 1961; Brewer, 1979;
Deutsch, 1949b; Dion, 1979; Fiedler, 1967; Hensley and Duval, 1976;
Kalin and Marlowe, 1968; Oakes, 1983; Sherif, 1967; Turner, 1981b).
It is also known that the different reference groups to which any
individual belongs tend to become psychologically important in different settings: in other words, ingroup membership and its effects have a
'contextual' basis, are situation-specific – just as one would expect if
the salient ingroup membership was a function of and so varied with
the available social comparisons (Boyanowsky and Allen, 1973;
Minard, 1952; see chapter 6). A recent study by Wilder and Shapiro
(1984) demonstrated this point very clearly: they found that by varying
the available outgroup different social identities became salient and
brought into play different social norms. Finally, of course, there are
the data already cited showing that imposing social categorizations
upon people in the absence of other social relations (and outside the
laboratory that the 'external designation' of people as members of some
social category, Cartwright and Zander, 1968, p. 56) is sufficient for
ingroup bias and group cohesion (Turner, 1984; see chapter 5).

The self-categorization theory has as yet little that is especially
distinctive to say about the internalization of preformed ingroup-
outgroup categorizations. If, as seems reasonable, one conceptualizes

the self-concept as a system of self-attitudes, and self-categorizations as the cognitive component of that system, then the problem of internalization may be regarded as in essence a problem of attitude change. That is, it can be hypothesized that people change their social definitions of themselves in the same way that they change their other beliefs and attitudes. It may be supposed, therefore, that changes in self-definition will tend to follow the established empirical laws of attitude change and social influence (see Gergen, 1971). Thus the primary modes by which people internalize group memberships are likely to be (1) simply as a result of persuasive communications from credible, prestigious, or attractive others (or in the terms of the present theory, from others with whom they identify), and (2) on the basis of public behaviour as group members leading to private self-attitude change.

Two experiments (Turner, Hogg, Oakes and Smith, 1984) were conducted to test the latter hypothesis. A major prediction of the interdependence theory is that group members should become more cohesive to the degree that group membership is associated with rewards and less cohesive to the extent that it mediates costs or deprivations (Lott and Lott, 1965). There is much evidence, however, that groups which experience failure or defeat and therefore mediate negative outcomes for members can under certain circumstances become more cohesive. Turner et al. proposed that need satisfaction is not a necessary condition for group formation and hypothesized that under conditions of group failure and defeat and high personal responsibility for one's actions (i.e., where the self is strongly invested in the action and the action is internally attributed to the self) members will tend to identify more with their group (define themselves more as group members) in order to explain and justify their actions (i.e., behaviour leading to negative outcomes). In other words, just as one may infer one's attitudes from one's public behaviour (a self-attribution process) – especially to the degree that it is costly and rewards cannot provide an alternative explanation of the action – or change one's attitudes in order to justify some negatively valued action (a dissonance-reduction process), so one may identify with a group, change one's self-definition, to make sense of and justify public behaviour as a group member which has negative outcomes.

Specifically, they predicted that under conditions of high personal responsibility ingroup identification would be enhanced more by costs than rewards associated with group membership, but that the opposite would be found under conditions of low personal responsibility (here the subjects would simply tend to identify more with a positively valued group). They assumed that ingroup identification would produce intragroup cohesion (in line with the hypotheses presented below). The results supported these predictions. In the first study, group members with high choice about continuing with a group task became more cohesive after failure than success on the task, whereas the opposite was the case under low choice. In the second study, people who committed themselves to their group membership became more cohesive after defeat than victory in an intergroup competition, but more attracted to their group after victory than defeat if they had not made such a commitment. There was some interesting suggestions, too, in line with the identification interpretation that self-esteem varied with intragroup cohesiveness. Apart from confirming that mutual need satisfaction in the form of success or victory on group tasks is not necessary for group formation and cohesion, these studies illustrate how existing knowledge of attitude change processes (specifically derived here from attribution and cognitive dissonance research) can be employed to explain the internalization of pre-formed ingroup-outgroup categorizations. Nevertheless, a fully adequate treatment of this issue must await a systematic review and integration of research on attitude change, the self-concept and identity and social categorization.

The salience of self-categories

Whereas group formation refers to the formation and internalization of self-defining social categorizations, the issue of salience refers to the conditions under which some specific group membership becomes cognitively prepotent in self-perception to act as the immediate influence on perception and behaviour. The two are related but not the same. An individual who defines him- or herself as an 'Australian', for example, may never think about nationality for days at a time, yet if that self-definition did not exist as a latent identity, it could hardly become salient in relevant settings (e.g., Waddell and Cairns, 1986). Oakes (see chapter 6) has recently discussed and researched the salience problem in some detail and what follows will summarize some of her main conclusions.

It can be hypothesized (adapting Bruner, 1957):

H.6 That the salience of some ingroup-outgroup categorization in a specific situation is a function of an interaction between the 'relative accessibility' of that categorization for the perceiver and the 'fit' between the stimulus input and category specifications.

Thus, given two equally 'fitting' categories, the more 'accessible' one will become salient and, given two equally 'accessible' categories, the one that better 'fits' the perceptual data will become salient. In general, salience depends upon both accessibility and fit. Accessibility is defined as 'the readiness with which a stimulus input with given properties will be coded or identified in terms of a category' (Bruner, 1957, p. 133): the more accessible the category the less input required to invoke the relevant categorization, the wider the range of stimulus characteristics that will be perceived as congruent with category specifications and the more likely that other less accessible categories which also fit stimulus input will be masked. Two major determinants of accessibility are past learning of what tends to go with what in the environment, its 'redundant structure', and the person's current motives. So, for example, given equal fit, people would be more ready to perceive somebody as 'French' if they were in Paris (learned expectations about the environment) and were looking for a French person (current motives).

The idea of fit simply refers to the degree to which reality actually matches the criteria which define the category. For example, a person would not be perceived as 'French' if he or she did not look, speak, or act in the ways the perceiver stereotypically defines as 'French'. Oakes (1983) defines and measures fit as the degree to which the similarities and differences perceived between people or their actions correlate with some classification (Tajfel, 1969b). This is identical with the idea of meta-contrast proposed here (assumption 7): of the various ways of categorizing the same people in a setting (e.g., 'male/female', 'black/white') that categorization will become salient which is associated with the largest meta-contrast ratio (which maximizes perceived inter-category differences and minimizes intra-category differences). It is also closely related to Rosch's (1978) concepts of 'cue validity' and the 'basic level' of categorization (the level which maximizes the intra-category similarities) except that, as here, the basic level of categorization of social interaction is assumed to be variable across social contexts.

Two important features of social category memberships are that the degree of internalization of or identification with an ingroup-outgroup membership, the centrality and evaluative importance of a group membership in self-definition, is a major determinant of accessibility, and that fit has a normative content (i.e., behaviour must be in line with the stereotypical norms that define the category: 'radicals' do not just behave differently from 'policemen', they do so in a definite, appropriate, political direction). There is good evidence, for example, that prejudiced people (for whom being 'white', say, is very important) are readier to categorize in racial terms than the unprejudiced, but that this depends as much on the actions or expressed attitudes of others as on their physical characteristics (see Brown and Turner, 1981; Tajfel, 1972a; and, in particular, Boyanowsky and Allen, 1973, for a nice demonstration of the interaction between perceiver prejudice and the behavioural and task context in determining salient racial categorization). Thus Oakes (1983) restricts the concept of fit to the degree of correlation between social behaviour and group membership in a *normatively consistent direction*.

There is a large literature on the empirical determinants of social category membership salience and Oakes concludes from her review of this literature and her own experimental research (see chapter 6) that there is good support for the interactional hypothesis above. One limitation is that most data concern the perception of others rather than the perception of self as group member. However, there are some studies demonstrating variations in the salience of group memberships in self-perception (e.g., Dion Earn and Yee, 1978; Hogg and Turner, 1987; Oakes and Davidson, 1986). There are likely to be at least some overt differences in the perception of self and others – e.g., a tendency to attribute more positive traits to the former – but it seems unlikely that this will imply a fundamentally different underlying process (as opposed to merely a difference in the antecedent variables governing operation of the process).

The consequences of depersonalization

The consequences of depersonalization are hypothesized to be the various phenomena of group behaviour. The application of the self-categorization theory to such phenomena requires explanation of how they may be derived from the depersonalization process. Sub-theories of, for example, group cohesion, social co-operation and influence need to be developed consistent with existing empirical generalizations but also productive of distinctive, testable predictions and clearly derived from the depersonalization process. This is a very large task since all of these so-called sub-areas are research fields in their own right, with their own theories, bodies of data and particular issues. The strategy followed here is, first, in the remainder of this chapter, to illustrate the basic ideas of the application of the theory to the phenomena of social attraction and co-operation. Secondly, in the next chapter, to present the sub-theory which has been at the forefront of our preoccupations and that has been developed in most detail, that of social influence, and, by deriving from it an analysis and explanation of group polarization, to show its integrative and predictive value and by implication that of the general theory too. Thirdly, the next four chapters will look at particular traditions of theorizing and research from the perspective of the theory and present illustrative empirical work directly stimulated by it.

Group cohesion, interpersonal attraction and ethnocentrism

Group cohesion is defined for present purposes as mutual attraction between ingroup members, ethnocentrism as ingroup members' positive evaluation of the group as a whole and interpersonal attraction as favourable attitudes towards an individual person (including one's personal self) or towards people as unique, differentiated persons. Attraction, 'liking', etc., are all employed specifically to indicate positive attitudes towards others in the sense of evaluations rather than emotional or affective states (Lalljee, Brown and Ginsburg, 1984), i.e., they represent appraisal from the perspective of social norms and values. Also, no causal distinction is made between attraction to others and self-evaluations: it is assumed that the self is evaluated at some level (resulting in high or low self-esteem) by the same process that leads to liking or disliking for others.

The basic hypothesis is that people are evaluated positively to the degree that they are perceived as prototypical of the self-category in terms of which they are being compared. It is assumed:

A.10 That self-categories tend to be evaluated positively and that there are motivational pressures to maintain this state of affairs.

A.11 That self and others are evaluated through a process of social comparison in terms of their membership of the (relevant) next more inclusive self-category.

A.12 That, therefore, self and others are evaluated positively to the degree that they are perceived as prototypical (representative, exemplary, etc.) of the next more inclusive (positively valued) self-category (in terms of which they are being compared).

The hypothesis will seem more familiar in the language of the 'ideal self'. In essence it is being proposed that in any specific setting where some evaluation of self and others is taking place one's ideal self is the most prototypical instance of the positive self-category in terms of which people are being compared, and that attraction to others is a direct function of their perceived similarity to one's ideal self in that specific situation. Thus if one is evaluating some individual colleague at work, one might tend to evaluate him or her in terms of the shared self-category of 'colleague'. In which case, assuming that 'colleague' is a positively valued category, that individual will be perceived as an attractive person and liked to the degree that he or she is perceived to approximate one's ideal collague, i.e., is a better colleague than others. Alternatively, somebody may be comparatively derogated as 'not acting like a colleague'. Or, suppose one is confronted with an out-group member, a member of some negatively valued nonself-category (at one level of abstraction), a 'bureaucrat' for example, then the same principle applies: to the degree that he or she is perceived as proto-typical of the negatively valued outgroup (which is in effect the same as being perceived as unrepresentative of the higher order self-category which includes both ingroup and outgroup), then he or she will be disliked.

There is an infinite regress in this derivation of an individual's value in that a person is evaluated positively to the degree that he or she approximates the ideal member of a positive group; one's ingroup is evaluated positively to the degree that it is assumed to be prototypical of one's positively valued definition of humanity, and even one's attitude to humanity may be conditioned by the extent to which it lives up to some more abstract ideal. This does not mean that people cannot evaluate themselves or ingroup members negatively. On the contrary, one's personal self may compare unfavourably with other ingroup members in terms of a positively valued ingroup self-category, and some ingroup category may be perceived less favourably than some outgroup in terms of one's definition of ideal human beings. Or some ingroup may be perceived as less prototypical of and thus compare favourably in terms of a negatively valued superordinate category. For example, one may be ashamed of one's countrymen and women during war in terms of one's beliefs about what is appropriate behaviour for human beings, just as one may be proud that at least one's country is not as bad as some others in its lack of social morality, and so on. All the various discrepancies between levels in the evaluation of self and others are possible. In any specific instance what matters is the value of the prototype that is being used as the standard: one likes people that represent positive categories or that are less representative of negative categories.

However, it *is* assumed that negative self-evaluation is an aversive motivational state which instigates psychological activity to restore self-esteem and that by and large self-categories do tend to be positive (and are probably more likely to be so the more superordinate they are). Why this should be so can be explained speculatively in many ways, but it can suffice simply to note that it has long been recognized that the concept of 'value' is bound up with the very nature of 'self' (e.g., Sherif, 1936). The present theory suggests that there is a real sense in which the 'valuing' of oneself or others as positive or negative is much the same thing as appraising the degree to which they are 'self' or 'not self' at some higher level of abstraction. It is not suggested that all comparison need be in terms of self-categorization and be self-referring, but it is suggested that, to the degree that it is not, it will cease to be evaluative (although the link between the evaluative connotations of some comparative judgement and self-identity will often be indirect and implicit). This general perspective will become clearer as it is related to the different forms of attraction.

It follows directly from the nature of depersonalization that the salience of an ingroup-outgroup categorization increases the mutually perceived prototypicality of ingroup members on the stereotypcial dimensions defining the ingroup category. Therefore, to the degree that the ingroup category is positively valued, it will increase mutual attraction between members. It is hypothesized:

H.7 That group cohesion or mutual attraction between ingroup members is a function of mutually perceived similarity (identity) between self and others in terms of the defining characteristics of the ingroup self-category.

H.8 That group cohesion is produced and increased by factors which lead to the formation and salience of shared ingroup memberships.

Some supportive evidence (see Lott and Lott, 1965) is that the perceived similarity of others to self in terms of attitudes, values, goals, experiences and explicit group membership is probably the most powerful single determinant of attraction yet identified. Experimentally manipulated attraction to others is found to lead to the perception or assumption that they are similar to oneself and in particular to one's ideal self. Also, as would be expected from the hypothesis that attraction follows from shared group memberships, liking tends to reciprocal: it appears that one identifies with people who like oneself – perhaps because this in itself will normally imply at least one shared attitude. And, as already noted, other variables likely to induce perceptual unit formation such as proximity and social interaction, common fate, common goals, or simply perceiving oneselves as 'belonging together' are reliable determinants of intragroup cohesion. The meta-contrast between groups implied by intergroup competition and conflict has the predicted effect on intragroup attraction. The social categorization of people into groups in isolation from other variables leads to mutual attraction (even where their personal characteristics are unknown) and attraction to others has been shown to increase as a function of contexts which make shared reference groups salient (e.g., Boyanowsky and Allen, 1973; Burnstein and McRae, 1962; Feshbach and Singer, 1957; Minard, 1952), while group formation can reverse patterns of friendship based on personal attractiveness (Sherif, 1967).

As group cohesion reflects shared prototypicality, so interpersonal attraction and personal self-esteem follow perceived differences in or the relative prototypicality of ingroup members. It is assumed that group cohesion (shared mutual liking between members) and interpersonal attraction (liking for members in terms of their individual differences, the evaluation of a member as superior or inferior to others) are conceptually distinct forms of attraction that co-exist within a social group predominating according to the relative salience of ingroup-outgroup and interpersonal categorizations. It is hypothesized:

H.9   That the attractiveness of specific individual persons (including one's personal self) depends upon their perceived prototypicality in comparison with other ingroup members (relative proto-typicality).

H.10 That the personal attractiveness of an individual is not constant, but varies with the ingroup membership providing the frame of reference, the defining dimensions of ingroup membership employed for interpersonal comparison and the specific others with whom the person is compared.

Where outgroup members are compared, they tend to be personally less attractive to the degree that they are relatively prototypical of a negatively valued outgroup (or less prototypical of a positively valued, more inclusive self-category). Evidence for hypothesis 9 is provided by data that people are more attracted to ingroup members perceived as better than their fellows in some way relevant to or important for the group – such as in terms of relative status or prestige, valued personality traits, their relative success, correctness, or competence in some group task or activity, and in general the degree to which they conform to group norms and role expectations (Lott and Lott, 1965). It is important to note that relative prototypicality in this context is primarily to do with the extent to which one's behaviour is normative for the group (i.e., conforms to or exemplifies some valued, stereotypical characteristic of ingroup membership) rather than simply having some physical or formal attribute. Terms such as 'success', 'competence' and 'correctness' do not indicate any concrete set of behaviours. They are value judgements, made by the group of the degree to which a member or the actions of members conform to its norms of activity, belief, or attitude. The assumption that conformity to or deviation from attributes and actions perceived by the group as ideal, appropriate, or desirable is a major determinant of the receipt of attraction and approval or rejection has been unquestioned in the conformity field since its inception.

Support for hypothesis 10 is provided by the studies already cited demonstrating different patterns of acceptance of others as a function of the reference group context and also by findings of variation in personal self-esteem as a function of the comparative context (Gergen, 1971) and in the evaluation of others according to group activities (e.g., Sherif, 1967, reports that a boy previously derogated as a bully by his group became more popular and gained in prestige for the very same physical talents once the stage of intergroup conflict began). These hypotheses reject the idea of intrinsically rewarding or attractive personalities and the very notion of the perception of personality as a constant. They argue that the perception of an individual's personality in a given setting (their distinctive personal characteristics) is largely determined by interpersonal comparisons made on situationally relevant dimensions of the ingroup membership(s) defining the frame of reference (see chapter 6).

Ethnocentrism is explained similarly to interpersonal attraction but at one level of self-categorization higher. It is hypothesized:

H.11 That ethnocentrism, attraction to one's own group as a whole, depends upon the perceived prototypicality of the ingroup in comparison with relevant outgroups (relative prototypicality) in terms of the valued superordinate self-category that provides the basis for the intergroup comparison.

H.12 That the attractiveness of some ingroup is not constant but varies with the superordinate self-category that provides the frame of reference for intergroup comparison, the specific dimensions of intergroup comparison employed and the specific outgroups with whom the ingroup is compared.

Ethnocentrism and group cohesiveness, therefore, are different sides of the same coin. One refers to the value of the ingroup perceived by members in comparison with outgroups and the other to ingroup members' mutual attraction on the basis of the value of shared ingroup membership. Ethnocentrism is not intended in a necessarily pejorative sense – it is merely the equivalent of personal self-esteem at the level of the ingroup self-category. Evidence for these hypotheses is provided by research on the social identity theory of intergroup behaviour (e.g., Brewer and Kramer, 1985; Brown, 1984; Tajfel, 1978, 1982a, 1982b; Turner and Giles, 1981b). This theory, it will be recalled, proposes that attraction to (a positive evaluation of) one's group and therefore a positive social identity is a function of its positive distinctiveness from other groups. The concept of 'positive distinctiveness' is equivalent to the relative prototypicality of the ingroup on valued dimensions of intergroup comparison. Since we have hypothesized that people are motivated to maintain a positive self-evaluation and that this is a function of their relative prototypicality at any given level of self-other comparison, it may also be assumed that there is a general tendency to seek positive distinctiveness for oneself at any salient level of self-categorization, i.e., to create and enhance favourable differences between oneself and ingroup members where intragroup differences comprise the frame of reference, between ingroup and outgroup where intra-human differences comprise the frame of reference and so on (Espinoza and Garza, 1985, and Sachdev and Bourhis, 1984, for example, show how variations in the salience of ingroup-outgroup categorizations, manipulated by majority-minority relations in both studies, can affect the level of competitive intergroup behaviour).

Two final hypotheses relate the different forms of attraction:

H.13   That the more salient is some relevant ingroup-outgroup categorization, the less will self-esteem and attraction to ingroup members reflect individuals' relative personal status within the group and the more they will reflect the relative status of the ingroup compared to the outgroup.

H.14   That, therefore, interpersonal attraction and group cohesion tend to be inversely related in the sense that the perception and evaluation of ingroup members in terms of their personal differences works against mutual attraction based on the mutual perception of identity as group members (and vice versa).

The latter hypothesis does not mean that specific individuals will necessarily be evaluated differently as the frame of reference changes – changes from an intra- to an intergroup frame of reference will most affect the evaluation of low status members of high status groups and high status members of low status groups. Relative status is a further term for positive distinctiveness, i.e., any positive comparative difference between individuals (personality differences, prestige, popularity) or groups (power, wealth, success). The point of hypothesis 14 is that as some shared group membership decreases in salience and intragroup comparisons tend to replace intergroup comparisons, so attraction within the (sociological) group should tend to become less mutually positive and more one-sidedly related to a hierarchy of personal popularity. Some relevant data are that intergroup conflict and competition produce positive attitudes to ingroup members who, as individual persons, have played a negative and detrimental role in the group (e.g., Fiedler, 1967; Kalin and Marlowe, 1968; Myers, 1962; Sherif, 1967) and the general fact of the distinction between interpersonal attitudes and attraction to the group (Brown and Turner, 1981; Cartwright, 1968).

The self-categorization analysis, therefore, appears compatible with much current evidence. One problem is that many of the same data are often cited as support for the need satisfaction theory of attraction. In fact, however, when one looks carefully at the latter interpretation, one finds that it tends either to be tautological or to be based on data where need satisfaction is confounded with shared group membership and conformity to group norms. It tends to be assumed *a priori* that any 'attractive' characteristic, person, or event must be rewarding in the sense of satisfying a need, but there is usually no independent attempt to show that a specific need has been satisfied and has resulted in the attractiveness of the satisfying state of affairs. Thus the need satisfaction explanation is often circular: an individual is said to demonstrate 'competence', 'intelligence', etc. – which in fact are already positive value judgements – and hence is 'liked', because these traits are 'attractive'; they are attractive because these things, it is claimed, help us to satisfy our needs, which can be inferred from the fact that they are 'rewarding', 'likeable' attributes. One begins with a positive evaluation and infers one's explanation from what has to be explained.

In addition, there is an untenable equation (or confusion) between the process of *social evaluation*, i.e., of social approval and disapproval, of appraisal from the perspective of one's values and *liking* some stimulus in the specific sense of *needing* it. These are not the same: one may like something at the same time that one disapproves of it and positively value something that one does not like. A sexual deviant or alcoholic, for example, may disapprove of their own needs and the things and people which satisfy them (and in this sense are liked); one may approve of hard work, but find it singularly unattractive. It cannot be assumed, therefore, that one 'values' people or things which satisfy one's needs – this must be demonstrated. The problem of social attraction (and social attitudes in general) is fundamentally the problem of attributing 'value' to people.

At this point it may be useful to return to the issue of whether interpersonal attraction is sufficient for group formation. In one sense it should now be clear that the idea of interpersonal attraction producing group formation is a contradiction in terms, since the former implies the salience of personal differences between people. However, all forms of social attraction are assumed to derive directly or indirectly from identification and shared group membership and so imply the existence of some ingroup category which can rapidly be brought into salience. Theoretically speaking, manipulations of 'interpersonal' attraction are often no such thing, but rather the manipulation of some variable which informs subjects that they will find some group or collection of people attractive or that they and some partner will be mutually attractive. In other words, empirical manipulations often emphasize that attraction between two or more subjects is shared and mutual in contrast with their relations to others. From the perspective of self-categorization theory such operationalizations are much the same as implicitly putting people into a group or calling attention to a shared group membership. Putting the issue practically, therefore, it can be said that attraction to others (in the widest sense) *is* a sufficient condition for group formation and belongingness, if only because such attraction will always be associated with, induce, or imply the perception of identity or similarity between oneself and the attractive others. What self-categorization theory denies is that attraction could be shown to produce group formation where it was demonstrably unconfounded by a process of self-other identification.

The most distinctive theoretical feature of the self-categorization analysis of group formation and cohesion is the idea that they depend upon the perception of self and others as a cognitive unit in contrast to yet others within the psychological frame of reference and not upon mutual interpersonal attraction and need satisfaction. To close this section some distinctive empirical predictions are derived from this view:

1 that (as in the social categorization paradigm) neither mutual need satisfaction nor interpersonal attraction are necessary conditions for group formation and cohesion;

2 that shared deprivations, costs, or frustrations (as well as the shared experience of rewards and gratifications) may provide a basis for perceived identity and hence mutual attraction between people;

3 that salient ingroup membership and, therefore, cohesion have a situational or contextual basis, varying with the psychological frame of reference (the pool of relevant comparable others) and the available meta-contrasts between people on relevant dimensions of comparison;

4 that interpersonal attraction and the very perception of personality are derivative of reference group membership and also vary with the reference group context;

5 that mutual attraction between people is sufficient for group formation in the sense that it will always tend to be associated with, imply, or induce some degree of perceived similarity between self and others; and

6 that the satisfaction of a need by others unconfounded with shared identity and conformity to shared norms (an example might be the forced feeding of a political prisoner on hunger strike by prison authorities) will not produce attraction to the others.

Social co-operation

The explanation of co-operation is a much simpler business. To the degree that the self is depersonalized, so too is self-interest. It may be hypothesized:

H.15 That the perception of identity between oneself and ingroup members leads to a perceived identity of interests in terms of the needs, goals and motives associated with ingroup membership.

Such an identity of interests may be assumed to imply (1) an empathic altruism whereby the goals of other ingroup members are perceived as one's own (Hornstein, 1972), and (2) an empathic trust whereby other ingroup members are assumed to share one's own goals. It is suggested that intragroup co-operation will follow from the shared and mutual perception by ingroup members of their interests as interchangeable. In consequence, it is proposed:

H.16 That factors which tend to enhance the salience of shared ingroup memberships will tend to increase the level of intragroup co-operation (and intergroup competition).

H.17 That factors which tend to personalize or individuate intragroup relations (or lead to the categorization of others as outgroup members) will decrease mutual co-operation (and increase inter-personal competition).

Factors likely to personalize intragroup relations are those which lead ingroup members to feel private, isolated, separate, distant, anonymous, different, and so on. Those likely to increase co-operation are, as we know, similarity, common fate, proximity, social interaction, intergroup competition, reduced social distance, and so forth. The earlier review demonstrates that by and large the evidence fits these hypotheses extremely well. They also make some interesting distinctive predictions. For example, it is argued that social co-operation reflects not an interdependence of separate, personal self-interests, but a cognitive redefinition of self and self-interest and hence has a strong element of altruism, and that the effect of anonymity is often to privatize and hence personalize and not to de-individuate as is usually supposed (in other words, that it is individuation rather than de-individuation which decreases the level of co-operation, see Colman, 1982). Some recent evidence that, as hypothesized, increasing the salience of a shared social identification raises the level of social co-operation (in a commons dilemma paradigm) is provided by Kramer and Brewer (1984).

Conclusion

Three metatheoretical points about the self-categorization theory may be noted. First, it demonstrates that the postulate that psychological processes belong only to individuals is fully compatible with the idea of a psychological discontinuity between individuals acting as 'individuals' and as group members. Group behaviour is psychologically different from and irreducible to interpersonal relationships and yet this need involve no metaphysical notions of a group mind. If the theory proves valid, then the group has *psychological reality* in the sense that there is a specific psychological process, a self-categorization or self-grouping process, which corresponds to and underlies the distinctive features of group behaviour.

Secondly, it is not being argued that groups are purely psychological or that group behaviour is primarily a product of psychological causes. On the contrary, groups are social phenomena that require social analysis (with distinctive contributions from many sciences from biology to history). The self-categorization theory is intended only as a contribution to understanding the social psychological basis of group behaviour. Moreover, the social psychological structures implicated, ingroup-outgroup categorizations in the self-concept, are themselves reflections and products of social activity; they depend upon social processes just as we have argued that some forms of social behaviour depend upon them (Turner and Giles, 1981a). In Asch's phrase, the social self-concept is a socially structured field in the mind of the individual.

Thirdly, there is a long tradition in social psychology which regards group functioning as a regression to more primitive, irrational, or instinctual forms of behaviour. Terms for group phenomena with derogatory connotations include 'de-individuation', 'diffusion of responsiblity', 'risky shift', 'group think', 'conformity', 'prejudice' (for negative intergroup attitudes), 'group pressure' and 'stereotyping'. The self-categorization theory takes a different view: it sees ingroup identification as an adaptive social-cognitive process that makes pro-social relations such as social cohesion, co-operation and influence (unity of action and attitudes) possible. It is assumed that acting solely in terms of one's personal uniqueness is not an unalloyed good, and that the psychological group is precisely the adaptive mechanism that frees human beings from the restrictions of and allows them to be more than just individual persons.

4

The Analysis of Social Influence

Introduction

The dominant theory of informational influence was outlined in chapter 2. It will be recalled that the basic ideas are that people depend on others for information to reduce uncertainty, that uncertainty is a direct product of the objective ambiguity of the stimulus situation, and that people are influenced (move towards others) in so far as others' responses are perceived to provide valid evidence about reality.

Some of the important predictions of the theory are that people conform more to similar others (with whom they are more likely to compare) and to expert, competent, or credible others (people likely to possess and who can be trusted to transmit valid information), that conformity increases with stimulus ambiguity, task difficulty, or complexity, and with any other factor likely to increase the subjective uncertainty of the person or their informational dependence on the group (e.g., their lack of ability, previous failure, low self-esteem).

The other major process of social influence in the current view is that of normative influence or conformity to others' expectations to gain social approval and avoid rejection, i.e., public compliance for extrinsic rewards and to avoid costs rather than because one is concerned with the content of the influence attempt. It is assumed that the power of others (their capacity to mediate rewards and costs for one) creates a need for their social approval and a fear of their disapproval, that this need comes into play under conditions of surveillance by the others, i.e., where one's actions are public and identifiable, and hence that, under such conditions, one will tend to develop a fear of being different and comply with their positive expectations ('group pressure').

The main predictions of this process are of increased conformity to the degree that one is interdependent with or attracted to others (more dependent for rewards and desirous of approval), that one acts publicly and so can be held responsible for one's actions, that pressures are clearly communicated and nonconformity liable to attract sanction and in so far as any factor enhances the normative dependence of the person on the group (e.g., attraction to group goals, insecurity, fear of rejection).

The predictions of these two processes have received extensive support (Allen, 1965, 1975; Allen and Wilder, 1977). Several variables, however, can be interpreted as increasing conformity through both processes (e.g., the degree of group cohesiveness) and there has long been suspicion that there is a certain amount of redundancy in the two-process formulation. Nevertheless, the distinction between informational and normative influence has remained for three seemingly immovable reasons: to express and explain (1) the difference between private acceptance of influence and mere behavioural compliance, and the distinctive effects of (2) stimulus ambiguity and uncertainty on the former and (3) surveillance by the group on the latter.

Problems with the theory of informational dependence

The theory of informational dependence has generated so much apparently supportive research that it is often regarded as almost self-evidently true. Yet there are problems – even if we do not for the moment question the conventional interpretations of much of the data. First, the theory is individualistic in its implications (see Moscovici, 1976; Reicher,1982; Wetherell, 1983). It is important to be clear here that we are not saying that these were intended or would be explicitly endorsed by individual originators of or contributors to the theory. Still less are we seeking to undervalue the scientific importance of the ideas and research it has generated. On the contrary, this tradition of social influence research is surely one of social psychology's major achievements (and it will be seen that the self-categorization theory of influence is a direct development of it, and is no less so for being a critical development). The point of the following discussion is not to criticize the ideas or intentions of any individual theorist but the larger implications of the core theory as it exists or has come to exist as part of the consensual subculture of the science, and which, like it or not, play a role in the development of the science.

The individualistic tendencies of the theory (and the two-process conceptualization as a whole) may be summarized as follows. The basic distinction between the 'social/normative/group-based' and 'informational' aspects of influence (adhering to ingroup norms to maintain membership and facilitate movement to group goals is the essence of the normative process of influence) tends to equate the former with uninformative 'group pressure', 'compliance', or 'conformity' (as a blind, passive, irrational process) and imply a pervasive 'conformity conflict' between the (correct) individual and the (incorrect) group. Individual perception is assumed to have sovereign status, to be the primary, normal and most reliable method of achieving subjective validity. The 'physical' reality testing of Festinger (1950, 1954) is in effect individual perceptual testing and perception of the physical world is assumed to produce directly valid data because it is supposedly a directly individual activity. Social influence even in the restricted, non-normative form of informational influence is a secondary, substitute process that only comes into play as direct individual testing becomes difficult and is conceptualized as influence from others who act merely as technical extensions of one's individual sensory apparatus (like a pair of spectacles). Such influence is not, therefore, a 'group' process, but at best one of interpersonal 'averaging' in which individuals move towards each other as they exchange their separate, private stocks of wisdom – the whole, the social norm, arises from a summation of the individual parts and is not an emergent property. The latter idea is especially clear in the contrast made between 'averaging' and 'polarizing' effects in group decision-making where the former are equated with normal influence processes (see Singleton, 1979; Wetherell, 1983; Wetherell et al., 1985), but it is also evident in Kiesler and Kiesler's (1969, p. 26) statement that: 'Social influence, then, is a change in individuals induced by individuals', or Shaw's (1976, p. 11) definition of a group as 'two or more persons who are interacting with one another in such a manner that each person influences and is influenced by each other person'. Individuals are assumed to be persuasive by virtue of the (asocial) valid information they possess (e.g., majorities, leaders, experts, etc.) and recently, especially in polarization research, the validity of information is assumed to be an interactive property of informational content as it matches the perceiver's cognitive structures, and persuasion is seen as a function of the cognitive processing of information. Thus even the social element of informational influence has been reduced to an intra-individual cognitive process.

Throughout, individual perception is assumed to be primary, valid and normal, whereas social influence is secondary, unreliable, indirect, abnormal and coercive and is useful only in default and in so far as it functions as an extension of individual perception. It takes little effort to realize that such a one-sided picture of the social basis of cognition and subjective validity is implausible. For example, how could one understand in these terms the functioning of science as a social institution (a social-cultural process of 'knowing') and the interrelationship between the cumulative development of shared scientific knowledge and the activities of the individual researcher?

Secondly, there are major empirical problems. The theory has failed: (1) to deal adequately with the facts of minority influence (Moscovici, 1976; Mugny,1982), (2) to provide an elegant, heuristic explanation of group polarization (a refutation of the interpersonal averaging theory of norm formation), (3) to make sense of the distinctive features of social influence in crowds (Reicher, 1982, 1984a; see chapter 8), and (4) to account for the classic data from the Sherif (1936) and Asch (1952) conformity paradigms. With respect to the latter, we have argued that the Asch study refutes the hypothesis that subjective uncertainty reflects objective stimulus ambiguity and demonstrates that such uncertainty arises as a social product of disagreement between people. It was concluded from the discussion of this issue in chapter 2 that whereas the accepted theory is that stimulus ambiguity produces uncertainty, which leads to dependence on others for information, mutual influence and the formation of shared norms, and that social influence and the emergence of norms represent the beginning of group formation, the classic data actually imply that uncertainty is a social product of disagreement with people categorized as identical to self. The perception of others as an appropriate reference group for social comparison creates the shared expectations of agreement necessary for the arousal of uncertainty and mutual influence. The point was made that psychological group formation in these experiments seems to be at the beginning of the influence process, and seems to function as its precondition as much as its product (the similarities in beliefs, attitudes and values which are produced by social influence will, of course, reinforce existing and may tend to create new group affiliations).

In contrast to the informational dependence conception, the self-categorization theory of social influence specifies that the very possibility of influence depends upon the shared, social categorical nature of the self (i.e., psychological group formation) and that individual perception and consensual validation are functionally interdependent processes.

The self-categorization theory of social influence

The link between the depersonalization process and social influence is the idea that it is the social (and human) identity perceived between self and ingroup members which both leads people to tend to agree and also to expect to agree in their reactions to or judgement of the same stimulus situation. If, as in the well-known formula, behaviour is a function of an interaction between the person and the situation, then it also follows, in a collective version of the formula, that identical or similar people in an identical or similar situation should tend to display the same behaviour (social consensus, agreement, uniformity). It can be assumed that people have implicit, 'practical' knowledge of this 'collectivized' formula in the sense that they would perceive as cognitively inconsistent disagreement between themselves and others perceived as *identical in respects relevant to the making of the judgement* about some identical or shared stimulus situation (see the earlier explanation of the uncertainty and cognitive conflict experienced by Asch's subjects).

A second fundamental idea – taken from Kelley (1967) but also expressed by others including Asch (1952) and implicit in Festinger (1950) – is that social consensus or agreement leads to the external attribution of the shared response, i.e., a shared response is perceived to reflect some external, public invariance in the situation: it is perceived as *objectively* required, correct, valid, demanded, appropriate, etc. (there is a whole plethora of terms for describing the property of a response of providing evidence about objective reality). From this perspective the social influence process (as embodied in the phenomena of social conformity, persuasion, group polarization, minority influence, etc.) is believed to originate in the need of people to reach agreement with others perceived as 'interchangeable' in respect of relevant attributes (psychological ingroup members in the given situation) about the same stimulus situation in order to validate their responses as correct, appropriate and desirable (reflecting the requirements of the objective situation rather than subjective biases and errors). This process can be conceptualized as one of 'referent informational influence' (Turner, 1982): the behaviour of others provides information about appropriate attitudes and actions in so far as it exemplifies the norms of some reference group (an ingroup self-category). It is not the informational content *per se* of others' actions which is persuasive but the degree to which that content is validated social psychologically by its participation in an ingroup consensus.

In an earlier statement (Turner, 1982) the process was summarized in three stages: (1) individuals define themselves as members of a distinct social category, (2) they form or learn the stereotypical norms of that category; they discover that certain ways of behaving are correlated attributes of category membership, that certain appropriate, expected, or desirable behaviours are used to define the category as different from other categories, and (3) they assign these norms to themselves along with other stereotypical attributes of the category – and thus their behaviour becomes more normative – as their category membership becomes salient. This formulation is useful in relating normative behaviour directly to the salience of self-categorization, but it fails to address the issue of subjective validity and explain how the stereotypical attributes of ingroup categories become normative.

The two basic ideas above, however, allow the application of social identity ideas directly to the classic issues of social influence. The resulting theory can be summarized by five major hypotheses all united by the same basic assumption that agreement with similar others subjectively validates our responses as veridical reflections of the external world:

H.18 That subjective validity (Festinger, 1950; Kelley, 1967), one's confidence in the objective validity of one's opinions, attitudes, beliefs, etc. (also termed subjective certainty, competence, correctness, etc.) is a direct function of the extent to which similar people (in relevant respects) in the same stimulus situation are perceived, expected, or believed to agree with one's own response.

H.19 That, conversely, subjective uncertainty is a direct function of the extent to which similar others are not perceived, expected, or believed to respond similarly to oneself in the same stimulus situation.

H.20 That uncertainty reduction may be accomplished by: (a) the attribution of the disagreement to perceived relevant differences between self and others, and/or (b) the attribution of the disagreement to perceived relevant differences in the shared stimulus situation, and/or (c) mutual social influence to produce agreement.

H.21 That the magnitude of the mutual pressures for uniformity between people is a product of (a) the degree of relevant similarity mutually perceived between them, (b) the degree to which the shared stimulus situation is perceived to be similar, (c) the extent of perceived, expected, or believed disagreement about that stimulus situation (subjective uncertainty), and (d) the importance of subjective validity to the group (i.e., the extent to which being right is perceived to matter in this instance).

H.22 That the direction of effective influence within the group (who successfully influences whom) is a function of the relative persuasiveness of the members, which is based on the degree to which their response (their arguments, position, attributes, experience, role, etc.) is perceived as prototypical of the initial distribution of responses of the group as a whole, i.e., the degree of relative consensual support for a member.

In the case of hypothesis 21 the overall magnitude of uniformity pressures can be assumed to be a multiplicative product of all the relevant variables such that if the value of just one variable is zero for any individual, then that person will experience no subjective pressure for agreement. Thus where there is no subjective uncertainty, there will be no pressure to agree because, by definition, agreement will already be complete (this is similar to Festinger's, 1950, idea that uniformity pressures in a cohesive group increase with the degree of discrepancy between members on relevant issues).

These hypotheses are solutions to the major problems of social influence (posed here from a conformity perspective) derived from a unified theory. The debts owed to earlier theorists will be readily apparent in, for example, the role of consensual validation (Festinger, 1950), external attribution (Kelley, 1967), the interchangeability of perceivers (Asch, 1952) and the idea of uncertainty as a social product of disagreement rather than as a simple reflection of stimulus ambiguity (Moscovici, 1976). However, the debt to previous work should not disguise just how different from other theories the present ideas are.

Thus in contradistinction to the theory of informational dependence, Festinger's (1950) distinction between physical and social reality testing and indeed that between the nonsocial and social environment (Allport, 1924) of individual action are rejected. It is assumed that *all* subjective validity rests upon a perpetual interaction between the data of individual perception (which whether of 'things' or people reflect a socially mediated cognition) and a social process of co-ordinating, checking, matching and negotiating a shared, publicly invariant and hence veridical picture of the world. The 'facts' of individual perception and judgement – that the earth is a globe, that an elephant is larger than a mouse, that one line is longer than another as measured by a ruler – are themselves social norms, based on the prior or current, explicit or implicit agreements of appropriate reference groups. The lone individual checking or extending his or her senses with some technological device is not asocial but employing at all times internalized norms and the device is merely a condensed, material expression or symbol of some prior consensus (Moscovici, 1976). This does not deny the independent informational value of individual cognition nor does it imply that social norms are arbitrary and infinitely malleable – to say that individual perception of the world is socially mediated is not to say that the world is socially constructed (except in this particular sense). A materialist perspective is adopted here that the external world exists independently of individual perception, that the function of consensual validation is to validate the objective, veridical character of one's perceptions and that it has such a power because of and not in opposition to the soundness of judgement of the individuals comprising the consensual group (see Allen, 1975). The point is simply that the agreement of several reliable individuals is self-evidently more likely to reflect an objective, public feature of the external world, whereas for any single individual, however reliable, their individual personality provides an alternative explanation of their judgement. The individual activity of 'seeing' and the social process of validation need to be kept analytically distinct at the same time that we understand that they are mutual preconditions and functionally interactive for human beings.

The latter is a difficult point: the question arises, for example, of why should not stimulus ambiguity as well as intragroup disagreement produce subjective uncertainty? Surely a lack of objective structure in the stimulus world also creates uncertainty? The essential point is the need to distinguish analytically between the individual 'percept' (what the person sees) and the issue of the *validity*, of the *correctness*, of that percept. The latter issue *cannot* be resolved within the confines of the individual sensory process but requires social psychological activity, and moreover can *only* be raised by what the individual sees 'directly' becauses in fact at all times the individual acts as representative of society, making assumptions about what others are or are not likely to see and whether others are or are not likely to agree. 'Subjective uncertainty' as employed in social psychology refers fundamentally to the evaluative status of sensory data, to validity, not to perceptual content. Subjective uncertainty and what can be called 'perceptual ambiguity' are, therefore, quite distinct: people may be certain of what they see but uncertain of whether what they see is correct, or, alternatively, certain that they are correct in seeing a stimulus as perceptually ambiguous. In one sense people can never doubt what they see – it is directly given experience; what they can doubt is the correspondence between what they know they see and the objective world (a correspondence that is never given directly in experience – as idealist philosophers have long since pointed out). Thus perceptual ambiguity can give rise to subjective uncertainty, not in the way that has been previously assumed, but only in so far as the person does not perceive, believe, or expect that like-minded others will also see a perceptually ambiguous stimulus. In most instances in the research literature what is meant by 'stimulus ambiguity' is in fact a setting where subjects believe that there is an objectively valid, unambiguously correct answer, but do not expect an immediate consensus.

The distinction between normative and informational influence (Deutsch and Gerard, 1955) is also rejected. Social influence (not power, coercion, compliance) is based upon the social normative processes that validate the informational content of others' responses; information is not self-validating. The theory explains the 'informational value' of a response (not the direct informational content but the degree to which that content is perceived to provide evidence about/is attributed to reality, i.e., its perceived validity or correctness) as a direct reflection of the degree to which it is prototypical of an ingroup consensus (i.e., a norm) and the subjectively 'normative' aspect of a response, the feeling that one *ought* to so act, as deriving from its perceived correctness. Compliance and 'group pressure' are assumed to reflect not 'normative' influence from an ingroup, but 'counter-normative' influence from a psychological outgroup, people with whom one would not expect to agree. Social norms are the basis as well as the product of influence: a response is persuasive to the degree that it represents and participates in some shared, consensual reaction stereotypically associated with an ingroup self-category and hence is perceived as valid, correct, competent (i.e., having informational value), which in turn leads to its perception as appropriate, desirable, expected, something one ought to believe or do (i.e., normative in the subjectively prescriptive sense).

The theory, therefore, unifies the normative and informational aspects of influence and integrates private acceptance and public compliance as reactions to (and determinants of) the ingroup or outgroup membership of others. The theory also explains and reinterprets the other major empirical generalizations in the conformity area – to do with the importance of (1) unanimity, consensus and social support, (2) reference group membership, (3) the public-private dimension of responding, (4) uncertainty and 'stimulus ambiguity', and (5) relative competence and correctness (see Allen, 1965, 1975, and Allen and Wilder, 1977, for reviews).

Thus hypothesis 18 explains the well-attested impact of social consensus on the influence process, but, unlike Festinger's (1950, 1954) analysis, does not restrict the role of consensual validation and social reality testing to settings in which physical reality testing is difficult or impossible. Further, unlike in Kelley's (1967) theory, it is not consensus in the abstract that leads to the external attribution of shared responses, but only the agreement of members of relevant ingroup self-categories. The findings that people tend to conform more to reference group members – others with whom they are interdependent, or to whom they are similar or attracted – are explicable in terms of the similarity of perceivers and stimulus setting implied by these variables (e.g., people interdependent with respect to some goal will tend to share the same perspective on an issue and hence should be more likely to agree). Similarly, that greater conformity occurs in public than private makes sense given that public settings represent 'shared social fields', settings where both social and stimulus identity are maximized and apparent. Although, therefore, we can agree with the traditional analysis that public conformity to outgroup norms may represent mere compliance, the distinctive predictions are made that ingroup norms may be more persuasive and lead to greater internalization when people are responding in public, and that an effect of privatization may be to reduce the influence of others by leading to the perception of personal differences. Hypothesis 19 is consistent with the effects of 'stimulus ambiguity' and uncertainty in increasing susceptibility to influence, but, as we have discussed, explains and redefines the former as 'normlessness' – uncertainty is created in settings where stimuli are confronted for which ready-made normative responses are unavailable and hence there is likely to be disagreement with others.

The hypothesis (22) explaining relative influence within the group summarizes much data that individuals who are and who are perceived as more competent, attractive, popular, able, successful, certain, confident, and so on, are both more influential and more resistant to influence than others, but derives these 'individual' differences from past, present and anticipated relative consensual support. Just as a consensual viewpoint is persuasive, so some group members are more persuasive than others, since their responses better embody that consensus. This idea gets away from the unwarranted assumption that consensus is all or nothing (the degree of intragroup consensus is a variable – easily quantifiable by means of the meta-contrast ratio – which implies complete unanimity only at one extreme) and begins to show how the process of consensual validation is compatible with leadership and minority influence.

Hypothesis 22 also provides the theoretical basis for explaining group polarization as a normal case of intragroup influence and conceptually unifying the phenomena of social conformity and group polarization. This is the issue that has been selected to illustrate in detail the usefulness of the proposed social influence hypotheses and substantiate some of the above points. The basic analysis is presented in the next section – to illustrate how it follows from the self-categorization theory – summarized and related in detail to the research context and relevant data in chapter 7 (see too Wetherell, 1983; Wetherell et al., 1985). It should be borne in mind that the quantitative mechanics of the theoretical analysis to be outlined are just as relevant to the earlier discussion of group cohesion and interpersonal attraction, for example, as they are to social influence.

The explanation of group polarization

Several reviews of the group polarization phenomenon are available (e.g., Lamm and Myers, 1978; Myers and Lamm, 1976). Group polarization is usually defined as the tendency of the average response of group members on some dimension to become more extreme towards the initially preferred pole after group discussion (or some related manipulation) than the average of their initial individual responses. The problem is that the traditional conformity conception of intragroup influence (deriving from the work of Allport, 1924, Sherif, 1936, and Asch, 1956, but not necessarily their own theorizing) expects that in forming a group consensus or group norm members should tend to converge on the average of their initial individually held judgements. Theories of polarization, therefore, have tended to look for some process other than social conformity to explain the effect.

Nevertheless, researchers have still sought the explanation in some importantly modified conceptualization of the processes of social influence, such as social comparison or the exchange of persuasive information (reviewed in chapter 7), and contemporary analyses usually emphasize one or other of these (as if) contrasting approaches. After more than 20 years' research (since Stoner, 1961), neither approach would seem to have furnished a completely satisfactory explanation, although both have attracted some empirical support.

A major omission has been the failure to provide a unified analysis which would show how the phenomena of social conformity (in the sense of convergence on the pretest mean of the group) and group polarization can be theoretically integrated so that it is possible to specify in advance the conditions under which either should occur. This is the alternative approach taken here (Turner and Oakes, 1986; Wetherell et al., 1985): to reconceptualize social conformity (social influence) to show how it embraces both convergence on and polarization of the mean under different conditions As throughout this book, the term 'conformity' has no implications of blind, sheep-like obedience, but indicates the process by which people shift towards some shared social norm.

There are three parts to the self-categorization analysis of group polarization: (1) the nature of stereotypical and prototypical attributes of ingroup categories, (2) the process of referent informational influence, and (3) the variation in the relative prototypicality of ingroup responses as a function of the social frame of reference.

Stereotypical and prototypical attributes of social categories

Assumption 7.1 is that the basic cognitive principle underlying category formation is that of meta-contrast. It follows from this principle that any given dimension of social comparison is more stereotypical of a given classification into ingroup and outgroup to the degree that it is associated with (produces) a higher meta-contrast ratio (MCR) than other dimensions. For example, to the degree that comparison in terms of political attitudes between black and white South Africans produces a higher contrast between perceived ingroup-outgroup differences and perceived intragroup differences than comparison in terms of attitudes to the arts or religion or eating meat, then the more stereotypical is that attribute of the black/white classification (usually labelled by the appropriate pole for each group, e.g., radical or left-wing for blacks and conservative or right-wing for whites).

Similarly, the prototypicality of any ingroup member is the degree to which he or she exemplifies or is representative of some stereotypical attribute of the group as a whole – also defined and operationalized by means of the meta-contrast principle. The greater the MCR produced by dividing the mean difference perceived between the ingroup member and outgroup members by the mean difference perceived between the ingroup member and other ingroup members on one or more relevant dimensions of comparison (i.e., relevant stereotypical dimensions), the more prototypical is that member of the ingroup category as a whole (on those dimensions). The higher this prototypicality ratio for a given ingroup or outgroup member compared to other ingroup or outgroup members, the greater his or her relative prototypicality.

The important point about prototypicality as defined here is that although it will tend to increase with intragroup similarities and intergroup differences, it is not related to either of these relations in isolation or in addition, but to their interaction. Thus the most prototypical member (simply referred to as the prototypical member where appropriate) need not be the person most similar to/least different from other ingroup members (defined by the mean intra-class position, i.e., the position that by definition minimizes the differences between group members), since a less similar member may yet be more different from the contrasting outgroup (this will be illustrated concretely below).

The relative prototypicality of an individual varies with the dimension(s) of comparison and the categories employed. The latter too will vary with the frame of reference (the psychologically salient pool of people compared) and the comparative dimension(s) selected. These phenomena are relative and situation-specific, not absolute, static, or constant. Also, unlike in Rosch (1978), categories are not defined simply by 'prototypes' or 'best exemplars' – the reverse also applies that prototypes are defined by the given categories, in turn a function of the relevant dimensions selected for comparison.

Referent informational influence

Simply stated, the theory of referent informational influence refers to the idea that we tend to perceive as normative – and conform to – the stereotypical attributes defining some salient ingroup identity. The basic assumption is that the informational value of a response, the perceived validity of its informational content, is subjectively equivalent to the degree to which it is perceived as exemplary of an ingroup norm (consensus). It is argued that convergence on the pretest mean and polarization both represent conformity to the ingroup norm embodied in the relevant stereotypical attribute or position of the group.

As we have seen, the theory is based on two fundamental notions. First, that in reaction to some stimulus one only expects to agree with others categorized as similar or identical to oneself, in respects perceived as relevant to the task – one experiences no subjective pressures to agree with people categorized as different from oneself, as outgroup members, since their difference explains the disagreement and by implication their incorrectness. Secondly, that shared or consensual responses tend to be attributed externally to the public, objective world and hence are perceived as *objectively* demanded, appropriate, or required, i.e., objectively valid. The shared, consensual responses of ingroup members are 'persuasive', i.e., intrinsically compelling as to their own validity, because they imply the reality which explains them (in being shared they are only explicable as a valid reflection of the 'common ground' of reality). The shared world is psychologically experienced as the real objective world. (This is the case with ingroup members at least, where the perceivers are fundamentally valued; an alternative explanation of dissenting, shared behaviour is the wholesale denigration of an outgroup.)

Since the stereotypical response of ingroup members to some stimulus is the consensual position, the one that displays intragroup agreement and divergence from outgroup members, then it is also by definition the normative position. Furthermore, just as some response is more normative the more that ingroup members are perceived, expected, or believed to agree with it, so it follows too that the responses of different ingroup members are perceived as more or less valid to the degree that they are prototypical of the existing consensus. The most prototypical response (argument, position, member, etc.) – the one that best represents and exemplifies the agreement of ingroup members – will tend to be perceived as most correct and be most valued: it will embody the (most) normative response in a given context. It may be assumed that in intragroup discussion members perceiving themselves to be less correct shift towards the more correct, but that there is no opposite tendency for the more correct to feel persuaded by the less correct. Thus it is hypothesized that relative influence is mediated by the perceived relative protoypicality of members and that pressures for mutual agreement within a group lead to convergence upon the most prototypical member. The initial responses of all ingroup members contribute to defining the prototype, but different ingroup members will appear to be more or less influential to the degree that they embody the prototypical opinion. Conformity to the stereotypical ingroup position, therefore, implies convergence on the most prototypical member.

The relative prototypicality of responses and the social frame of reference

It follows from the above definition that the relative prototypicality of responses varies with the frame of social-comparative reference. It can be shown that whether the most prototypical position coincides with or differs from the ingroup mean is determined by the relationship between the initial distribution of ingroup responses and the total pool of responses comprising the frame of reference.

First, it needs to be noted that the response dimension employed in polarization research (of whatever kind, e.g., attitude scales, probability ratings, person perception judgements, etc.) is always a dimension of social comparison, a relative ordering of the real or imagined responses of different people to the same stimulus. It is, in fact, a symbolic representation or operationalization of the psychologically salient social frame of reference for a given behaviour. It specifies (and tends to define) the varying responses of the (culturally or situationally appropriate) pool of others with whom both subjects and researchers will compare the subject's response. Thus the reference dimension provides information about the responses of comparable others, and, in fact, to the degree that the reference dimension and the initial distribution of ingroup responses are not identical, directly specifies the responses of outgroup members (scale values not endorsed by ingroup members). The 'outgroup' need not be a polar opposite; in a given context it may be defined as comprising any psychologically relevant other not belonging to the ingroup. It becomes possible, therefore, to use the relationship of the ingroup responses to the reference dimension as a heuristic operationalization of the intragroup and intergroup differences perceived by subjects (ingroup members) or that they may have been induced to perceive by the provided frame of reference.

Secondly, a simplifying assumption needs to be made about the form of distribution of responses represented by the reference dimension and perceived by ingroup members. An assumption that seems to correspond closely to the idea of an equal interval scale is that approximately equal numbers of people are perceived at each scale value. This is the one made here (others are possible and in certain conditions may be more appropriate). For the purposes of calculation each position not occupied by an ingroup member will be construed as the response of an outgroup member (since MCRs are based on mean perceived differences, absolute numbers are unimportant). We can now calculate the perceived relative prototypicality of ingroup members directly from their scale positions. For example, on the following seven-point scale, where A, B and C indicate ingroup responses, the remaining four scale values may be construed by definition as outgroup responses (O):

$$
\begin{array}{ccccccc}
\text{O} & \text{O} & \text{A} & \text{B} & \text{C} & \text{O} & \text{O} \\
-3 & -2 & -1 & 0 & +1 & +2 & +3
\end{array}
$$

Using the formula above, B is plainly the most prototypical member since the meta-contrast ratios are $2.5/1 = 2.5$ for B (i.e., the mean difference between B and outgroup members divided by the mean difference between B and ingroup members), but only $2.5/1.5 = 1.67$ for A and C. The 'outgroup' need not be one group; outgroups with opposing positions as in this example may be treated as one unit from the perspective of defining the ingroup.

Now the average difference between any scale value and the remaining values must increase as the distance between that value and the midpoint of the scale increases. It can be shown in consequence that, for any initial distribution of ingroup responses, as the mean deviates from the midpoint of the scale towards one pole then the difference in perceived prototypicality of members closer to or further from that pole will increase (in favour of the more extreme members). For example, in the distribution of responses (or people) above where the mean = the scale midpoint, A and C are equally prototypical – by symmetry the average intra- and intergroup difference is the same for both. However, if A, B and C are moved towards one pole as follows:

$$
\begin{array}{ccccccc}
\text{O} & \text{O} & \text{O} & \text{A} & \text{B} & \text{C} & \text{O} \\
-3 & -2 & -1 & 0 & +1 & +2 & +3
\end{array}
$$

then, by definition, the average intragroup difference (1.5) is still the same for A and C, but the average intergroup difference of C is greater than that of A (the ratios are now $2.25/1.5 = 1.5$ for A, $2.75/1 = 2.75$ for B and $3.25/1.5 = 2.17$ for C). The response of B on the group mean is still the most prototypical position, but the important point is that more extreme responses now tend to be perceived as more prototypical than moderate ones.

In general it is the case that as the difference between the initial mean and the psychological midpoint of the scale increases, the more extreme responses will gain in relative prototypicality over the less extreme and the more likely it is that the most prototypical response will be more extreme than the mean. In practice, the prototype will differ from the mean either where no ingroup member holds the mean position or where the distribution of ingroup responses is asymmetrical. A gain in the relative prototypicality of extreme responses is, in fact, conceptually equivalent to a tendency towards an asymmetrical distribution. Therefore, the general probabilistic relationship is that as the mean-midpoint discrepancy increases, the greater the relative prototypicality of extreme compared to moderate responses, the more likely it is that ingroup responses will be distributed asymmetrically and the most prototypical response differ from the mean.

In any individual case, of course, the specific configuration of ingroup responses will determine whether the prototype differs from the mean. For example, on the following scale:

$$
\begin{array}{ccccccc}
\text{O} & \text{A} & \text{B} & \text{C} & \text{D} & \text{O} & \text{O} \\
-3 & -2 & -1 & 0 & +1 & +2 & +3
\end{array}
$$

a symmetrical distribution of ingroup responses around the mean (-0.5) nevertheless produces a more extreme prototype of -1 at B (the respective MCRs for A, B, C and D are A = 1.67, B = 2.26, C = 2 and D = 1.17), since no individual actually holds the mean position of -0.5.

An example of an asymmetrical distribution is as follows:

O	O	O	A	O	B	C and D
-3	-2	-1	0	+1	+2	+3

where C and D are more prototypical than B despite the latter's holding the mean position at +2 (the MCRs being A = 1.75/2.66 = 0.66, B = 3.25/1.33 = 2.44 and C = D = 4.25/1.33 = 3.19). This example illustrates how as the ingroup's views approach one pole so the relative prototypicality of more extreme positions is enhanced by an increase in their intragroup similarities as well as their intergroup differences.

It needs to be stressed that the general psychological principle proposed is independent of the specific numerical assumption made that the reference dimension reflects a flat distribution of people across the scale; it is equally compatible with normal or bimodal distributions of responses comprising the frame of reference. The important point is that as a group approaches the extreme of the relevant frame of reference the intragroup similarities and intergroup differences of extreme members will increase compared to moderate members making them more prototypical. This point can in fact be grasped intuitively relatively easily, because the analysis is consistent with our everyday sense of social or political polarization – as where, for example, opposed left-wing and right-wing factions of a political party or reforming and conservative wings of some established institution are said to 'polarize', meaning become more extreme in their views in opposition to each other.

In summary, it is hypothesized (1) that both conformity (convergence on the pretest mean) and polarization represent convergence on the most prototypical ingroup position, (2) that polarization, depolarization, or conformity will occur depending simply on whether the prototype is more or less extreme than or coincides with the pretest mean, and (3) that the extent and direction of any discrepancy between the pretest mean and the prototype is determined by the perceived relationship between the initial distribution of ingroup responses and the total pool of responses employed as the salient frame of reference. The prototypical position will tend to coincide with the initial, pretest mean of the ingroup responses where the latter tends to coincide with the psychological midpoint of the salient judgemental or reference dimension, but will tend to be more extreme than the mean in the same direction the more that the mean differs from the midpoint.

Some of the distinctive points made by this analysis are that shared identification with a group is a precondition for polarization; that the extent and direction of polarization will depend upon factors determining the formation and salience of relevant ingroup-outgroup categorizations; that polarization is not merely a 'sample' effect (see chapter 7) but is an effect of influence within the specific group, and represents conformity to a polarized ingroup norm; that 'conformity' in the sense of convergence on the pretest mean and polarization express the same process of conformity to the ingroup norm, and that which will occur is not determined by whether judgements are factual, physical, or evaluative, but simply by the relationship of the ingroup's initial distribution of responses to the social frame of reference; and that in principle (in practice there are methodological and other problems) the degree of polarization may be directly predicted for a specific group from a quantitative analysis of the degree of discrepancy between its pretest mean and the most prototypical position.

The point that there are practical methodological problems in testing some of these expectations with respect to naturally functioning groups (they can all be tested experimentally) is worth expanding. Our analysis explains how the process of referent informational influence leads directly to the prediction of polarization under certain conditions. It shows why the most normative position is sometimes polarized beyond the mean. However, in all this, the expectation that subjects will converge on the prototypical position depends on the background assumption that conditions for mutual influence within a group are optimal. *Given* that group members converge, we have tried to explain how the endpoint of that convergence may vary. The determinants of intragroup convergence have been identified as the degree of identification with the relevant ingroup category (perceived similarity to group members on relevant dimensions), the perceived similarity of the stimulus situation, members' subjective uncertainty about the correctness of their response and the importance to the group of reaching agreement.

These factors will rarely be optimal in any specific group and so full agreement and maximum polarization will usually be unlikely. There will appear to be a degree of attitudinal inertia due to lack of experimental control over relevant background variables. A related problem in making specific predictions within an interacting group is that conformity to the polarized ingroup norm is only one way of reducing uniformity pressures. Alternatives are simply to reduce the other factors which make for uniformity pressures, e.g., to cease to identify with the polarized ingroup member or the ingroup as a whole, to persuade oneself that the issue is not important enough to change one's mind about, and so on. This kind of effect is very likely to occur when the group contains people with strongly opposing views. It will tend to produce what looks like convergence on the mean when in fact group members are merely not moving or not moving very much.

The basic determinants of social influence also have implications for the perception of relative prototypicality. The persuasiveness of a response will rarely be based on a single modality of comparison such as the response dimension (although our analysis has stressed this one modality because we believe that ultimately it is the fundamental one). The degree to which a member is perceived as prototypical on related stereotypical attributes of ingroup membership, or has been proved correct in the past, or has been legitimized as leader by some social mechanism, for example, may all have some effect on persuasiveness. It must suffice here to note that relevant background differences between ingroup members in perceived relative competence (leadership, correctness, confidence, ability, etc.) will tend to enhance or attenuate predicted polarization, depending on whether such differences correlate positively or not with the differences between members' responses in being prototypical of the immediate ingroup consensus.

This identifies a pervasive source of error in making predictions across different groups, since background individual differences between members are inevitably uncontrolled. Further problems are to do with the salient level of social identification, compliance and recidivism. Specific predictions of convergence or polarization assume that people identify with the particular discussion group in which they find themselves. They may do so, but at a higher level of abstraction than realized. Subjects who are university students, for example, may define their relevant ingroup category as 'students', 'young people', 'radicals', etc. What is perceived as prototypical of the specific discussion group may not be perceived as prototypical of the higher level identification, and, in fact, different higher level identifications may be characterized by opposed norms. A discussion group of American university students a while ago might have been relatively 'hawkish' about the Vietnam war but nevertheless have polarized to a more 'dovish' position if confronted with the different views of the student community or youth as a whole, or have become even more hawkish in so far as they defined themselves as 'American patriots' (cf. Eiser and Stroebe, 1972). The direction of shift will depend upon the content and the level of the ingroup identification that is actually salient in the specific setting. Interesting predictions can be made that the same group of people on the same issue will polarize in opposite directions depending on the level of identification and the relevant frame of reference that can be manipulated (e.g., 'liberals/conservatives' versus 'liberals/radicals').

Another point is that subjects may tend to revert to some more customary identity or frame of reference during the individual posttest than that salient in group discussion producing a degree of 'recidivism'. There may also be an element of compliance in arrival at the group consensus, given lack of identification, producing a degree of recidivism at the posttest. However, even if the discussion group represents a psychological outgroup and subjects are only complying behaviourally, the norm of that outgroup should still tend to be predicted by its prototype and the degree of recidivism might be expected to be relatively constant across groups. Thus there should still tend to be a positive relationship between the group consensus and the posttest.

Conclusion

Polarization has represented a direct challenge to the informational dependence theory of social influence. This theory explains the formation of social norms as an interpersonal process in which individuals exchange their private stocks of information and, it has been implicitly assumed, converge upon the mean of their individual positions. It also implies that group formation is the result of mutual dependence for information and the creation of shared norms. The group is not a distinctive social psychological process nor any kind of distinctive theoretical entity, but is simply a convenient descriptive term for summarizing, amongst other things, the relations and products of interpersonal influence. The notion of a social norm as the simple mean of individual members' positions fits excellently the individualistic thesis that the group is a collection of individuals behaviourally but not psychologically changed by their interrelations.

The polarization phenomenon, however, has implied from LeBon onwards that the group process produces distinctive, emergent normative tendencies, inexplicable as derivatives of the individual properties of members. Putting people into a group seems to 'add on' something to their individual views, leading to extremitization – the relations between members seem in some puzzling way to be mediated by their membership in the group, producing social norms with 'whole-properties' different from the sum of their parts. It is no accident that Floyd Allport, the champion of individualism, was the first modern researcher to report and explain social conformity as a process of mutual interpersonal convergence, whereas the original term for polarization, the 'risky shift', and related explanations, alluded to concepts of diffusion of responsibility, loss of personal moderation and self-control and de-individuation, harking back directly to the ideas of LeBon and McDougall of a distinctive group psychology. Polarization, then, is a testing ground for alternative metatheories of the relationship of the individual to the group and has long been a conundrum for the dominant theory of social influence (the efforts to explain it in purely informational terms notwithstanding, see chapter 7).

In light of these considerations, the implications of the self-categorization analysis are apparent. It is assumed that social influence is a psychologically distinctive intragroup process, not an interpersonal one, and that shared ingroup membership and associated norms are preconditions for mutual influence as well as outcomes. The proposed theory is interactionist in character, explaining social norms and values as emergent (i.e., irreducible) properties of group formation. The most prototypical (normative, valued) position is not the sum or mean of ingroup responses, nor an individual property of the member holding it, but is a higher order, category property, reflecting the views of all members and, indeed, the similarities and differences between them and in relation to others. The prototypical member's persuasiveness, perceived competence, leadership, the perceived validity of their information, etc., are mediated by and based on his or her membership in the group as a 'whole'. The prototypical position is a product of social relations in interaction with the psychological processes (of categorization, comparison, etc.) which represent them. It is accepted throughout that action as group members is psychologically different from action in terms of one's personal self because it represents action in terms of a social categorization of self and others at a higher level of abstraction.

5

Social Identity and Group Cohesiveness

(Michael Hogg)

Introduction

This chapter will look at the relationship between psychological group formation and group cohesiveness from the contrasting perspectives of the interdependence and self-categorization theories (referred to alternatively as the social cohesion and social identity models, Turner, 1982). It will be argued that traditionally in social psychology the social group has been described as a psychological entity by means of the concept of cohesiveness and has gradually been equated with this concept. Furthermore, group cohesiveness actually refers almost exclusively to and in effect has been reduced to interpersonal attraction. The result has been the disappearance of the group as a theoretical entity distinct from processes of interpersonal attraction. This is particularly so because, as will be seen, interpersonal attraction is implicitly conceptualized as the process underlying group belongingness in a wider variety of analyses than is usually acknowledged.

The limitations of this approach are articulated in the context of a metatheoretical critique and the alternative implications of the self-categorization theory are presented – that psychological group formation/social identification is a distinct process from that of attraction, that group cohesiveness differs from *interpersonal* attraction in being a special kind of *intragroup* attraction (based upon the salience of shared social category memberships) and that the basic causal direction (but not the only one empirically) is from ingroup identification to attraction rather than vice versa. The latter part of the chapter is devoted to a series of experimental studies which address the relationship between social identity and group cohesiveness and explore the role of the process of self-categorization in psychological group formation.

Group cohesiveness: traditional perspectives on the social group

In the 1940s social psychology experienced a rapid growth of interest in the dynamics of small group functioning (see Cartwright, 1979; Festinger, 1980; Marrow, 1969). A term was required to describe the essential quality of a group which sets it apart from a mere aggregate of individuals: a term to capture both the objectively observable phenomena and subjectively experienced feelings of closeness, *esprit de corps*, 'we-ness', solidarity, unity, etc., associated with a group. 'Group cohesiveness' was adopted to serve this purpose (e.g., French, 1941; Lewin, 1952), and with Festinger and his colleagues' systematic scientific conceptualization of the term, it very soon became the cornerstone concept in the analysis of small group behaviour – a position which it has not noticeably relinquished (see Blumberg, Hare, Kent and Davies, 1983; Kellerman, 1981).

Group cohesiveness is defined as 'the resultant of all the forces acting on the members to remain in the group' (Festinger, 1950, p. 274) or the 'total field of forces which act on members to remain in the group' (Festinger, et al., 1950, p. 164) and is considered to be determined by the attractiveness of the group and its members, and the extent to which the group mediates goals which are important for the members. The cohesiveness of the group as a whole is defined as the average magnitude of the forces acting on all the individual members. The background to this analysis is Lewin's (1948, 1952) field theory: the *group* quality of cohesiveness, the way in which groups appear to vary along a dimension 'from a loose "mass" to a compact unit' (Lewin, 1948, p. 84), is reciprocally determined by the *individual-psychological* quality of cohesiveness, where the latter is regarded as the psychological representation in the individual's 'life space' of inter-individual forces of attraction and repulsion within the group.

Although the concept of group cohesiveness permits and encourages different operationalizations (e.g., Festinger et al., 1950; Lewin, 1952), overwhelmingly it has been operationalized as, and identified theoretically with, attraction between individual group members, i.e., interpersonal attraction. This is as clear in early (e.g., Back, 1951; Berkowitz, 1954; Downing, 1958; Newcomb, 1953; Pepitone and Reichling, 1955; Schachter, Ellertson, McBride and Gregory, 1951) as in more recent work (e.g., Knowles and Brickner, 1981; Nixon, 1976; Wolf, 1979), and is well documented by review articles. For all practical purposes cohesiveness refers only to interpersonal attraction (see Cartwright, 1968; Hogg, 1985a; Lott and Lott, 1965; McGrath and Kravitz, 1982; Turner, 1982, 1984; Zander, 1979). The latter is 'the "cement" binding together group members' (Schachter et al., 1951, p. 229) and therefore the *sine qua non* of group belongingness; as Bonner, (1959, p. 66) puts it: 'without at least a minimal attraction of members to each other a group cannot exist at all'. This rapid restriction of the concept of group cohesiveness has been accompanied by an equally rapid and complete abandonment of its background in Lewinian field theory.

What remains is the belief that a collection of individuals is not a group unless and until a degree of mutual interpersonal attraction has arisen and that the stronger the attraction the more 'cohesive' is the group. The generation of group behaviour depends therefore upon the affective dynamics of interpersonal attraction and the determinants of attraction become the antecedents of psychological group formation.

This idea of group cohesiveness embraces a distinctive model of the social group, the 'social cohesion' model (Hogg, 1985a; Turner, 1982, 1984), that likens the group to a molecule in which individual atoms are people and inter-atomic forces interpersonal attraction (e.g., Kellerman, 1981; Raven and Rubin, 1983, p. 405). (In turn, this represents a manifestation of the wider, well-documented tendency in social science to adopt physical or biological metaphors as models of social processes, see Kellerman, 1981; Pepitone, 1981.) The social cohesion model traces the emergence of the 'inter-atomic' forces of interpersonal attraction to the multitude of factors which are known to determine liking (e.g., co-operative interdependence to achieve shared goals, attitude similarity, physical proximity, common fate, shared threat/a common enemy, being liked or approved by the other, attractive personality traits, success in group tasks, etc.): the latter are usually thought to produce attraction by means of some direct or indirect process of 'reinforcement' or satisfaction of individual needs. It is taken for granted that one is attracted to or likes people who are 'rewarding' and that a 'reward' is some action, attitude or attribute of oneself or another that satisfies a need (desire, drive, motive, etc.). Thus it follows that a collection of people come together to form a group, spontaneously or deliberately, to the degree that they have needs capable of mutual satisfaction and in this sense are *dependent* upon one another.

As stated in chapter 2, then, the fundamental hypothesis is that people who depend upon each other (which need not be an exclusive dependence) to satisfy one or more of their needs and who achieve or expect to achieve satisfactions from their association develop feelings of mutual attraction and hence become a group. Although some theorists are more explicit than others as regards the importance of interdependence as the key to association, there is wide acceptance of the Gestalt assumption that the 'wholeness' of the group, despite what may be very different 'parts' (i.e., members), reflects the interdependence of those 'parts'. The differences between theorists are largely to do with how explicit an emphasis is placed on interdependence, what antecedents or aspects of interdependence are stressed and whether or not interpersonal attraction is credited explicitly with a direct role. Even where a researcher makes no mention of interpersonal attraction as important for group formation, but stresses instead some kind of interdependence or other relation between people, the idea will often be implied in their understanding of the effects of interdependence. To substantiate these points, let us now briefly review a selection of important treatments of the group.

In general, theories of the group tend to fall into one of two camps – respectively stressing explicit inter-individual interdependence (e.g., Lewin, Sherif, Deutsch) or inter-individual similarity as the basis of attraction (e.g., Festinger, 1954). Lewin (1936, 1948, 1952) introduced an influential definition of the social group as a collection of individuals who are interdependent in forming a dynamic system: 'The essence of a group is not the similarity or dissimilarity of its members, but their interdependence. A group can be characterized as a 'dynamical whole'' (1948, p. 84). Cohesiveness (as mutual forces of attraction within the group) is also considered to be a fundamental quality of the group (e.g., 1952, p. 162), and so interdependence and cohesiveness co-vary and both relate to need satisfaction: need satisfaction is the motive for interdependence and the more complete the latter, the greater the need satisfaction and the greater the group's cohesiveness.

The Sherifs (Sherif, 1967; Sherif and Sherif, 1969) consider co-operative interdependence in the pursuit of shared goals that cannot be achieved by an individual alone to result in the establishment of a well-defined group structure (i.e., role relations and shared rules of conduct). The group is defined in terms of co-operative interdependence and objective social structure and it is this that distinguishes a group from a mere aggregate of individuals. However, psychologically speaking, the crucial process is repeated positive inter-individual interaction: group formation proceeds 'from interaction among unrelated individuals to the stabilization of role-status relations and norms' (Sherif and Sherif, 1969, p. 132). Mutual need satisfaction through co-operative interaction imbues the group members with positive valence and so makes the group attractive and encourages members to remain within it. Although Sherif (1967) argues that there is more to group formation than the development of spontaneous personal friendships and shows how intragroup attraction developed from co-operative interaction can overturn such friendships, his theory, nevertheless, rests upon the implicit idea that individual members become attractive – and the group therefore cohesive – to the degree that they contribute through inter-individual interaction to the attainment of one's goals.

Deutsch's (1949a, 1973) analysis is extremely similar except that the emphasis is placed on goals rather than activity, and the language comes directly from Lewin's field theory. Goals which can only be achieved through the co-operation of individuals ('entities') are 'promotively interdependent' and 'an entity will acquire positive valence . . . [become attractive] . . . if that entity is seen to be promotively related to need satisfaction' (Deutsch, 1949a, p. 138), i.e., an individual will 'accept, like or reward' (p. 138) another's actions which achieve promotively interdependent goals and this in turn will generalize to liking for the actor (see p. 146). It is clear that the promotive interdependence of individuals is believed to create attraction between them through need satisfaction. It is also clear, therefore, that interpersonal attraction is at the heart of the group as a psychological entity, since the psychological group comprises individuals who 'perceive themselves as pursuing promotively interdependent goals' and whose cohesiveness is determined by 'the strength of goals perceived to be promotively interdependent and . . . the degree of perceived interdependence' (p. 150). The basic message is that interpersonal attraction is the psychological force responsible for group belongingness and that its emergence can be traced to mutual need satisfaction through co-operation for promotively interdependent goals.

There is an ambiguity in the Lewinian approach (and that of the Sherifs too) to interdependence and interpersonal attraction that is well reflected in the views of Cartwright and Zander (1968). On the one hand the stress on the group as a dynamic system of interdependent members implies strongly that there are properties of the group as a whole – such as cohesiveness – which cannot be reduced to mere interpersonal relations, but, on the other hand, there is a theoretical failure to explain how attraction to the group could be generated by any process that does not ultimately resolve itself into interpersonal attraction. Thus Cartwright and Zander adhere to the interdependence theory of the group, are explicit in their recognition of the role of cohesiveness and seek to restrain the tendency to identify it solely with interpersonal attraction, but, despite an extremely detailed treatment, there is no definite indication of what alternative process is being suggested.

Social exchange approaches (Homans, 1961; Kelley and Thibaut, 1978; Secord and Backman, 1964; Thibaut and Kelley, 1959) are characterized by an emphasis on the cost/benefit aspects of social relations. They reduce interaction to the transaction of rewards and costs and simply state that interaction and hence the group continues to the extent that rewards outweigh costs. Cohesiveness is considered to be an essential quality of groups and its magnitude 'will be greater to the degree that rewards are experienced in belonging to the group' (Thibaut and Kelley, 1959, p. 114). However, since the unit of analysis is a dyad, cohesiveness in practice is interpersonal attraction based on interpersonal rewards. Secord and Backman (1964), too, make it clear that by cohesiveness is meant mutual interpersonal attraction.

Still emphasizing interpersonal rewards and costs, but with the analysis explicitly grounded in reinforcement theory is the work of the Lotts (Lott, 1961; Lott and Lott, 1961, 1965). Interaction which mediates goal achievement or is rewarding in some other way is reinforcing and hence results in interpersonal attraction. Cohesiveness is then defined as 'that group quality which is inferred from the number and strength of mutual positive attitudes among the members of a group' (Lott, 1961, p. 279).

Interpersonal interdependence is also central to equity theory (Berkowitz and Walster, 1976). This approach defines the group in terms of 'equitable' (i.e., fair, just, etc.) interdependence between individuals: the perception of inequity creates pressures for its reinstatement or for the termination of interdependence, in which case the group has disbanded. It is assumed that equitable interdependence creates interpersonal attraction which functions to produce group cohesiveness.

In contrast to the treatments discussed so far, Festinger and Heider provide examples of theories which stress the role of similarities in attitudes and values between people in attraction and group formation. Festinger's social comparison theory (1950, 1954; Festinger et al., 1950; see Suls and Miller, 1977) argues that people affiliate with others in order to validate their opinions, attitudes and beliefs. If physical, nonsocial means of testing or evaluating our beliefs, abilities, etc., are unavailable, we rely on comparison with relatively similar others. The agreement of others, i.e., their *similarity* to us in attitudes, etc., gives us confidence in the correctness of our views and so satisfies a basic need to evaluate ourselves/know that we are correct. Since similar others are rewarding – in that they satisfy informational needs – we are attracted to them and affiliate with them. This idea has become a cornerstone of research on interpersonal attraction (e.g., Byrne, 1971). Festinger is explicit that we compare with other individuals, not groups, and that mutual interpersonal attraction reflecting shared attitudes is the basis of group formation. (The theory has also been extended by Schachter, 1959, to include emotions.)

Heider's (1958) theory rests on the principle of cognitive balance, which postulates a need within the organism for balance between different cognitions. He argues that positive sentiment relations (i.e., liking for others) and positive unit relations (a sense of togetherness, oneness, being linked, being the same) between individuals tend to go together. Interpersonal attraction and being in the same group are therefore inextricably linked. Heider's theory is somewhat different from the others in that attraction to similar others is seen to follow from a basic need for cognitive consistency and there is an implication that group membership need not merely reflect interpersonal attraction but could also directly produce it. Newcomb (1968), however, in his application of cognitive balance concepts argues that liking is more likely to lead to a positive unit relationship than vice versa.

Finally, social impact theory (Latané, 1981; Latané and Nida, 1980) specifies factors in a group which determine its impact on potential members – i.e., increase conformity, group belongingness and cohesiveness – and nominates: (1) group size – the larger the number of physically present others the greater the group's impact, (2) immediacy – the closer the others are in space and time the greater the impact, (3) strength of source – characteristics of the group and its members that are attractive to potential members. The first two factors seem to relate to social interaction and the last to interpersonal attraction; implicitly, therefore, the theory appears to be based on an interpersonal interdependence model of the group.

In this section it has been shown how interpersonal attraction lies at the root of a wide array of superficially diverse conceptualizations of the social group. Current definitions of the social group (as can be seen in most contemporary social psychology texts) employ an admixture of components drawn from these theories. The group is essentially a numerically small face-to-face collection of individuals interacting to perform a task or to fulfil shared goals. The members like each other and have role relations with respect to each other which emerge from intragroup structural divisions developed in the fulfilment of the group's purpose. A product of the continued interaction is a sense of identity as group members. However, the fundamental process for the psychological formation of the group and the degree of cohesiveness of the group is interpersonal attraction.

Group cohesiveness: theoretical and empirical limitations

Theoretical limitations of the concept of group cohesiveness stem from the *type* of theory it has come to represent. The reduction of what was intended as a group quality to an interpersonal process of attraction and the determinants of group formation to the antecedents of interpersonal relations has attenuated the independent theoretical status of the concept and the group itself (cf. Albert, 1953; Eisman, 1959). Research on intragroup cohesiveness has disappeared into the study of a different phenomenon. Furthermore, the adoption of and tendency to reify the 'molecular' metaphor (e.g., Kellerman, 1981) of the relationship between the individual and the group has tended to obscure the point that, psychologically, people in groups, unlike atoms in molecules, can contain the whole within themselves, i.e., that they can cognitively represent the group to themselves and act in terms of that cognitive representation (see chapter 1).

The disappearance of the group as a theoretically distinct entity is nicely enunciated in Steiner's (1974) cry, 'Whatever happened to the group in social psychology?' and his (1983) follow-up, 'Whatever happened to the touted revival of the group?' (see also Smith and White, 1983), and is attributed to pragmatic and ideological considerations by Cartwright (1979), Festinger (1980), Pepitone (1981) and Triandis (1977). Not surprisingly, sociologically oriented social psychologists (e.g. Heine, 1971) register disbelief that experimental social psychology has reduced the complexity, variety and historical significance of social groups to individuals' liking for each other.

Holding in mind the metatheoretical critique, some more specific theoretical weaknesses can be cited. Adherence to a 'molecular' model has entailed the use of sociometric choice (Moreno, 1934) as the predominant method of charting who likes whom within the group in order to arrive at the cohesiveness of the group as a whole. This method has limitations (Golembiewski, 1962), of which perhaps the most relevant is that it is unidimensional (A.I. Cohen, 1981; Hare, 1962), i.e., it fails to allow for a qualitative distinction between sociometric choice as an indicator of friendship and as an indicator of attraction between group members (Hagstrom and Selvin, 1965; Scott, 1965). The same criticism can be directed at the use of Bales's (1950) 'interaction process analysis' method to study communication patterns in small groups. This method stresses the *quantity* of communication directed by one person to another in terms of categories based on task management functions and the valence of socio-emotional reactions, but makes no allowance for any qualitative distinction between intragroup and interpersonal relations.

A second problem is that it is not possible to select one unique conceptual definition of cohesiveness for the purposes of operationalization. As originally defined by Festinger and colleagues, the concept encompasses a number of different sources of attraction (to the prestige of the group, its task, members' traits, etc.) and lends itself to a number of, in principle, equally valid operationalizations, which research has since revealed in general not be be significantly correlated (Bovard, 1951; Eisman, 1959; Jackson, 1959; Ramuz-Nienhuis and Van Bergen, 1960). A group which is cohesive by one definition may not be by another. Since no one operationalization covers all aspects of group cohesiveness, interpersonal attraction constitutes at best an incomplete or partial explanation (cf. Gross and Martin, 1952).

Third is the issue of motives or motivation in group formation: why join a group? The frequently encountered sentiment that joining a group entails 'sacrifice of individual freedom' (e.g. Gergen and Gergen, 1981) suggests that groups suppress individuality and that individuality is superior, antithetical and ontogenetically prior to group behaviour. If this is so, then why do people join groups? The answer, as we have seen, is usually in order to satisfy needs – ranging from specific goals to supposedly fundamental drives for affiliation (Watson and Johnson, 1972), reinforcement, identity (Knowles, 1982) and information validation. The first point to be made here is that these needs in themselves represent 'reasons' for (although no doubt valid ones) rather than 'causes' of group membership (in Buss's, 1978, sense of that distinction): no causal *process* for psychological group formation is directly stated. The implicit process is, as argued in the previous section, interpersonal attraction – the force that binds people into a group.

The second point is that individuals' needs, aims, goals, attitudes, beliefs, etc., are largely socially acquired cognitive constructs. Thus although they may well act as motives for affiliation, there is also an important sense in which they must be considered as determined by one's group memberships (e.g., Christians have similar beliefs because they are Christians as well as being Christians because they have similar beliefs). In emphasizing such factors as belief/attitude similarity or shared goals as bases of group formation the traditional approach often seems to beg the question of the origin of beliefs, attitudes, goals. etc., and hence the origin of such similarities in the first place. In so far as group memberships (in the widest sense) determine similarities between people, then, they also determine inter-individual bonds and variations in cohesiveness and are not merely an effect of purely individual motives and needs.

The fourth and perhaps the most serious problem with cohesiveness as interpersonal attraction is that of group size. The concept was developed to address a certain type of group, the numerically small face-to-face predominantly task-oriented group, and hence the field is referred to as that of *small* group dynamics. However, although most researchers restrict the concept's applicability accordingly, others are less cautious and give the impression that interpersonal attraction is experimental social psychology's explanation of the group independent of size.

Defining the group in terms of number creates serious problems in specifying precisely the parameters of small group dynamics and cohesiveness (cf. A. I. Cohen, 1981). For example, Shaw (1976, 1981), although convinced that less than ten individuals is a small group and more than 30 is a large group, is driven to maintain that a cohesive 25-person group is a small group whereas a non-cohesive 15-person group is not a small group. So for 'small' we should read 'cohesive', and we are left with no independent criterion of the range of applicability of the social cohesion model.

The sensible solution to this dilemma is to accept that mutual face-to-face interaction between individuals (a phenomenon which is by definition restricted by number as well as time and place) entails behaviours perhaps uniquely dependent on such conditions, but also to recognize that there may be some other process independent of these specific circumstances responsible for group behaviour *sui generis*. Interpersonal attraction may have relevance for the analysis of small group phenomena, but it is plainly inadequate as an explanation of a large audience, crowd, nation, or any group for that matter in which interpersonal interaction between all members is not possible.

That cohesiveness as interpersonal attraction merely redescribes interpersonal relations within groups which are small enough to allow interpersonal interaction rather than addresses truly intragroup phenomena is suggested by the way increasing group size (within the small group purview) reduces the cohesiveness of the group as a whole. As the group gets larger, structural divisions emerge to create subgroups and friendship cliques, which although internally cohesive tend to lower overall or average cohesiveness (Gerard and Hoyt, 1974; Kinney, 1953; Porter and Lawler, 1968). Increasing size dictates structural subdivisions and supposedly weakens cohesiveness because it makes personal relations between all group members increasingly difficult.

But, increasing group size is also reputed to magnify the impact of the group on the individual and strengthen adherence to group norms according to Latané's social impact theory (1981). Thus we find that increasing group size apparently weakens cohesiveness under certain conditions but increases conformity under others. The determining factor may be the extent to which group belongingness does or does not reflect frequency and ease of face-to-face, interpersonal relations – they may be closely related in some small groups, but they cannot be equated with each other.

A fifth difficulty also stems from attempts to distinguish between small and large groups. A common distinction is between groups on the one hand and 'categories' and 'roles' on the other, where 'category' typically refers to large-scale affiliations such as nationality, sex, or religion and 'role' to an individual's position in a group such as leader, gossip, joker, etc. However, role is also employed to refer to position within the small group based on large-scale group membership (e.g., sex, ethnicity, class, education). The implication is that small group dynamics deals with the impingement of large-scale category memberships and intergroup relations on the functioning of small, *ad hoc* collections of individuals in face-to-face relations by reference (a generally theoretically unelaborated reference) to the concept of behavioural role. The social cohesion model, therefore, is reduced to juggling with two largely separate and unintegrated sets of concepts, where the social identity model would explain behaviour in terms of the complexities (e.g. identities at different levels of abstraction, varying with the frame of reference, overlapping or cross-cutting each other, etc.) of the same identity process.

Despite these theoretical limitations the group cohesiveness concept has survived relatively unscathed – no doubt because on the whole it has proved useful. Some term has been needed to summarize the empirical relationships between what has been presumed to be interpersonal attraction (e.g., Lott and Lott, 1965) and the 'cohesiveness' of the group in the sense of the impact of group membership and belongingness. The evidence shows that in general attraction between individuals in a small group increases their productivity (Schachter et al., 1951) and performance (Goodacre, 1951), increases conformity to group norms (Festinger et al, 1950), improves morale and job satisfaction (Exline, 1957; Gross, 1954), facilities intragroup communication (Festinger et al., 1950), solidifies intergroup barriers (Knowles and Brickner, 1981), reduces intragroup hostility and directs it towards an outgroup (Pepitone and Reichling, 1955), and increases feelings of security and self-worth.

There are also, however, numerous empirical instances where the expected relationship between interpersonal attraction and its antecedents and the 'cohesiveness' of the group is not obtained. For example, proximity and interaction between people across an emotionally charged intergroup boundary may not increase cohesiveness (Grundlach, 1956), nor under conditions of forced affiliation (Festinger, 1953). Attitude similarity may lead to antipathy and differentiation rather than the usual attraction when it occurs across a salient ingroup-outgroup division (Byrne and Wong, 1962; Brown and Turner, 1981) and may only lead to attraction within the confines of common category memberships (Kandel, 1978; Turner, 1982; cf. Allen and Wilder, 1975). Furthermore, Sole et al. (1975) found that altruistic helping only occurred where the similarity of others was so strong as to produce common category membership, not as a function of the liking it generated. Even co-operative relations and behaviour between people have been found not to be sufficient to generate social cohesion where they occur under conditions that fail to weaken the salience of existing ingroup-outgroup distinctions (Brewer and Silver, 1978; Doise Csepeli, Dann, Gouge, Larsen and Ostell 1972; see Turner, 1981b, for a review). A fundamental prediction of the interpersonal attraction theory is that rewards associated with the presence of individual group members (e.g., group success, victory in intergroup competition) should increase the degree of 'groupness', but in fact there is a substantial body of data that this need not be the case and that for example group failure can sometimes increase cohesiveness (Lott and Lott, 1965; Turner et al., 1984) – a finding consistent with much historical evidence. Turner et al. (1984) demonstrate that failure and defeat can increase group cohesiveness under certain conditions even where the members explain such outcomes internally in terms of their group membership. In reviewing data on the effects of intergroup co-operation and competition on social attitudes, Turner (1981b) and Worchel (1985) conclude that these variables may work not so much by directly affecting interpersonal relationships and feelings (as tends to be assumed in the Sherifs' summer camp studies, for example), but by defining or redefining the cognitive boundaries between groups (see, too, Brewer, 1979). Finally, there are the data already discussed in chapter 2 demonstrating that social categorization *per se* is sufficient for group behaviour and that interpersonal attraction (and interpersonal relations and attractive personal characteristics in general) are not necessary for group cohesiveness.

These disconfirming data and the social categorization studies in particular all strongly suggest the importance of social-cognitive processes of self-categorization and social identification rather than positive interpersonal attitudes and primarily affective relations between individuals in the development of group belongingness and cohesion. The traditional minimal group experiments, however, do not address themselves directly to this issue. In the remainder of this chapter we shall briefly summarize the main implications of the self-categorization analysis for the concept of group cohesiveness and describe a series of initial empirical studies.

The self-categorization analysis of group formation and cohesiveness

The self-categorization analysis reconceptualizes the social group in predominantly cognitive terms as a 'collection of individuals who perceive themselves to be members of the same social category' (Tajfel and Turner, 1986, p. 15), individuals who define, describe and evaluate themselves in terms of the social category and apply the ingroup's norms of conduct to themselves. The group is cognitively represented within the mind of the individual member and in this sense exists as a social identification.

The formation and internalization of a social categorization (often accompanied by some culturally conventional label such as 'black/white') to include the self – and function as a social identification producing group behaviour – is described as the process of self-categorization. Just as the categorization of physical objects and other people results in a perceptual accentuation of intra-category similarities and inter-category differences on dimensions believed to be associated with the categorization (Doise, 1978; Eiser and Stroebe, 1972; Tajfel, 1981a), so will the categorization of *self*: self will be perceived in terms of ingroup stereotypes, where stereotyping can be considered to operate in terms of evaluative status, prestige, emotional experiences, needs, goals, behavioural and attitudinal norms and personality or behavioural traits (Turner, 1982). Thus, self-categorization leads to stereotypical self-perception and depersonalization, and adherence to and expression of ingroup normative behaviour.

It has been explained in chapter 3 how depersonalization can produce intragroup cohesion in the sense of mutual attraction between group members. The salience of a shared ingroup-outgroup categorization increases the mutually perceived identity between ingroup members and their perceived dissimilarity from outgroup members. This mutually perceived similarity in terms of a positively valued ingroup category (and it is assumed that self-categories are generally – but not always – positive) leads to mutual positive evaluation between ingroup members and at the same time a tendency to dislike the members of the less valued outgroup. Depersonalization extends positive self-sentiments to other stereotypically identical members of the ingroup self-category.

This form of attraction between ingroup members represents cohesiveness proper, *intragroup* rather than *interpersonal* attraction (see Hogg and Abrams, in press). A basic point in the self-categorization analysis is that intragroup cohesion is distinguished from interpersonal attraction just as group behaviour in general is distinguished from interpersonal relationships. The latter reflect reactions to others in terms of their idiosyncratic, unique characteristics and individual differences, under conditions where personal rather than social identities are salient.

The social identity model differs radically therefore from the social cohesion model in so far as it contends that (1) the process of group formation cannot be reduced to the development of cohesiveness but embodies a distinct process of social identification, (2) there are different forms of social attraction and in particular that interpersonal liking is different from group cohesiveness, and (3) that group cohesiveness is an emergent property of group membership and social identification, i.e., it is in fact an outcome of and not the basis of ingroup identification (with the reservations expressed in chapter 3). Nevertheless, many of the supposed empirical determinants of interpersonal attraction (e.g., proximity, similarity, shared fate) are still considered important in group formation but are reinterpreted as leading to category formation or enhancing the clarity and salience of some ingroup category.

To conclude this section it should be emphasized that the social identity theory not only explains the role of social categorization *per se* in group formation and cohesiveness but also circumvents many of the theoretical limitations of the social cohesion model enumerated above, for example the problem of group size. The two approaches can be clearly contrasted over this issue.

The social cohesion model states that a collection of individuals (they must be few in number and engage in mutual interaction) becomes a group to the extent that it expresses an array of group behaviours, e.g., co-ordinated interaction, adherence to norms, mutual attraction, etc. The boundary of the group is set by those individuals physically present and the specific content as opposed to the form of the group's behaviour is determined by the relevant specific qualities of the members. Large-scale category-congruent behaviour, i.e., behavioural content which derives from 'groups' whose boundaries lie far beyond that of the specific small group, is generally labelled 'role' behaviour and excluded from the cohesiveness formulation or is treated as a cause of liking due to similarity of interpersonal attitudes. The *psychological* process of group formation, the process whereby the individual member becomes psychologically 'attached' to the group, is brought about by the development of bonds of mutual attraction between that person and the other members: attraction between members, cohesiveness and the group are theoretically identical.

In the social identity theory a collection of individuals – and there is no theoretical restriction on number – becomes a group to the extent that it acts in terms of a shared ingroup category. The content of the behaviour may be defined by the uniquely shared qualities of those present and the unique *raison d'être* of the aggregate, but it may also be determined by qualities of a far greater number of people than those present, e.g., the attributes of socially defined race or sex. So five individuals in a room have just as much become a group in that situation if they are behaving in terms of a large-scale category membership they share (such as race, sex, or religion) as if in terms of an emergent group whose norms and defining features are unique to that specific collection of five people (a friendship group, an experimental decision-making group, etc.). *Psychological* group formation is based on self-categorization in terms of the relevant category (whether small, *ad hoc*, face-to-face, short-lived experimental group or large-scale, widely dispersed, culturally produced social category). Group cohesiveness is the attraction between individuals mediated by their common membership in the group, a symptom of the degree of group formation and a theoretically distinct process from liking based on differing personal traits, reflecting a more inclusive frame of reference in the perception of self and others and the increased salience of a higher level of abstraction of self-categorization.

Social identification and attraction: empirical studies

The first major hypothesis of the self-categorization theory noted above is that a fundamental distinction can be made between psychological group formation, which is conceptualized as a process of self-categorization in terms of some ingroup-outgroup division, and attraction between ingroup members. The first studies reported here aimed to explore this point by manipulating independently the social categorization of subjects and social attraction in order to determine their effects on group behaviour. There are some relevant data from the minimal group paradigm but these studies do not vary attraction directly; they infer it from other variables.

Turner et al. (1983) employed the minimal group paradigm (based closely on the design of Billig and Tajfel, 1973) to compare experimentally the effects of social categorization *per se* and attraction between people in generating group behaviour – as monitored by subjects' use of distribution strategies (specifically ingroup favouritism and intergroup discrimination) in the allocation of points. It was hypothesized that group behaviour, and hence implicitly group formation, would be a function primarily of categorization, not attraction.

The subjects (80 school pupils aged 15–18) were informed that the experiment was concerned with decision-making. They first completed an 'interpersonal preferences' task, which involved looking successively at ten different pairs of photographs, taken of the other pupils taking part in their session, and privately indicating whom they preferred by choosing one photograph in each pair.

There were four separate sessions. Subjects were told that they had been assigned individual code numbers in the 40s or 50s for the remainder of the experiment (the non-categorization conditions) – in which anonymity would be crucially important – or were told that they would be divided into two separate groups, 'A' and 'B' (with corresponding code numbers in the 40s and 50s for A and B group members respectively), for the remainder of the study (the categorization conditions). Half the subjects in each of these treatments were told that code numbers (or group membership) were randomly determined by the toss of a coin (the random conditions), or that they were determined by information from the interpersonal preferences task such that pupils with code numbers in the 40s (or in group A in the categorization conditions) were 'the people that on the whole you liked' and those with code numbers in the 50s (or in group B in the categorization conditions) were 'the rest' (the criterial or affective conditions, where assignment of code number/group membership is ostensibly by an affective criterion) – the 'disliked' were not explicitly labelled as such for ethical reasons. Thus the independent variables were code number of the subject (40s versus 50s), the criterion of assignment of code numbers (random versus affective) and categorization or not on this basis (non-categorized versus explicitly categorized as A or B group). They were manipulated in a complete experimental design, with ten subjects randomly assigned to each of the eight conditions.

The subjects' main task was to distribute points between different pairs of anonymous individuals (one always with a code number similar to the subject's own, i.e., in the 40s or 50s, and one always different) on a series of allocation 'matrices' identical to those used by Billig and Tajfel (1973) and most minimal group studies. Each matrix presents 13 pairs of boxes containing a number of points, of which the subject has to circle one to indicate his/her choice. Taken together the matrices reveal the particular distribution strategies that are being employed, measured as the 'pulls' of strategies in relation to or against each other. In this study the strategies were fairness (F), seeking the 'maximum joint profit' of the recipients irrespective of who gained most (MJP), seeking 'maximum ingroup profit' or the maximum number of points for the person with a code number similar to one's own (MIP), and maximizing the difference in points awarded to the two recipients in favour of the person with a similar code number to one's own (MD). Ingroup favouritism or discrimination in favour of one's own group/similar others (MIP and MD) is assumed to be a reliable and characteristic expression of group formation. These matrices and strategies are described in more detail in Turner (1978) and Turner et al. (1979).

A brief questionnaire administered to the subjects after the point distribution task confirmed that they were unaware of the true purpose of the study and that the manipulations had been effective: the subjects were more aware of their group membership in the categorization than non-categorization conditions, and were more attracted to 40s than 50s people in the affective than random conditions (in the latter there was no difference). Also, as expected, responses on the point distribution task were found to reflect two relatively uncorrelated broad social orientations, favouritism towards the ingroup/similar others and discrimination against the outgroup/ dissimilar others and being co-operative and fair. The former tendency (the measure of ingroup formation) was the major dimension describing how subjects' responses varied.

The social cohesion model expects that subjects will favour attractive others, i.e., in the affective conditions people with code numbers in the 40s will favour similar others and those with code numbers in the 50s will favour dissimilar others (irrespective of the categorization variable). There should be no difference in the random conditions, where code numbers indicate nothing of people's prefer- ences. Thus group formation in terms of people's own code numbers should occur only amongst subjects who believe they are consensually attractive. The self-categorization theory also predicts that uncatego- rized attractive subjects will act as a group: according to the theory (see chapter 3) one will tend to assume that people one likes are similar to one self, that one shares common category memberships (which are the basis of the liking); the argument can also be made that since people generally tend to define themselves positively, as likeable people, they are in a sense justified in identifying more with subjects described as attractive than unattractive. The distinctive prediction of the self-categorization analysis, however, is that, once categorized explicitly into ingroup and outgroup, the subjects will favour mem- bers of their own social category even where categorization is explicitly unrelated to personal preferences (the random/categorization condi- tions) or groups them with unattractive others (the affective/ categorization/50s condition). Thus social attraction is a sufficient basis for group formation in so far as it leads to the perception of shared category membership, but explicit categorization is sufficient even without inter-member attraction.

Summarizing the results, analyses revealed that:

1 interpersonal similarities and differences (in terms of code num- bers) assigned on an explicitly random basis (the random/non- categorization control conditions) produced little or no discrimina- tion in favour of similar others;
2 both liked (40s) and disliked (50s) non-categorized individuals (the affective/non-categorization conditions) favoured attractive others (i.e., recipients whose code numbers were in the 40s);
3 social categorization on any basis, with attractive others, unattrac- tive others, or others selected by chance, (the categorization

conditions) increased favouritism towards similar others compared to non-categorization (the non-categorization conditions); and

4 members of disliked groups (the affective/categorization/50s condition) showed as much ingroup favouritism as members of liked groups (the affective/categorization/40s condition), and both discriminated more than members of randomly composed groups (the random/categorization conditions).

Thus the results were consistent with both the social cohesion and social identity theories in the non-categorization conditions – social attraction without explicit categorization led to group formation – but only with the latter theory in the categorization conditions – being categorized with unattractive as well as attractive people and also in a way unrelated to interpersonal preferences led to group formation. Interestingly, there was no greater identification with a positive than a negative group. It is particularly striking how disliked, non-categorized individuals favour the liked others, but, once categorized as a disliked group, express as much ingroup favouritism as members of liked groups. The apparent fact that people can identify with negatively distinctive groups suggests that it may be useful to distinguish between actually defining oneself as a group member (which may be a veridical and unavoidable cognition) and wanting to be a member: one may sometimes identify with groups of which one would prefer not to be a member. It may be assumed that, as was probably the case in the present experiment, members of such groups are strongly motivated to re-evaluate their category to achieve a positive social identity.

The second experiment (Hogg and Turner, 1985a) to be reported in detail was also conducted to unconfound the effects of social categorization and social attraction in group formation. In the last study people in the affective conditions are defined as *consensually* attractive or unattractive so that intergroup attitudes as well as intragroup attitudes are manipulated, e.g., 50s subjects not only know that they should tend to dislike each other but also that they like 40s people. The next study attempted to induce mutual liking or disliking between people independently of intergroup relations and in a way which did not imply some shared characteristic of the liked or disliked which could become an implicit basis of categorization (in the latter respect, however, it was almost certainly unsuccessful). A much more comprehensive array of measures of group formation was also employed.

Seventy-two university students were randomly assigned to six experimental conditions. These were formed by the manipulation of two independent variables, type of social categorization (non-categorization versus random categorization versus criterial categorization conditions) and social attraction (liking versus disliking for similar code number others). The experiment was introduced as an investigation into personality and decision-making and subjects were informed that they would be identified by a personal code number throughout. In the non-categorization conditions they believed that the code numbers had been assigned on the basis of their responses to a lengthy 'personality and friendship-choice' questionnaire, which they had completed at a pre-experimental session. The instructions stated: 'Any individual with a code number in the 30s would on the whole very probably tend to like (get on well with) and perhaps if given the opportunity become good friends with any other individual with a code number in the 30s — and any individual with a code number in the 40s would on the whole very probably tend to dislike (get on badly with) and not become friends with any other individual with a code number in the 40s.' No information was given, and it was stressed that no assumptions could be made, concerning affective relations between 30s and 40s.

Random categorization condition subjects were informed that they had been divided into two groups (X group with code numbers in the 30s and Y group with code numbers in the 40s) on the basis of the toss of a coin, but that pre-experimental session information revealed *incidentally* that those in the X group would tend to like each other and those in the Y group to dislike each other. In the criterial categorization conditions interpersonal liking or disliking were emphasized as being the explicit criteria of assignment to group X or group Y, i.e., people who would tend to like each other were explicitly assigned to form the X group and people who would tend to dislike each other were assigned to the Y group.

The subjects completed the same matrices to allocate points to people with code numbers in the 30s and 40s as in the previous study, followed by a questionnaire containing a large number of items relating to 'behavioural intentions' (e.g. co-operation, altruism), 'affective reactions' (e.g., liking, trust) and perceptions and evaluations of self and others (e.g., self-esteem, similarity). An analysis of the correlations between subjects' responses to these items and their point distribution strategies revealed a distinct dimension of behaviour which can be confidently attributed to the degree of ingroup identification with people of similar code numbers. The behaviours which co-varied in this way included ingroup favouritism/intergroup discrimination, the perception of similarity, attraction to and an intention to co-operate with ingroup members, dislike of the outgroup, perception of dissimilarity to and a competitive intention towards the outgroup.

Thus the subjects are faced with people with whom and between whom there should be mutual liking or disliking, either uncategorized into groups, categorized randomly, or categorized explicitly on the basis of their mutual liking or disliking. Again, the social cohesion model predicts that subjects will simply identify (as operationalized by the response dimension above) with people they like; there should be no effect of categorization. The social identity model expects that shared mutual attraction between people should lead to the assumption of mutual similarity and shared category memberships and so also predicts group formation in the liking conditions. However, it predicts effects of social categorization too.

In fact, the main result, obtained on the identification/group belongingness dimension, was of an interaction between the independent variables: subjects in the non-categorization conditions identified more with others they liked than disliked; this effect was enhanced in the criterial categorization conditions, but tended to be *reversed* in the random categorization conditions (i.e., randomly categorized subjects did not prefer liked to disliked others and indeed on some measures identified more with the latter than the former). Thus the manipulation of mutual liking and disliking within categories has perhaps not surprisingly had a bigger impact than varying consensual popularity, where even the disliked might still be able to assume a degree of reciprocal intragroup attraction. The most important feature of these data are that they begin to illustrate the distinction between interpersonal and intragroup attraction. The fact that responses to liked and disliked others are *enhanced* in the criterial categorization conditions – towards both greater acceptance and greater rejection – implies a categorization-depersonalization process: the others are reacted to in terms of the characteristics, good or bad, of the category as a whole, and hence there is a stereotypical accentuation of their positivity or negativity. The *additional* effects of criterial categorization compared to simple mutual like or dislike are evidently a function of the defining attributes of category membership and so cannot be reduced to interpersonal attitudes. On the other hand, randomly categorized subjects not only act as group members despite mutual dislike, because they are aware that their affective relations are incidental to common category membership, but their independent or unrelated mutual dislike seems to motivate them to a *stronger* assertion of group belongingness (as if in compensation).

Thus these subjects seem perfectly able to act and feel on the basis of a categorization of themselves which they know to be at odds with their tendencies towards individual friendships and dislikes.

A remaining issue is whether the finding of increased rejection of disliked others as a function of criterial categorization implies that after all attraction is necessary for group formation. Such an inference is contradicted by the random categorization conditions. Another possible explanation has to do with the distinction made in relation to the Turner, Sachdev and Hogg study between ingroup identification in the sense of acceptance of and action in terms of some self-defining social category and a positive evaluation of or a desire to be a member of some group. These subjects seem to be rejecting their group membership, asserting that they do not belong, but, paradoxically, the very force of their denial suggests that they are acting in terms of the imposed ingroup membership, assuming a greater mutual dislike because of it. It is probably sensible to bear two things in mind: first, that the artificial oppositon between intragroup attraction and identification created in this condition (which is not to say that real life does not provide analogous instances) implies that some kind of identity conflict may underlie their behaviour rather than a simple acceptance or not of group membership, and, secondly, that the fact that such conflicts can be created testifies to the usefulness of a conceptual distinction between self-categorization and social attraction.

A third study (Hogg and Turner, 1985b) examined more systematically the distinction between interpersonal and intragroup attraction. It attempted to test the idea that social attraction is sufficient for group behaviour only under conditions where it is associated with or implies some shared characteristic, some mutual similarity, which can act as the basis of ingroup-outgroup categorization. Where others are *personally* attractive in that they possess positive but individually unique attributes, but do not share any salient common trait, then group belongingness will not be apparent.

The study manipulated three independent variables in a complete factorial design – the implicit versus explicit categorization of subjects into groups, the personal likeableness versus dislikeableness of others and the shared positive versus negative distinctiveness of ingroup from outgroup members – to create eight experimental conditions. It employed a version of the minimal group paradigm and was introduced as being an investigation of the formation and cognitive storage of impressions of other people. Seventy-two 16–17-year-old school pupils were randomly assigned to experimental conditions.

They were either implicitly categorized into groups (the non-categorization conditions) through the assignment of individual code numbers in the 20s or 30s or explicitly divided into groups (the categorization conditions) through assignment of group labels and code numbers corresponding to group membership. They were then given time to form impressions of ingroup and outgroup members by studying a booklet which described each of the four other ingroup members and each of the five outgroup members in terms of combinations of three personality traits – ostensibly obtained from their responses to a personality questionnaire administered the previous week. Personality profiles were carefully constructed to operationalize the other two independent variables: both ingroup and outgroup members were described in terms of unique combinations of either one dislikeable and two likeable traits (the personal likeableness conditions) or one likeable and two dislikeable traits (the personal dislikeableness conditions). At the same time, either one positive trait was shared in common by ingroup members and one negative trait by outgroup members or vice versa, making the ingroup and the outgroup either positively and negatively distinct from each other respectively in terms of some trait shared within groups and differing between them or negatively and positively distinct respectively (the stereotypical and depersonalized positive versus negative distinctiveness of the ingroup conditions).

Subjects completed the minimal group point distribution task as before and then a questionnaire assessing group-related behaviours (ratings of similarity to, liking and preference for the ingroup and outgroup as a whole), interpersonal behaviour (the same ratings but for selected individual profiles from ingroup and outgroup) and self-esteem. These two types of ratings reflected an attempt (which later analysis revealed to be generally successful) to operationalize the distinction between group and interpersonal behaviour – ingroup favouritism and group ratings and preferences representing the former, and fairness and interpersonal ratings and preferences the latter. It was expected that group formation or group-related behaviours would occur primarily where an explicitly categorized ingroup was positively distinctive from the outgroup independently of the personal attractiveness of members and that the latter would be relevant primarily for determining interpersonal attitudes.

The results generally upheld these expectations. There was evidence that the independent variables had been successfully operationalized and it was found, amongst other results, that explicitly categorized subjects faced with positively distinctive ingroup others tended to express differential intergroup behaviour favouring the ingroup, whereas the personal likeableness variable tended to affect interpersonal but not intergroup attitudes, i.e, subjects tended to express a positive orientation to likeable individuals irrespective of their group membership but this had no effect on their group behaviour.

These results are inconsistent with the idea that group formation is a simple matter of interpersonal attraction: such a view predicts an effect only for personal likeableness. The fact that the obtained effect for likeableness emerged only on interpersonal measures underscores the point that the interpersonal attraction notion of group cohesiveness merely tends to redescribe interpersonal behaviour and fails to deal with the qualitatively different aspects of relationships made possible by group membership. The results support the idea that group formation is determined by self-defining cognitive meta-contrasts between people in the form of explicitly designated category memberships or implicit category information contained in highly stereotypical similarities and differences. It is important to understand in this context that the positive distinctiveness of ingroup members, as operationalized here, does not affect the overall attractiveness of members but merely refers to whether an element of that attractiveness is shared within the group and different between groups (i.e., it indicates whether a trait is associated with a high meta-contrast ratio in a direction congruent with self-esteem).

So far the studies reported have sought to demonstrate that social categorization can produce group behaviour independently of social attraction in that group formation can be shown with unattractive or randomly assigned others. The last study to be described explored more directly the process of self-stereotyping and depersonalization by which self-categorization is hypothesized to produce collective behaviour and intragroup cohesion. It is therefore relevant to the prediction that cohesion is an effect and not a cause of group formation.

Hogg and Turner (1987) manipulated independently the variables of sex of subject and the situational salience of sex category membership (low versus high salience). It was hypothesized that high salience would transform idiosyncratic personal behaviour (i.e., individual differences in behaviour) into unitary collective behaviour in terms of shared sex category membership, and that the specific form and content of this behaviour would be predictable from the nature of the relations between the sexes for the relevant population and in the specific context of the experiment.

Subjects (74 male and 66 female university students) were assigned to single-sex dyads (low salience of sex category membership) or four-person mixed-sex groups of two males and two females (high salience) for the purpose of an unstructured and spontaneous competitive *interpersonal* (intra-sex) or *intergroup* (inter-sex) debate. In the dyads in the low salience conditions the experiment was presented as being concerned with individual differences in debating style, and the members of each dyad held opposing viewpoints. In the high salience groups the experiment was presented as being concerned with differences between the sexes in debating style and there was intra-sex agreement and inter-sex disagreement within each group on the topic of debate. Sex was never mentioned in the low salience conditions but referred to continually in the high salience conditions. Thus sex category membership was made more salient amongst the groups than dyads by explicit references to category membership, treating subjects as representatives of their sex, and creating a strong intergroup meta-contrast in the former (high differences between compared to low differences within the sexes) and a strong interpersonal meta-contrast (high differences between persons and within sexes compared to low differences within persons) in the latter. This procedure for operationalizing salience is theoretically consistent with hypothesis 6 in chapter 3 (and the more detailed analysis presented in chapter 6) and is empirically grounded in previous research (e.g. Doise and Sinclair, 1973; Van Knippenberg, Pruyn and Wilke, 1982).

After the subjects had actually conducted the debate they completed a questionnaire eliciting self-ratings on sex-stereotypical dimensions selected (on the basis of pilot data) from Bem's (1974) sex-role inventory. There were also questions monitoring self-definition in terms of sex (the extent to which they felt they had acted as typical men or women would in a discussion), self-esteem and liking for opponents. This was followed by a restricted set of minimal group point distribution matrices.

At an earlier pre-experimental session the subjects' own *individual, situation-specific* (i.e., how they believed a typical member of their sex would behave in the dyad or group debate situation – depending on their experimental condition) stereotypes of their sex were elicited and their self-ratings on these dimensions were obtained. These individual stereotype dimensions were employed to measure stereotyping in the study and so it was possible to measure changes in the self-ratings of subjects on their own personal stereotype of their sex (although analysis confirmed that these were also social stereotypes proper in that they tended to be shared).

Analysis revealed that the salience manipulation had the predicted effect. The high salience subjects defined themselves as typical members of their sex more than did low salience subjects, and also tended to stereotype themselves more in terms of the attributes which they personally believed defined their sex category. The latter finding varied interestingly with sex: high salience males tended to stereotype themselves more on both positive and negative but less on neutral items, but high salience females more on positive and neutral but less on negative items. Salience also produced ingroup favouritism and dislike of opponents amongst the females but the opposite result amongst the males. Thus the males seemed ambivalent about themselves and unwilling to show ingroup bias, whilst the females seemed more conventionally ethnocentric and discriminatory. A clue to this pattern of results may be found in the fact that salience increased the self-esteem of males but lowered it for females. It may be that in our society defining oneself as a male in this kind of situation provides one with a positive social identity and so reduces the need to assert one's positive distinctiveness and be discriminatory, whereas the opposite may be true for females. In any case, the important points are that the salience of sex category membership influences self-perception and self-evaluation in line with the relevant self-categorization and produces sex differences in behaviour and attitudes which can be attributed to the real status and power differences between the groups in society and to individuals' subjective beliefs about the legitimacy and stability of such intergroup relations (cf. Kramerae, 1981; Tajfel and Turner, 1986).

Further weight is added to this conclusion by the fact that salience of sex category membership actually seemed to change the subjects' speech styles. Hogg (1985) presented extracts from the tape-recorded debates to male and female listener judges and was able to conclude that in groups both males and females adopted a more masculine speech style than in dyads and that this effect was much more pronounced for female speakers. This finding is consistent with Giles's (1984) speech accommodation theory, which explains speech style shifts in face-to-face encounters in terms of the intergroup context and the operation of self-presentational motives related to social identity in the situation.

Conclusion

This chapter has argued that the dominant treatment of psychological group formation in social psychology rests upon the concept of group cohesiveness and that in practice the latter refers almost exclusively to what has been defined as interpersonal attraction, i.e., to attraction between individuals causally unmediated by any shared group membership. Such attraction is believed to derive from the capacity of others to satisfy one's needs. This approach has been criticized and the self-categorization analysis of group cohesiveness advocated as an alternative. The latter implies that group formation cannot be reduced to social attraction — being primarily a process of self-categorization, that interpersonal differs from intragroup attraction and that, theoretically, group cohesion is fundamentally a symptom and not a cause of group belongingness. Social attraction between people is not necessary for group formation but it can be sufficient where it is associated with, implies, or tends to induce the perception of shared social identity.

The empirical studies described examined the relationship between attraction and identification. The first three studies (Turner et al., 1983; Hogg and Turner, 1985a, 1985b) all show that social categorization is sufficient for group formation in the absence of attraction between members or even where members dislike each other. The first two suggest that attraction without explicit categorization into groups can also lead to group behaviour. The social cohesion model can explain the latter finding but not the former, but the social identity theory is consistent with both (there is much evidence to support the contention that a person described as attractive will tend to be perceived as similar to oneself). The third study confirmed that the important role of attraction in this respect is not simply to do with whether individuals are personally likeable or an affective process but to do with the perception of common category membership and shared attributes. Both the second and the third studies provided evidence for the generation of evaluative reactions to others on the basis of their group membership independently of their attractiveness as individuals. Another way to summarize the causal role of attraction in group formation implied by these data is to say that intragroup attraction or group cohesiveness, i.e., attraction that is empirically or operationally inseparable from awareness of identity, enhances group belongingness but that personally unique or differentiated qualities, no matter how attractive, reduce it. This, of course, is as much a conceptual point as an empirical one. The last study (Hogg and Turner, 1987) demonstrated that enhancing the salience of a social category membership did increase self-stereotyping and self-definition and produce attitudes and behaviour in line with the content and meaning of those categories in society, and so provided support for the depersonalization process hypothesized to underlie the generation of group cohesion from group membership.

The purpose of the research described in this chapter has been to disentangle the theoretical and empirical implications of the self-categorization theory from the traditional treatment of the group cohesiveness concept. For this reason it has been necessary experimentally to oppose operationalizations of attraction and identification. It should not be forgotten, therefore, that the self-categorization theory is in fact a theory of attraction as well as of group formation and implies fundamentally that the two processes are intimately linked – indeed, from the viewpoint of the theory attraction to others is in one sense merely the evaluative aspect of identification. From this perspective the research to date has barely scratched the surface of the novel hypotheses that remain to be tested. For example, there is a need to re-examine the evidence for the need satisfaction theory of liking now that an alternative conceptualization of variables is available – much of this evidence has been accepted by default. Similarly, since variations in the social frame of reference change the level of abstraction of self-categories and modify the relative prototypicality of ingroup members (see chapters 3, 4 and 7), these variations alone predict changes in people's situational attractiveness. Such changes would be evidence against the widely shared ideas of attractiveness as a personality trait or as the result of an interpersonal process. These frame of reference effects are consistent with some data but remain to be demonstrated systematically.

6

The Salience of Social Categories

(Penelope Oakes)

Introduction

This chapter discusses the conditions and processes responsible for increasing the salience of specific ingroup/outgroup categorizations. Whilst such an understanding of the determinants of salience is obviously central to the development and heuristic value of the self-categorization theory this is not a new research issue created by the emergence of the theory. There is a long tradition of research into the effects and determinants of social group membership salience which can be traced back at least as far as 1947 when Festinger published a paper on the salience of religious identity in the first volume of *Human Relations*. There is , therefore, a fairly rich empirical store to draw upon but unfortunately almost no theoretical development. Our own work has attempted to rectify that situation through the development of a hypothesis of social group membership salience which integrates past research in the context of the self-categorization theory.

That context makes appropriate a somewhat different approach to the salience problem than might otherwise have been adopted. The core assumption of the theory is the idea that self-conception varies across levels of abstraction or relative inclusiveness. The salient level of abstraction determines the content of self-perception, which in turn determines the form of social behaviour. It is not that some special, unusual conditions prevail which shift perception and cognition from a customary focus on personality and individual differences to 'something else' underlying group behaviour, but rather that social perception and cognition exhibit a *general* variation in the level of abstraction at which they operate. Thus, the salience of social categorizations and group memberships becomes a general problem of social perception, no more and no less of a special issue than those associated with individual person perception and impression formation. The research question becomes correspondingly 'basic' – what determines the salient level of social perception? – rather than the more specialized issue, 'what makes social group memberships salient?', to be addressed within the confines of group theory and research.

The reader should not be surprised, therefore, to find that the attempt to understand the determinants of salience involves basic theories of perception (Bruner, 1957) and social perception (Heider, 1958) as well as the tradition of group membership salience research. Specifically, the salience hypothesis to be proposed is an adaptation of some ideas from Bruner's classic paper on the functioning of categorization in perception, 'On Perceptual Readiness' (1957). In developing that hypothesis we became aware of some striking similarities between Bruner's approach to perception and Heider's (1958) original conception of the attribution process. This led to the development of both theoretical and empirical links between our approach to social category salience and attribution theorists' attempts to predict the content of social perception.

We shall begin with a brief overview of the accumulated research on social group membership salience, then outline Bruner's hypothesis and, in the light of the research reviewed, our adaptation of it to the salience of social categorization in social perception. We shall then develop the attributional perspective and describe our own research designed to test both the general salience hypothesis and its attributional implications.

Before proceeding, however, a brief note on our definition of the term 'salience' is necessary. There has been much recent discussion of 'stimulus salience' (e.g., Higgins and King, 1980; Taylor and Fiske, 1978) and it is important to avoid a potential confusion between different uses of this term. By a salient group membership we refer to one which is *functioning psychologically* to increase the influence of one's membership in that group on perception and behaviour, and/or the influence of another person's identity as a group member on one's impression of and hence behaviour towards that person (e.g., Brewer, 1979, pp. 318–19; Hamilton, 1979, p. 59; Kramer and Brewer, 1984; Turner, 1982, p. 36; Wilder and Shapiro, 1984). The term salience is *not* being used to refer to some 'attention-grabbing' property of a stimulus (e.g., Taylor and Fiske, 1978). Stimulus salience in this attentional prepotency sense may function as a causal antecedent of the psychological salience of a group membership in our sense (Taylor, Fiske, Etcoff and Ruderman, 1978), but this is an empirical question and it is important to maintain the distinction between the two ideas. In this chapter the salience of a group membership is its current psychological significance, not the perceptual prominence of the relevant cues.

Overview of past research on social group membership salience

Group membership salience research has passed through three fairly distinct periods: considerable theoretical interest and research activity in the late 1940s and the 1950s, a marked waning of theoretical interest but continuing sporadic, fairly isolated research activity in the 1960s and early 1970s, then a renewal of both theoretical and concerted empirical effort in the late 1970s through to the present.

Early interest in the salience problem reflected the preoccupation with groups and group membership which characterized the beginnings of the discipline of social psychology. Recognizing both the social and the psychological reality of groups, several researchers stressed the determining influence group membership could have on social behaviour and consequently urged more attention to the salience problem (e.g., Festinger, 1947; Hartley, 1951; Lewin, 1935; Newcomb, 1951). The early studies concentrated on religious group memberships and manipulated salience through what Charters and Newcomb (1952) refer to as 'vivid reminders' of group membership. Subjects were made unambigously aware of a particular group affiliation through such procedures as open and public group identification, or being told that they were participating in the study as group representatives (Charters and Newcomb, 1952; Festinger, 1947; Kelley, 1955; Lambert, Libman and Poser, 1960). The dependent variables included ingroup bias and conformity to ingroup norms. Whilst providing convincing evidence of the validity of the salience phenomenon – individuals' social attitudes and behaviour did change when their awareness of a group membership was increased – these studies also revealed its complexity in that even the relatively strong salience manipulations involved did not always produce effects on ingroup bias, increased conformity to group norms, or whatever, that were easily predictable. As Kelley (1955, p. 286) suggested, the effects of 'vivid reminders' may depend upon an interaction with other factors such as the strength of group identifications or the specific content of relevant group norms.

The one exception to the concentration on religious group memberships during this early period was a study by Bruner and Perlmutter (1957) which looked at national identity and confirmed their hypothesis that social categorization would become more salient in a 'comparative context' (i.e., where two or more categories appear simultaneously, either actually or symbolically) than under conditions which do not allow or encourage an intergroup comparison (see also Bochner and Ohsako, 1977; Bochner and Perks, 1971; Doise Deschamps and Meyer, 1978; Wilder and Shapiro, 1984). The major empirical generalization to be drawn from the research findings which accumulated during the 1960s and early 1970s builds on this foundation. Several different lines of evidence combine to suggest that the sharper the contrast afforded by an intergroup comparison, the more salient ingroup identification tends to become. Another way of putting this is that the relative 'separateness and clarity' (Rosch, 1978) of a categorization – i.e., the extent to which individuals may be perceived as different between and similar within categories – is positively related to its salience. Both chronic and acute variations in separateness and clarity appear to influence salience, i.e., it has an effect as both a 'state' and a 'trait' variable.

Evidence supporting this generalization comes from three main sources. The first is research on the effects of intergroup competition and co-operation on the salience of ingroup identification. The intuitively plausible and often assumed relationship is a straightforward one between competition (or rivalry and conflict in general) and increased salience, and co-operation and decreased salience. The finding is, however, that whilst competition does reliably increase salience (e.g., Myers, 1962; Ryen and Kahn, 1975), co-operation does not always decrease it. Indeed, ingroup membership can be as salient in co-operative as in competitive intergroup encounters (Brewer and Silver, 1978; Doise et al., 1972; Rabbie and Wilkens, 1971). The extent to which competition and co-operation can work to enhance or diminish the separateness and clarity of the relevant categorization has been identified as the general mechanism underlying these various findings (Brewer, 1979; Dion, 1979; Turner, 1981b; Worchel, 1979). An element of rivalry or explicit competition obviously increases the separateness of the categories and thus reliably increases salience, whereas co-operation only decreases salience to the extent that other factors which could maintain awareness of the intergroup distinction are not present. Worchel's imaginative experiments (Worchel, Andreoli and Folger, 1977; Worchel, Axsom, Ferris, Samaha and Schweitzer, 1978) clearly illustrate this point. In the 1978 study, for example, four-person groups engaged in co-operative intergroup interaction with both groups wearing white laboratory coats, or one group wearing white and the other red. A main effect for similarity of dress indicated that intergroup co-operation led to greater intergroup attraction when both groups wore the same colour coats. There were also interaction effects demonstrating an inhibition of intergroup attraction when the groups were dressed differently. Thus, a clear physical difference between the groups maintained the separateness and clarity of the categorization, mitigating the potential effects of the co-operation.

The second source of evidence for the influence of separateness and clarity on salience comes from research on 'collective' versus 'individual' intergroup encounters. Doise and his colleagues have conducted several studies comparing encounters between two or more members of each of two groups ('collective' encounters) with those in which only one representative from each group is present (individual' encounters), the reliable finding being that group membership is more salient under collective than individual conditions (e.g., Doise and Sinclair, 1973; Doise and Weinberger, 1973; see also Dustin and Davis, 1970; McKillip, DiMiceli and Leubke, 1977). Doise (1978) interprets the difference between individual and collective encounters as due to the operation of a 'convergence effect' associated with the cognitive effect of categorization (Tajfel, 1959, 1969b). Category boundaries are blurred in individual encounters because the two participants converge towards each other, whereas in collective encounters within-group convergence occurs, accentuating the difference between the categories. Doise further suggests that it is the perception of intra-category similarity which produces within- rather than between-group convergence in collective encounters. The two people involved in an individual encounter can perceive themselves as similar or different in any number of ways, whereas in a collective encounter the awareness of shared identity within both groups works to 'bring the categorization process to bear on clearly defined dimensions associated with the two memberships represented' (Doise, 1978, p. 199). Consequently, *both* groups must provide at least two representatives for the increase in intergroup differentiation, and hence salience, to occur (see Doise and Girourd, reported in Doise, 1978, pp. 199–201).

Thirdly, several studies address the relationship between separateness and clarity and category salience more directly. Treating separateness and clarity as a trait variable, Buss and Portnoy (1967) found that a comparison between Russia and America made American subjects' national identity more salient than did a comparison with Canada. They conclude that 'the greater the difference between reference group and comparison group . . . the greater is the individual's feeling of being a member of the reference group; that is, the more salient is group identity' (1967, p. 108). Studies by Brown and Turner

(1979), Hensley and Duval (1976), Kramer and Brewer (1984), Sole et al. (1975) and an impressive series of studies by Wilder (1978, 1981; Wilder and Thompson, 1980) indicate that contextual variations in the relative clarity of a categorization are positively related to variations in salience. Wilder's general hypothesis is that the 'individuation' of group members can blur group boundaries and thus reduce group membership salience (e.g., Wilder, 1981, p. 235). In two experiments (1978) he divided subjects into groups and then created a situation in which they required additional information from the outgroup in order to complete a task. The outgroup was either completely co-operative, completely unco-operative, or partially co-operative in one of two ways. In the partially co-operative/group condition the ingroup received help from half of the outgroup acting as a unit. In the partially co-operative/individual condition, on the other hand, this help came from half of the outgroup acting explicitly as individuals. The primary dependent measure was reward matrices as used in the minimal group paradigm, and, as expected, subjects were most discriminatory in favour of their own group in the completely unco-operative condition, least so in the completely co-operative condition. Between these two extremes, there was significantly less ingroup favouritism in the partially co-operative *individual* condition than when the partial help came from a sub-*group*.

There is, in summary, considerable evidence that the (chronic and/or acute) separateness and clarity of a categorization is positively related to its salience. The degree of differentiation between categories has often been referred to as the distinctiveness of the categorization (Buss and Portnoy, 1967; Tajfel, 1972a; Tajfel and Turner, 1979). Rosch's equivalent term 'separateness and clarity' has been used in order to avoid confusion between the empirical generalization just drawn and an influential approach to salience which has emerged during the most recent period of theoretical interest in the problem: the distinctiveness hypothesis (McGuire, McGuire, Child and Fujioka, 1978; Taylor et al., 1978). Distinctiveness here refers to the relative numerical infrequency, rarity, or novelty of a stimulus within a given context; the more novel or infrequent the stimulus the more distinctive it is said to be (e.g., Taylor, 1981, p. 94). Drawing from work on object perception it is assumed that novel, distinctive stimuli have an inbuilt, automatic capacity to attract attention (McGuire et al., 1978, p. 512; Taylor and Fiske, 1978, p. 280). Applied to social category memberships this produces the hypothesis that where a cue to a category membership constitutes a novel stimulus it automatically attracts attention, making the relevant membership salient. Thus, in general terms, it is hypothesized that *numerical minority* category memberships should be particularly salient, the smaller the minority in relation to the majority the greater the salience of minority (but *not* majority) membership. More specifi- cally, and in line with the current popularity of information- processing explanations for social behaviour, it is suggested that the psychological mechanism underlying minority salience is the automa- tic functioning of a perceptual bias directing perceivers' attention towards novel stimuli.

As the most current and influential hypothesis of social group mem- bership salience, the distinctiveness hypothesis occupied our own first efforts at an understanding of the salience problem (Oakes, 1983; Oakes and Turner, 1986). We shall simply summarize the main points and outline one of our own experiments (Oakes and Turner, 1986). The first point to note is that there is surprisingly little sound empirical support for contextual distinctiveness as a predictor of social category membership salience. The kind of robust and generally posi- tive relationship between numerical minority status and salience which would be expected if an automatic perceptual bias towards novelty mediated minority effects is not evident from a survey of relevant studies (e.g., Dion et al., 1978; Etzkowitz, 1971; Moscovici and Paicheler, 1978). McGuire and Taylor's own research into the effects of novelty on the salience of ethnic (McGuire et al., 1978) and sex (McGuire, McGuire and Winton, 1979; Taylor et al., 1978) category memberships has produced results consistent with the distinctiveness hypothesis but open to plausible alternative interpretations (detailed in Oakes and Turner, 1986). Our own experiment followed up a suggested alternative interpretation of results from the Taylor et al. (1978) study of sex category membership salience. Taylor et al. varied the sex composition of a stimulus group over seven conditions, from single-sex groups of six men or six women through the intermediate proportions to the 'solo' conditions, i.e., one man and five women or one woman and five men. Subjects rated the stimulus group on several dependent measures including evaluations of each member on dimen- sions of sex stereotyping, with a positive relationship between the relative distinctiveness of a stimulus individual's sex category mem- bership and its salience being one of the main predictions. This predic- tion was not supported on the stereotyping measures, but the result on one dependent measure was consistent with it. For each member of the group subjects were asked 'if this person had seemed to play any special role in the group and if so, what that role was (open-ended)' (Taylor et al., 1978, p. 786). Responses were blind-coded for sex stereotyping and a test for a linear trend in proportions revealed a marginally significant effect ($p < .09$) indicating that more sex-typed roles were imputed to male and female stimulus individuals the fewer the other members of their sex there were in the group.

The alternative interpretation of this result focuses on the specific questionnaire item involved. Subjects were asked 'if this person had seemed to play any *special* role in the group.' For a role to qualify as special it needs to be clearly different from those played by the other group members – doing what everyone else is doing is not special. Thus, in effect the subjects were being asked to differentiate the individual under consideration from all the others. For a solo male, gender is a clearly differentiating characteristic and so stereotypically male behaviour would count as a 'special' contribution. Likewise, stereotypically female behaviour would appear particularly special in the solo female condition. In other words, task requirements (answering the 'special role' question) rather than a perceptual bias towards novel stimuli may have mediated Taylor et al.'s result.

This possibility was investigated in an experiment employing tape-slide presentations similar to those created by Taylor et al. in which the distinctiveness of a target male stimulus individual's sex category membership was varied over five conditions (i.e., one male/five females through the intermediate proportions to five males/one female). In addition, a simple task variable was manipulated. Half the subjects were asked to focus on and describe the one male target (the 'individual' task orientation), whilst the other half gave a description of each member of the stimulus group (the 'collective' task orientation). It was predicted that the individual task orientation would mediate a positive relationship between distinctiveness and salience; a distinctive male identity could distinguish the target from the rest of the group in much the same way as it could define as individual as special in Taylor et al.'s study. Collective task subjects, on the other hand, were expected to rely on the sex categorization most heavily in the balanced, three male/three female stimulus group condition, where it was maximally differentiating for all of the individuals they had to describe.

In support of the hypothesis the task variable had marked effects on the salience of the target's sex category membership. More specifically, the prediction for the collective task condition was confirmed (maximum stereotyping in the three male/three female stimulus group), whilst individual task subjects described the target most male stereotypically where his sex category membership was most dintinctive, as predicted, *and* where it was *least* distinctive (in the one male/five female and five male/one female stimulus group conditions). There was, in summary, no evidence of any automatic tendency to focus on distinctive category memberships.

A second notable feature of research in this area is a failure to address the important distinction between 'minority group' in a numerical sense and 'minority group' in a sociocultural sense (Tajfel, 1981a). Indeed, the absence of a clear distinction between these two ideas has been responsible for some of the difficulty in interpreting results and, more interestingly, leads us into a parallel distinction between numerical and sociocultural distinctiveness. Tajfel (1981a) has argued that 'the perceived clarity of the boundary separating in common the members of that group from others' (p. 314) is a crucial factor in the development of subjective sociocultural minority status. Thus sociocultural minority/majority categorizations are associated with a high degree of separateness and clarity; because of their social significance, rich, polarized stereotypes develop. In many cases what could superficially be identified as an effect of numerical minority distinctiveness on salience may in fact depend upon the sociocultural distinctiveness (separateness and clarity) of the categorization involved; a single black amongst whites (or vice versa) may 'stand out' and attract attention because of the social significance and hence perceived separateness and clarity of the racial categorization rather than because of the perceptual significance of novelty.

Finally, one major metatheoretical problem with the distinctiveness bias as a mechanism determining the salience of group memberships is that it makes no attempt to link that salience with the realities of the social context in which it occurs. Regardless of individuals' actual behaviour and the meaning or significance of that behaviour for the perceiver, if a particular category membership is novel it is supposed automatically to become salient. Clearly, that salience, with its consequences for the perceiver's behaviour, could be entirely inappropriate. In this way, the assumptions underlying the distinctiveness hypothesis tend to deny the validity and adaptiveness of the perception of group behaviour: it is the product of a capricious perceptual bias rather than functionally related to the realities of the social context, individuals' behaviour within that context and the current goals and motives of the perceiver (see Sherif, 1951). It was a sense of dissatisfaction with this aspect of the distinctiveness hypothesis which led us to adopt Bruner's explicitly functional approach to the salience of categorization in perception.

Before going on to discuss Bruner's ideas, however, there is one final point to be made from the review of group membership salience research. Thus far we have concentrated on the cognitive-structural aspect of social categorization, the grouping of individuals on the basis of similarity and difference. Less attention has been paid to the specific dimensions on which that similarity and difference is perceived, i.e., the content or meaning of social categories. Although the pioneers of salience research placed a good deal of emphasis on content in both their manipulations and interpretation of results (e.g., Festinger, 1947, pp. 76–7; Herman and Schild, 1960; Kelley 1955), very little subsequent work has looked at the effects of category content on salience, either directly or indirectly. One notable exception is a paper by Boyanowsky and Allen (1973) which reports two experiments demonstrating the effects of content on the salience of racial identity. Boyanowsky and Allen were interested in whether or not prejudiced white subjects would conform less to an incorrect or unpopular white majority when provided with a black social supporter. They found that conformity was reduced when the judgements to be made did not touch on the norms which, for prejudiced subjects, defined the distinction between black and white. However, when the judgements concerned opinions 'integral to identification with the ingroup' (p. 413), highly prejudiced subjects conformed to the unpopular white majority rather than agree with the black supporter, i.e., they acted on the basis of race rather than interpersonal similarity.

The relative dearth of evidence that category content affects salience is a result of insufficient attention to content by salience researchers rather than the insignificance of this variable. Indeed, our own research confirms the important role played by content in the salience process; it is to the theoretical background to that research that we now turn.

Category salience as a product of 'accessibility × fit'

Before outlining our salience hypothesis we need to make explicit two assumptions (based on the self-categorization theory) which underly our approach to the salience problem. First, we assume the social and psychological reality of groups and group behaviour – social groups do exist, individuals do identify with social groups, i.e., perceive themselves as group members, and they do behave as group members rather than as individuals under certain conditions. Following from this, it can be further assumed that there are circumstances in which perceiving the self and others in terms of a given ingroup/outgroup categorization is entirely appropriate and indeed highly adaptive (Turner, 1985; Vinacke, 1957). This raises the possibility of a *functional* relationship between the salience of a given ingroup/outgroup categorization and the context of that salience such that individuals will tend to perceive themselves and others as members of given social categories to the extent that it is appropriate (in view of the realities of the situation they are in and their goals and motives within that situation) to do so.

Such a functional relationship between categorization and its context is implicit in the self-categorization theory (e.g., Turner, 1985, pp. 93–4) and is, in fact, generally assumed by researchers of the categorization process (e.g., Bruner, 1957; Rosch, 1978; Tajfel, 1972a, 1980). The above points, therefore may hardly seem to need stating. However, given the popularity of the distinctiveness hypothesis, which, as we have seen, treats salience as the product of an automatic bias triggered by factors potentially quite unrelated to the current social and psychological relevance of that categorization (the relative novelty of particular cues), the functional assumption needs to be made explicit from the outset. Moreover, it was the congruence between this functional perspective on social category membership salience and the assumption underlying Bruner's (1957) analysis of categorization in perception which led to the recruitment of his general salience hypothesis for the causal analysis of our own more specific problem.

In 'On Perceptual Readiness' Bruner presents a particularly clear expression of the functional approach to perception in general and the categorization process in particular. For Bruner, categorization is an inalienable aspect of perception, serving the perceiver through its ability to guide, order and simplify. Its essential role is to produce as accurate and veridical a representation of reality as possible whilst steering that representation away from currently irrelevant detail and towards what is relevant and important for present purposes. Given that reality is always too complex to be 'known' completely, categorization helps ensure that we know what we need to know.

How does it do this? Bruner's answer is an interactional hypothesis of the processes determining categorization in any given context. He argues that the 'capture' of a stimulus by a category depends on an interaction between the relative 'accessibility' of that category within the perceiver's repertoire and the 'fit' between input and stored category specifications. Accessibility refers to the relative 'readiness' of a given category to become activated; the more accessible the category the less input required to invoke the relevant categorization, the wider the range of stimulus characteristics that will be perceived as congruent with category specifications and the more likely that other less accessible categories which also fit stimulus input will be masked. The two major determinants of accessibility discussed by Bruner are the current tasks, goals and purposes of the perceiver, and the likelihood of particular types of objects or events occurring in the perceiver's present environment; my 'taxi' category would be particularly accessible if I were in a hurry to get somewhere and standing at a taxi rank. Whilst accessibility thus ensures that perception is appropriately selective, gearing categorization to the demands imposed by changing motives and circumstances, fit – the match between actual stimulus characteristics and category specifications – ties it firmly to reality. However 'ready' I might be to see a taxi, I do not until something with at least some requisite characteristics appears. Bruner suggests that, in general, given two equally accessible categories, that which best fits input will become salient, and given two equally good fits, the more accessible category will become salient.

In order to tailor Bruner's general hypothesis to the specific problem in which we are interested – the salience of particular categorizations at the social, ingroup/outgroup level of abstraction – it is necessary to relate his concepts of accessibility and fit to the functioning of social categorizations. Our task is (1) to specify the factors determining relative accessibility for social categories (which make perceivers more ready to use one social categorization rather than another), and (2) to distinguish the conditions under which a given social categorization is perceived as fitting stimulus input from those under which it is not. Our own research, and consequently the remainder of this chapter, concentrates on the conditions of fit rather than the determinants of accessibility. We shall begin, however with a brief discussion of the relative accessibility of social categories.

The relative accessibility of social categories

In general terms relative accessibility translates quite straightforwardly to the social domain; there will be variation across both contexts and perceivers in the latent readiness of given social categorizations to become activated. Bruner's two major determinants of relative accessibility, current goals and circumstances, are also applicable to social categorization. There is some evidence that subjects' task orientation can influence social categorization (Oakes and Turner, 1986; see C. E. Cohen, 1981, for similar conclusions in personality research), and the early vivid reminder manipulations of group membership salience can be seen as attempts to vary the situation-specific relative accessibility of the categorization concerned.

Some recent research has identified information-processing factors which may affect category or 'construct' accessibility (Higgins and

King, 1980; Wyer and Srull, 1980). Higgins and King, for example, add recency and activation, 'salience' (i.e., prominence and attentional distinctiveness) and the relationship to other accessible constructs to Bruner's determinants of accessibility. Such factors clearly can affect the relative accessibility of stored constructs (Higgins, Rholes and Jones, 1977), but, as social rather than purely cognitive constructs, social categories have some distinctive characteristics and functions (Tajfel, 1972a, 1981a), with implications for the factors likely to determine their relative accessibility. Their role in self-conception suggests that the relative centrality or importance of a particular group membership to an individual's self-definition will be a major determinant of its relative accessibility for that individual (e.g., Boyanowsky and Allen, 1973). A closely related point is that the current emotional or value significance of a given ingroup/outgroup categorization is likely to influence its relative accessibility (Tajfel, 1972a; Tajfel and Wilkes, 1964). This effect may be evident throughout a culture, for some groups within a culture, or for some individual group members. Thus, the black/white categorization is chronically accessible in South Africa. In other countries it may be more accessible to groups involved in the politics of race relations (members of anti-apartheid groups or fascist political parties) than to others not so involved, and more accessible to racially prejudiced individuals, both black and white, than to the non-prejudiced. It can be suggested that these sorts of factors are likely to be the major determinants of relative social category accessibility (Tajfel, 1980) and future salience research may be profitably addressed to the systematization of our understanding of just how such factors influence relative accessibility.

When does input fit a social categorization?

As already noted, the concept of fit in Bruner's hypothesis ties the categorization process to reality. It takes account of the fact that categories represent real-world invariances and co-occurrences (Rosch, 1978) and are activated to make sense of those invariances when they appear in the perceptual field. (Accessibility takes into account the perceiver's capacity to pay attention to, and indeed his or her interest in, only some of the invariances perceivable at any one time.) In defining fit for social categorizations the task is to specify the characteristics of the social invariances to which the ingroup/outgroup level of categorization corresponds.

It is hypothesized that fit for social categories comprises the degree to which the people under observation maximize the perceived differences between and similarities within categories. As one way of operationalizing this idea, fit can be thought of as the degree to which observed similarities and differences between people (or their actions) are perceived as *correlated with* a division into social categories (Tajfel, 1969b). Thus, of the various ways available of categorizing a collection of individuals (e.g., male/female, black/white, English/American) the best-fitting categorization will be that with which observed similarities and differences in individual characteristics, expressed attitudes, behaviour, etc., correlate most highly.

This definition of fit relates directly to the principle of meta-contrast outlined in chapter 3 – that within a given frame of reference any collection of stimuli is more likely to be categorized as an entity to the degree that the differences between those stimuli (on relevant dimensions of comparison) are perceived as less than the differences between that collection and other stimuli. The meta-contrast ratio, the ratio of perceived inter-category differences to intra-category differences, is equivalent to the degree of (bi-serial) correlation between category membership and observed similarities and differences: the higher that correlation, the higher the meta-contrast ratio for the comparison. As noted in chapter 3, several major theoretical analyses of the categorization process have emphasized the idea of intra-category similarities and inter-category differences as fundamental to categorization. In particular, Rosch (1978) introduces the probabilistic concept of 'cue validity', which describes the extent to which the defining attributes of a category are common to category members but not shared by members of other categories: 'the validity of a given cue x as a predictor of a given category y (the conditional probability of y/x) increases as the frequency with which cue x is associated with category y increases, and decreases as the frequency with which cue x is associated with categories other than y increases . . . The cue validity of an entire category may be defined as the summation of the cue validities for that category of each of the attributes of the category. A category with high cue validity is by definition more differentiated from other categories than one of lower cue validity' (1978, pp. 30–1). She notes that categories with high cue validity provide the most information with the least cognitive effort because they allow the perceiver to move quickly and confidently from 'cue to categorial identity' (Bruner, 1957) with little danger of misidentification. The 'diagnosticity principle' in Tversky's (1977; Tversky and Gati, 1978) feature-matching theory of similarity, Campbell's (1958) 'coefficient of common fate' as the basis of 'perceived entitativity' and Tajfel's (1969b, 1972a) discussion of categorization in terms of a correlation between continuous attributes and a discontinuous classification all stress the importance of a clear differentiation between categories. Further, as we saw above, the major empirical generalization to be drawn from past research on group membership salience is that the relative separateness and clarity of a social categorization is closely related to its salience, and separateness and clarity are simply ways of describing the degree of correlation between people's actions and a division into social categories. There is, therefore, both a theoretical and an empirical basis for the hypothesis that the degree of similarity perceived between individuals identifiable as members of one category and difference perceived between individuals identifiable as members of different categories defines the conditions of fit.

However, this is merely the cognitive-structural aspect of fit; the definition must at the same time take into account the behavioural content or social meaning of ingroup/outgroup categorizations. Perceiving a person as 'English', for example, does more than define him or her as similar to or different from other people; it defines similarities and differences on specific, normatively appropriate dimensions. Ingroup/outgroup categorizations represent the *direction* of similarities and differences and their specific behavioural and normative *content*, and, therefore, it is similarities and differences which are socially meaningful in terms of and congruent with the content of the defining dimensions which fit the categorization. To define fit for social categories more precisely, therefore, it comprises the degree to which observed similarities and differences between people (or their actions) are perceived to correlate in a stereotype-consistent manner with a division into social categories.

It should be emphasized that fitting input with a social categorization is situation-specific. We are not discussing whether given social categorizations are more or less highly correlated with differences in attitudes or behaviour in a chronic, acontextual sense (although the same ideas can be applied to this end), nor suggesting that a given attitude or behaviour is always perceived as related to the norms of one particular category. On the contrary, perceived *structural fit* always depends upon the contrast of differences between categories with differences within categories for individuals and behaviour currently under consideration. Similarly, the *normative fit* between a given characteristic or action and a given categorization depends on the intergroup comparison being made and on context: what is normatively relevant to one category membership in one context may be irrelevant, or relevant to a different membership, in another context. This is an important point because one of the primary distinguishing characteristics of *social* categorization is that its object can transform itself: people act differently in different situations, varying the 'cues' for categorization available, and the current meaning of those cues. Thus, in contrast with Rosch (1978), we see the 'basic', most useful and informative (and hence salient) level of categorization as highly contextually variable rather than fixed.

To summarize, it is hypothesized that the salience of a social categorization depends upon an interaction between its relative accessibility and the fit between input and category specifications. Fit for social categories comprises both structural and normative elements: input fits a social categorization to the extent that (1) observed similarites and differences between individuals (or their actions) are perceived as correlated with a division into social categories (i.e., the higher the meta-contrast ratio), and (2) that correlation is on dimensions comprising and in the direction consistent with the normative content of the categorization. Given equal accessibility, that categorization which maximizes the normatively consistent correlation between observed similarities and differences and category memberships will become salient.

Before discussing research testing this salience hypothesis it will be useful briefly to examine the salience problem from an attributional perspective.

Group membership salience and attribution

The foundations of what has become known as attribution theory grew from Heider's lifelong interest in basic processes of perception (Heider, 1983). As outlined in *The Psychology of Interpersonal Relations* (1958), Heider's attributional approach to perception shares some central features with Bruner's categorization analysis. First, both theorists conceive of perception as the reference of unique, potentially infinite surface events to some known underlying invariance; a category in Bruner's analysis, a 'dispositional property' in Heider's. Secondly, this reference of perception to an underlying invariance was seen as an essential, inalienable aspect of psychological functioning in both accounts. Bruner held that 'all perceptual experience is necessarily the end product of a categorization process' (1957, p. 124), and Heider has commented quite recently that 'Attribution is a part of our cognition of the environment. Whenever you cognize your environment you will find attribution occurring' (in Harvey, Ickes and Kidd, 1976, p. 18). A third closely related shared assumption is that categorization/attribution imparts *meaning* to perception (which is why each serves such an essential function). Bruner comments: 'whatever is perceived . . . achieves its "meaning" from a class of percepts with which it is grouped' (1957, p. 124). In Heider's words, 'the invariances of the environment . . . give meaning to what [man] experiences and it is these meanings that are . . . precipitated as the reality of that environment to which he then reacts' (Heider, 1958, p. 81).

Thus, for both Bruner and Heider, the meaning or identity of what is perceived depends upon the specific invariance to which it is referred, making the prediction of that process of reference essential for a proper understanding of perception. As we have seen, Bruner developed his 'accessibility × fit' hypothesis for this purpose and we have been able to adapt it for predicting reference to the social, ingroup/outgroup level of invariance. How does work on attribution processes fit in with this analysis?

The major work specifying the conditions of attribution has been done by other theorists attempting to produce more tractable, hypothesis-generating formulations from the broad sweep of Heider's insights (Jones and Davis, 1965; Kelley, 1967). This inevitably involved a certain narrowing of focus, and one important idea of Heider's which took a central place in subsequent theoretical developments was his distinction between 'personal' and 'environmental' attributions. In particular, Kelley's formulation focused directly on the person/environment dichotomy. His 'ANOVA' model attempted to specify the conditions under which a person's response to a stimulus would be attributed to 'something about' the stimulus (an external attribution) rather than 'something about' the person (an internal attribution), or circumstantial factors. The model outlined three now familiar criteria on which decisions about causal allocation would be based: distinctiveness, consistency and consensus. His predictions were generally upheld in experiments by McArthur (1972), and have been supported by many studies since (see Kelley and Michela, 1980). In general, a person's response to an entity (e.g., John laughs at the comedian) is attributed to the entity (the comedian) rather than the person (John) when it is distinctive (John doesn't laugh at any other comedian), consistent (in the past John has almost always laughed at the same comedian) and consensual (almost everyone who hears the comedian laughs at him). Person attributions, on the other hand, occur when the response is non-distinctive, consistent and non-consensual. Inconsistent responses tend to be attributed to the particular circumstances in which they occurred.

For present purposes, what is of interest is the way in which Kelley conceptualizes the consensus variable to deal with collective, shared behaviour. Consensus is all-or-nothing in the theory (Lalljee, 1981). There is either total agreement (i.e., at least implicitly, across social category boundaries) or the actor differs from everyone else. In the first case the conclusion is that some constant feature of the external world must be responsible for the consensus (entity attribution), in the second that something in the actor's individual personality must underly his or her deviance from the consensus. Because conditions of *collective* agreement and disagreement, of collective similarities and differences, do not feature in Kelley's theory, neither does the possibility of a person attribution which is not individual and idiosyncratic.

The importance of the consensus variable as formulated by Kelley has been questioned by some attribution theorists (Nisbett and Borgida, 1975; Nisbett, Borgida, Crandall and Reed, 1976; see Kassin, 1979). However, the fundamental assumption it embodies – that only idiosyncratic behaviour is deliberate, internally motivated and therefore attributable to the person, shared behaviour must be externally constrained – is widely accepted. Kassin (1979) describes it as 'one of the more intuitively appealing' (p. 1966) assumptions of Kelley's theory. The same assumption is expressed in a different way in Jones and Davis's (1965) 'correspondent inference' development of Heider's ideas. Their theory concentrates on the 'person' side of Heider's dichotomy, attempting to account for the attribution of specific, stable, idiosyncratic personality characteristics on the basis of particular actions. Very briefly, the major components of the theory are the non-common effects of an action (i.e., those produced by the action which would not have been produced by any alternative(s) at the actor's disposal) and its assumed social desirability. It is hypothesized that when both the number of non-common effects produced by an action and its general social desirability are low, the perceiver can make the most 'correspondent inference', i.e., the most confident attribution of an actor's personality from their actions. In this account it is the operation of the social desirability or 'expected valence' variable which effectively limits person attributions to idiosyncratic behaviour; socially desirable and therefore socially shared behaviour does not attract person attributions. In Jones and McGillis's (1976) elaboration of the theory the specific prior probabilities which replace the earlier general social desirability variable include category-based expectancies which derive from perceivers' knowledge of the norms associated with given category memberships. It is assumed that normative behaviour, being expected and shared, does not provide information about the actor and thus does not lead to a person attribution.

These assumptions are entirely valid and appropriate given that

Jones and his colleagues are explicitly interested in the attribution of *personality* characteristics to individuals. The problem is, however, that as in Kelley's formulation no allowance is made for the possibility of any other type of person attribution. In effect, the basic distinction in attribution theory has come to be between *individual* (personality) and environmental explanations for events. 'Persons' (i.e., people) only exist as causal entities in terms of individual personality. This is, of course, in direct opposition to our own assumptions, specified in the self-categorization theory, about what 'persons' are. It is hypothesized in chapter 3 that, under specific conditions, self- and/or other-perception (and consequently behaviour) will refer to the social, ingroup/outgroup rather than personal, individual level of categorization. It can now be further hypothesized that the same conditions will produce *attributions to 'persons' (people) as social category members* rather than to personality (or external factors), i.e., a qualitatively distinct type (or level) of person attribution.

This is by no means the first time that accusations of individualism have been levelled at attribution theory (see Hewstone, 1983, for a brief review), and recent work has set out to demonstrate the influence of both social category memberships (e.g., Hewstone, Jaspars and Lalljee, 1982) and more general societal variables (Miller, 1984) on the ways in which we explain our own and others' behaviour. The present hypothesis extends this 'socializing' effort into the area of attribution theory as a basic theory of social perception rather than one more specifically concerned with explicit attempts at explanation (see Eiser, 1983). The suggestion is that social category memberships can be treated not only as an *influence upon* the attribution process but *as attributions in themselves*, as a distinct type of 'dispositional property', relating to *social* or *collective* invariances in people's attitudes and actions, to which perceptual reference can be made. To perceive people as social groups (different from other social groups) is implicitly to explain their behaviour in terms of their shared, collective, societal properties and not in terms of individual personalities, but it is nevertheless an attribution to internal psychological (social-psychological) causes.

Two experiments on salience and attribution

This section outlines two experiments (Oakes and Turner, 1987) conducted to test major aspects of the above analysis of salience – the hypothesized conditions of fit between input and a social categorization and link between salience and attribution to a social category membership.

The first study investigated the salience of sex category membership and manipulated the cognitive-structural aspect of fit – the degree of correlation between behaviour and sex category membership – whilst holding the normative or content element constant. The hypothesis was that sex category membership salience and attribution would be maximized where behaviour correlated with the sex categorization.

Subjects viewed a tape-slide presentation of a six-person stimulus group discussing a sex-relevant issue (Kogan and Wallach's, 1964, choice dilemma item concerning the proposed marriage of 'Mr M.' and 'Miss T.'). The experimental design manipulated two independent variables: the stimulus group comprised either three men and three women (non-solo conditions) or one man and five women (solo conditions), and the pattern of agreement on the issue was either three versus three (dissent conditions) or one versus five (deviance conditions) such that in the non-solo/dissent and solo/deviance conditions the correlation between observed behaviour and the sex categorization was maximized (the three men disagreed with the three women or the one man with the five women). In the non-solo/deviance and solo/dissent conditions either one man disagreed with two men and three women (the latter agreeing with each other) or two women and the one man disagreed with three women. The dependent variables were subjects' attributions (to situation/personality/sex category) for the opinion expressed by one male stimulus individual who appeared in every condition, and their description of that target on sex-stereotyped adjective scales. It was predicted that attributions to sex category membership and male stereotyping would be strongest and attributions to personality weakest in the correlated non-solo/dissent and solo/deviance conditions.

This prediction was confirmed in the non-solo/dissent (three men versus three women) condition, which produced the strongest attributions to the target's male identity, the weakest attributions to his personality and the most stereotypically male descriptions of him. Note that the inverse relationship between category membership and personality attributions supports the assumption in the self-categorization theory of 'a functional antagonism between the salience of one level of self-categorization and other levels' (chapter 3).

However, the predictions were only weakly confirmed in the solo/deviance condition (one man versus five women): there was a significant increase in attributions to the target's male identity compared to the non-solo/deviance condition, but no difference from the solo/dissent condition. Also he was actually described as most 'feminine' on the sex-stereotyped adjective scales. It seems likely that, despite out intention to control them in this experiment, normative factors were responsible for this result. The male target always argued in favour of the marriage of Mr M. and Miss T. In the absence of direct evidence that other men would agree with him (as in the non-solo/dissent condition) but with the correlation between sex and attitudes making the sex categorization the salient basis for evaluating his attitudes, his pro-marriage decision may have been perceived as counter-stereotypical and hence feminine. In other words, it appears that the disagreement between the target and the women and the specific issue made the sex categorization salient, but in such a way that its ready-made content was at odds with the behaviour of the stimulus individuals ('men are generally less interested in marriage than women'; see Douvan and Adelson, 1966; Leonard, 1980), which accentuated the perception of the target as a counter-stereotypical deviant from his male category membership (see Etzkowitz, 1971).

Following from this interpretation, the second experiment systematically manipulated both the structual and normative aspects of fit. It was hypothesized that attributions to and the salience of category membership would be maximized under conditions of both high structural and normative fit between behaviour and the categorization. The relationship of social category attributions to the traditional internal (personal)/external (entity, situational) dichotomy was also closely examined through an explicit test of the hypothesis that category membership attributions refer to an internal rather than external causal invariance but can, at the same time, be clearly distinguished from attributions to individual personality characteristics (as the inverse relationship between the two in the previous study suggests). To this end, conditions which should elicit each of the three types of attribution – entity, category membership and personality – were created.

The categorization of interest in this experiment was membership of the Arts or Science faculties for undergraduate university students. Subjects (science students) watched video presentations of six-person stimulus groups which ostensibly comprised three arts and three science faculty students. The stimulus individuals discussed their attitudes to university life, an issue on which, according to the stereotype of the arts/science faculty categorization ascertained in a pilot study, the two groups are clearly differentiated. Arts students are believed to be relatively frivolous and radical in their approach to university education, whilst science students are seen as conscientious and career-oriented. Normative fit was manipulated by means of the specific attitude expressed by the target stimulus individual, an arts student, which was either consistent or inconsistent with the arts faculty stereotype. The pattern of agreement within the stimulus group, i.e., the extent to which attitudes correlated with the arts/science categorization, constituted the manipulation of structural fit. There were three agreement conditions: consensus (all six stimulus individuals agreed), dissensus (the three arts students expressed one attitude whilst the three science students expressed the opposite view) and deviance (the target arts student disagreed with the other five stimulus individuals). The two variables of consistency and agreement were manipulated in a complete factorial design to produce six experimental conditions. In the inconsistent/dissensus condition, for example, the three arts students took a counter-stereotypical line (arguing for the science point of view) against the three science students (who argued for the arts point of view).

The major dependent variables were subjects' attributions for the target's attitude. There were three attribution measures. The first asked subjects to make a general person versus entity attribution to explain why the target expressed the attitude she did ('something to do with the kind of person she is' versus 'the objective facts of the case') which was followed by a question assessing the relative influence of her personality and arts faculty membership ('insofar as something about the kind of person she is was responsible, which of her characteristics was more important?' . . . 'something to do with her individual personality' versus 'something to do with the fact that she is an arts student'). Thirdly, subjects were asked how far they thought 'the presence of the other arts students' had influenced the target's expression of her opinions. The person/entity and personality/faculty membership items were repeated for the stimulus group as a whole.

It was predicted that the strongest entity attributions (i.e., to 'the objective facts of the case') would be made in the consensus conditions, where the entity (the discussion topic) elicited uniform reactions from the individuals present. No effect for the consistency variable was expected here. The strongest category membership attributions were expected in the consistent/dissensus condition where both the structural and normative aspects of fit were maximized. Personality attributions were predicted for the inconsistent/deviance condition where the target's behaviour was both idiosyncratic (in comparison to the others present) and counter-normative for her identity as an arts student (Jones and McGillis, 1976). In other words, the latter two conditions were both expected to produce attributions towards the 'person' pole of the initial, general scale, but then expected to produce divergent results on the second personality/faculty membership measure, confirming the hypothesis that category membership attributions refer to an aspect of the person rather than external causal factors but can, nevertheless, be clearly distinguished from personality attributions.

The 'presence of other arts students' measure was included to test the idea that the perceived influence of the target's fellow ingroup members would increase with the salience of the arts/science categorization. Wilder (1978) presents some results congruent with this expectation. He examined attributions made for an actor's agreement or disagreement with others where the actor was either categorized into a group with those others or appeared as one of an aggregate of unrelated individuals. It was predicted and found that stronger attributions were made to the 'presence of others' when the actor agreed within a group than when he agreed with an uncategorized aggregate. Wilder treats this as evidence for the *external* attribution of group behaviour on the basis of the assumption that shared behaviour is determined by external normative pressure rather than identification with ingroup norms (see Wilder, 1981, pp. 220–2). 'Other people', including other ingroup members, are of course 'external' to the actor as an individual person. However, following self-categorization theory, their influence on the actor could be seen as mediated by a *shared internalization* of or identification with a social group membership (and associated norms), rather than based on any process of external pressure. In this case, attributions to the presence of other ingroup members should be affected by the perceived salience of the shared ingroup identification over and above the simple presence of other ingroup members behaving similarly to the target. The present experiment afforded an opportunity to test such a hypothesis through a comparison of the strength of attributions to 'the presence of the other Arts students' in the consistent/dissensus condition on the one hand and the consensus conditions and the inconsistent/dissensus condition on the other, the prediction being that this attribution would be strongest in the consistent/dissensus condition (where the arts/science categorization should be most salient).

The salience of the arts/science categorization was also assessed by measures of perceived similarity and attraction. Subjects were asked how similar they thought the target was 'in her general beliefs, attitudes, values, etc.' to the other arts students and to the science students, and how well they thought the target would get on socially with each group. The greatest differentiation between the two categories (i.e., most similarity and attraction to other arts students and least to science students) was expected in the consistent/dissensus condition and the least in the inconsistent/deviance condition.

Our predictions were strongly supported by the results: entity attributions were strongest in the consensus conditions, category membership attributions in the consistent/dissensus condition and personality attributions in the inconsistent/deviance condition. Subjects thought the presence of the other arts students influenced the target most significantly in the consistent/dissensus condition, and results on the measures of intra- and intergroup similarity and attraction indicated that the arts/science categorization was most highly differentiated in this condition too (see Oakes and Turner, 1987, for a more detailed account).

These results provide good evidence that social categorizations become salient (as reflected in both category membership attributions and the degree of category differentiation) under conditions of cognitive-structural and normative fit (both these variables as well as the interaction between them produced effects) and that category membership represents a third type of attribution, distinct from entity and personality explanations. Further, it was clear that both personality *and* category membership attributions made reference to an aspect of the individual rather than to external factors. The latter hypothesis also received some indirect support from an interesting finding that subjects' impressions of the target were more favourable in the consistent/dissensus condition than in any other. If the target was perceived as complying with ingroup norms through the force of some external pressure in this condition, she would surely have created a somewhat unfavourable impression, and would have been evaluated most favourably in the inconsistent/deviant condition, where she resisted this pressure and asserted her own opinions. In fact, she was evaluated least favourably in the latter condition.

In sum, the results of the two experiments oulined here have well supported the major hypotheses. Two issues stand out as needing more empirical attention. First, given that we now have a better understanding of the conditions determining fit for social categories, the hypothesized interaction between accessibility and fit needs to be addressed by research. Secondly, the applicability of the interactional hypothesis to the salience of category memberships in *self*-perception must be investigated. Hogg and Turner (1987, see chapter 5) have presented some evidence of increased sex stereotyping in self-perception under conditions of gender salience. In the second experiment reported above subjects did provide self-descriptions on arts and science faculty stereotype adjective scales. Whilst there was significant evidence of self-stereotyping, this did not follow the stereotyping of the stimulus individuals in any straightforward manner (see Oakes and Turner, 1987). A more recent attempt to address the self-salience issue involving national identity amongst Australian students (Oakes and Davidson, 1986) again produced very significant self-stereotyping and some evidence that this was enhanced under conditions of best fit with the national category, particularly best normative fit. Interestingly, there was also some evidence of higher self-esteem amongst subjects in the high salience condition (see Dion et al., 1978; Hogg and Turner, 1987; Oakes and Turner, 1980). Clearly, in the context of the *self-categorization* theory this issue is a central one. The results thus far have been supportive rather than otherwise, but, none the less, the testing of the hypothesis in this sphere will remain a priority for some time to come.

Conclusion

This chapter has presented an interactional hypothesis of social category membership salience, from which some distinctive predictions have been derived, and supported by new research. Whilst there is more to be done, it is suggested that the approach outlined here represents a theoretically precise and empirically promising solution to the problem of predicting salience which has been noted in social identity research for some years (e.g., Brown and Turner, 1981, p. 42; Stephenson, 1981, pp. 192–3; Turner, 1982, p. 36).

The reported research findings also give credence to the functional perspective which underlies that hypothesis. It has been argued that, given the reality of groups and individuals' identifications with them, there would be conditions under which group-based perception (of both the self and others) would be entirely appropriate (and not a dysfunctional oversimplification and distortion of the uniqueness of individuals). In support of this line of reasoning, the research indicates that the situational salience of social categorizations is indeed finely tuned to their appropriateness as ways of interpreting individuals' actions in given contexts: the stimulus individuals' category memberships did become most salient when they demonstrated collective, normatively consistent and socially systematic uniformities of behaviour, when, it is not too much to say, they were, *in reality*, behaving as social groups. In other words, the subjects' perceptions of the stimulus individuals as group members were entirely valid, or, as Bruner (1957) would put it, 'veridical'. Thus, in contrast with the current view that perceiving individuals as group members – stereotyping – is a manifestation of social psychological errors, biases, illusions and irrationality (e.g., see Ashmore and DelBoca, 1981, pp. 28–9), the present analysis is firmly grounded in the view that there is behaviour in the real world corresponding to the social level of abstraction, which salience processes both reflect and help to make possible.

7

Social Identity
and Group Polarization

(Margaret Wetherell)

Introduction

This chapter continues the application of self-categorization theory to social influence, returning to look at the phenomenon of group polarization in detail. As we have seen, groups are said to polarize when the prevailing opinion extremitizes as a result of group interaction and discussion: like polarized molecules, group members become even more aligned in the direction they were already tending. More precisely, group polarization is usually defined as the hypothesis that the 'average postgroup response will tend to be more extreme in the same direction as the average of the pregroup responses' (Myers and Lamm, 1976, p. 603).

There are empirical and theoretical reasons why group polarization is an important site for social psychological investigations of group influence. Polarization effects are not isolated instances: they have been demonstrated in the laboratory with great regularity and reliability for a wide range of discussion items (e.g., controversial attitudes, gambling and risk-taking, ethical dilemmas, person perception, mock jury decision-making and even for matters of obscure fact, see reviews by Lamm and Myers, 1978; Myers and Lamm, 1976). In addition, there are obvious examples from outside the laboratory. Reicher's (1984a, see chapter 8) description of a 'riot', for instance, provides abundant illustrations of the process.

Such a pervasive phenomenon demands an explanation. Why should opinions and actions intensify in this way? It is not intuitively obvious that they should. Why do people not become more moderate or compromising through discussing an issue with their peers? Early empirical work and theorizing about group influence, in fact, typically found compromise effects across different tasks, i.e., convergence on the average pregroup response (Allport, 1924; Sherif, 1936). It was assumed that the function of influence is primarily a moderating or equilibrating one (Festinger, 1950). The more recent discovery of polarization upset this assumption. Although polarization generally represents a convergence of views (Singleton, 1979), it is an *extremitized convergence*: a regular deviation from the moderate position or mean of individuals' initial, prediscussion opinions. The phenomenon, therefore, also raises critical theoretical questions. Modern reconceptualizations of group influence must account for both convergence/compromise and convergence/polarization effects and explain under what conditions each can be expected.

It will be argued that currently favoured models of polarization are inadequate in this respect, that the difficulties can be resolved through the application of self-categorization theory, and a body of empirical research will be described in support of this alternative. We begin with some details of the methodology of the laboratory studies and the history of polarization research.

That history is a rather curious one and worth considering as a case study in the blinkering effects of dominant theories. In 1961 Stoner discovered that given choice-dilemmas to discuss (e.g., should Mr A. give up his secure but boring job for an exciting but insecure position) groups made more extreme, riskier decisions than individuals. The effect became known as the 'risky shift' and rapidly developed into one of the most popular research areas in group dynamics. During the first phase of the research these risky shifts tended to be seen as an exception to the general rule of group interaction effects, which were conceptualized as moderation and compromise on the average, and work focused on the special nature of risk-taking. This trend continued despite evidence that subjects in groups also became more cautious on some dilemmas (Brown, 1965). An overemphasis on one particular paradigm thus led to a misleading perspective on the problem (Cartwright, 1973). In 1969 Moscovici and Zavalloni demonstrated that group-induced shifts to more extreme positions occurred for more general attitude items as well. The term 'group polarization' became widely accepted as it became apparent that group discussion would enhance pre-existing tendencies in a large range of situations and was not restricted to choice-dilemmas and the risky shift.

A typical study employs a simple 'within-subjects' procedure. The responses of the same subjects are obtained and compared at three stages: (1) a *pretest* where the participants privately express their individual views on the issue(s), (2) a stage where the *consensus* reached by the group after discussion (or a related manipulation) is recorded (polarization also occurs, but usually to a lesser degree, if consensus is not required and members discuss without reaching unanimity, or indeed if subjects are exposed to each other's views but do not discuss, Cartwright, 1971), and (3) a *posttest* where members privately indicate their individual postdiscussion views. The same response scale is used on all three occasions, e.g., a seven-point scale from 'strongly agree' to 'strongly disagree' with some statement, or a choice of the odds of success required from 1 in 10 (risky) to 9 in 10 (cautious) before some course of action is recommended. Polarization is deemed to have occurred if there is a significant difference between the mean pretest and mean posttest response (or group consensus) in the same direction as the pretest trend (i.e., towards the closer pole of the scale). A shift in the opposite direction to the pretest trend would be a case of extremitization without polarization, defined here as depolarization.

Although once quite varied, explanations of polarization have tended in recent years to crystallize into two kinds: a persuasive arguments or informational influence model and a social comparison account. These have taken up two intuitively plausible ideas, namely, that members could become more extreme because (1) if they all share an attitudinal tendency, any new and persuasive material brought out in discussion might tend to reflect that tendency, and (2) their self-esteem is likely to be bound up with endorsing what seems to be the most socially desirable position. As will become apparent as these interpretations are reviewed, they reflect the informational and normative influence distinction described in chapters 2 and 4 and, although moderately successful empirically, they have left important questions in abeyance partly because of this intellectual heritage.

Persuasive arguments and social comparison
Theories and empirical data

The persuasive arguments analysis has been developed principally by Burnstein and Vinokur (1973, 1975, 1977; Burnstein, 1982; Vinokur, 1971; Vinokur and Burnstein, 1974, 1978a). They suggest that during the pretest stage subjects review all the arguments they are familiar with or that they can remember relevant to the issue and make a decision on this basis. In effect, they are retrieving the arguments they know from a 'cultural pool' of possible material. The balance of arguments retrieved (the proportion of 'pro' and 'con' material) and their persuasiveness (validity, relevance, lack of triviality) will determine the direction and extremity of subjects' opinions. Because subjects are generally from the same kind of background and thus have in common the same cultural pool of arguments, there is frequently a pretest trend towards one option.

Burnstein and Vinokur maintain that group discussion will then polarize this trend to the degree and *only to the degree* that the exchange of arguments throws up new persuasive material. They suggest that arguments are often partially diffused among group members, i.e., one person will remember two or three pro arguments, another two or three different pro arguments but not the first two or three, and so on. The combination of persuasive, partially diffused information through discussion would cause polarization as the members consider the new, previously unfamiliar pro arguments which persuade them of the even greater wisdom of endorsing that position.

Arguments need not be diffused in this way. Burnstein and Vinokur specifically predict that if all the group members retrieved exactly the same arguments then there would be no polarization; similarly, if a great many original 'anti' arguments were presented, then this would swing a group formerly pro on an issue towards the opposite view. These predictions are in line with their general claim that polarization depends on strictly informational criteria being met.

A problem arises here, however. Given that polarization is a much more common outcome than depolarization, their explanation will only work if they assume that new persuasive arguments arising in discussion are much more likely to favour the dominant than the non-dominant trend. Why should this happen? Burnstein and Vinokur would claim that material with polarizing rather than depolarizing effects is more likely because the very fact that a pretest trend exists demonstrates that people find those kinds of arguments more accessible or easier to retrieve from memory. But this seems an incomplete account of the conditions under which new material might arise. It seems equally plausible to argue that new material favouring the non-dominant pole is more likely to emerge because the few arguments that are retrieved or presented for this option are much less likely to be shared (representing, by definition, a minority viewpoint), whereas those favouring the dominant pole will probably be familiar to all.

It can be seen that the persuasive arguments model is highly cognitive in emphasis. Opinion shifts appear as quite rational with the individual and the group functioning rather like information-processing machines calculating the status and originality of material. Attitude changes are seen as genuine in the sense of being internalized or privately accepted and not merely public compliance with the group.

In contrast, social comparison theorists have developed a

motivational, affect-based analysis: self-presentational strategies of one kind or another are thought to be the cause. Several models have been articulated but all share the basic assumption that one side of a choice dilemma (e.g., the risky or cautious option) or pole of an attitude item is more socially desirable, valued, admired, or associated with positive characteristics such as ability than the other – hence the pretest tendency in a sample and the explanation of shifts.

One version claims that individuals become more polarized in groups because not only do they value more extreme responses but they have 'miscalculated' the likely extremity of their peers and, discovering that others are more extreme than themselves, need to shift to recover lost self-esteem (Levinger and Schneider, 1969). Alternatively, it has been suggested that extremity is rewarded by the group because it is perceived to be associated with ability (Jellison and Arkin, 1977) or that shifts result from members competing with each other to take up the most desirable, extreme positions to maximize their distinctiveness from others in a valued direction (Myers, Bruggink, Kersting and Schlosser, 1980; Lamm and Myers, 1978). Despite these minor differences social comparison theories can be treated as one coherent approach. They share the same assumptions – that people value extremity and shift to be evaluated more positively than their peers by themselves or others – and more or less stand or fall together.

Over the last decade or so a great deal of research has been conducted to test the central hypotheses of persuasive arguments and social comparison models. In general, in terms of weight of evidence, it seems persuasive arguments theorists have fared better.

Summarizing, first, the main points for their model: it has been demonstrated that there is a significant correlation between the pro/con balance of arguments raised in discussion and opinion shifts (Ebbesen and Bowers, 1974), and there seems little doubt that subjects spend their time exchanging substantive information (Vinokur, Trope and Burnstein, 1975). Persuasiveness ratings of arguments are also highly correlated with shifts, and there is a relationship between the balance of arguments subjects can note down on a pretest while thinking about an item (presumably retrieved from the 'cultural pool') and the pretest positions normally obtained across samples for that item (Vinokur and Burnstein, 1974). Vinokur and Burnstein (1974) have also managed to model mathematically the kind of shifts expected from a partial diffusion of arguments account of polarization and shown a good correspondence with actual *in vivo* shifts. Novel persuasive arguments presented to subjects to read are also more effective in changing opinion than non-novel persuasive ones (Vinokur and Burnstein, 1978a). One obvious weakness is the failure to demonstrate directly that in discussion it is the arguments alone and not some factor consistently associated with the material which cause polarization (cf. Pruitt, 1971).

For their part, social comparison theorists need to be able to demonstrate that (1) groups move in socially desirable/culturally valued directions, (2) subjects typically underestimate the extremity of other people's positions, and (3) mere exposure to others' positions (the opportunity for social comparison) produces shifts.

Evidence on the first point is mixed. It has been shown with the risky shift that more extreme, riskier responses are admired or seen as ideal (Levinger and Schneider, 1969), but for items which typically produce cautious polarizing shifts more cautious responses are not consistently and regularly admired (Fraser, 1971), as they should be if polarization depends on social desirability. Lamm, Schaude and Trommsdorff (1971) have demonstrated that large discrepancies between one's own initial pretest view and the admired response (say risk) also produces large polarization effects, which is strong support for social desirability. But, then, other studies (Vidmar, 1974; Vinokur and Burnstein, 1978b) have shown polarization for category width judgements, for example, and similar items where the notion of one response being more socially desirable than another in the culture is quite meaningless. In addition, it seems naïve subjects presented with a consensus in a group manufactured by confederates of the experimenter or through a tape-recording will conform to that consensus to the same extent whether or not it endorses the socially desirable position (Baron, Dion, Baron and Miller, 1971; Blascovich and Ginsburg, 1974; Cecil, Chertkoff and Cummings, 1970; Clark and Crockett, 1971; Roberts and Castore, 1972; the exception being Baron, Monson and Baron, 1973). The only possible conclusion here is that social desirability may motivate polarizing shifts but it does not appear to be a necessary determining condition.

Social comparison theory is on slightly stronger ground in the other two areas. Numerous studies have found that people responding on a pretest estimate that their peers will not be as extreme or polarized as themselves (e.g., St Jean and Percival, 1974); thus some (the moderates) must be 'miscalculating', giving them a reason for becoming more extreme in discussion as this mistake is revealed. However, those who are 'mistaken' in this way do not necessarily polarize the most (Lamm et al., 1971). Finally, on the last point, despite disputes over early attempts to establish the sufficiency of mere comparison with others for opinion shifts (Burnstein and Vinokur, 1977), a recent experiment (Cotton and Baron, 1980) would seem conclusively to have confirmed that mere exposure to other people's positions – the minimal condition for social comparison – is sufficient to bring about opinion change.

Both theories, therefore, have empirical support (albeit with some major loose ends in the case of social comparison theory). But, despite vehement attempts to establish the priority of the persuasive arguments explanation (see Burnstein and Vinokur, 1977, versus Sanders and Baron, 1977), a stalemate seems to have been reached. If the rapid decline in polarization research since the late 1970s is any indicator, the consensus among social psychologists working in group processes would seem to be that all directions appear to have been explored, even if no clear solution has emerged.

This view is a mistake. As we shall try to demonstrate, there is considerable scope for a new theoretical initiative. This will become obvious if we return to the theoretical bases of the persuasive arguments and social comparison analyses and point out the major unresolved problems.

Unresolved theoretical issues

The problems fall into several different categories but basically can be attributed to the general assumptions about group process and influence underlying persuasive arguments and social comparison models. They will be dealt with as a series of specific questions.

What makes a persuasive argument persuasive? According to Burnstein and Vinokur people are supposedly influenced in groups due to new and persuasive arguments. But what distinguishes a novel and persuasive argument? Burnstein and Vinokur's criteria can only be described as rudimentary, varying simply from the operational (arguments are persuasive when perceived as such by subjects) to the notionally cognitive (persuasiveness of arguments depends on the extent to which they are related to and the size of the internal information networks with which they make contact, Burnstein, 1982). In general, they refer in their theoretical statements to qualities of logic (validity and consistency), lack of triviality or redundancy, and originality.

The problems here are easily illustrated. Properties of arguments such as validity, triviality, or even originality do not exist in the abstract or, to use Tajfel's (1972b) phrase, in a social vacuum. A message from a group one supports and identifies with will be perceived quite differently than similar messages from a rival outgroup to which one is strongly opposed. As many different strands of research in social psychology have demonstrated, persuasiveness depends on one's perception of the source, situation and message, and one's own initial attitudinal position (Eiser and Stroebe, 1972; McGuire, 1985; McLachlan, 1985). Frequently, even the originality of an argument can be decisively redefined from discussion to discussion. It is more or less a truism in psychology to state that information will be actively constructed and reconstructed in different contexts (cf. Zavalloni and Louis-Guerin, 1979) and therefore the direction Burnstein and Vinokur's theory takes seems particularly iconoclastic. The point for polarization research would seem to be that any credible theory of group influence cannot avoid describing and explaining social contextual variations in argument persuasiveness.

Lamm and Myers (1978) have claimed that other, more flexible cognitive models such as Anderson and Graesser's (1976) information integration approach could accommodate a range of contextual effects. Although this approach has not been as systematically applied to polarization, the argument seems to be that individuals will combine various kinds of information such as the fact that an argument is in line with the dominant tendency in a group as well as the properties of arguments Burnstein and Vinokur stress (relevance, lack of triviality, cogency and novelty) and that these may be differentially weighted. In this way source effects (where the message is coming from) could be accommodated, also the persuasive effects of assertions without much content and the fact that material is often raised in a more dynamic fashion in a discussion than when simply read in a list of arguments (Lamm and Myers, 1978).

The crucial argument, however, is whether this incorporation of source and other effects is explanatory. The social psychological process still seems obscure. Cognitively speaking, arguments from political groups one supports may open up information networks to a greater extent than arguments from political groups not supported; information may be more persuasive on some occasions that others depending on congruency with the pretest trend, but we still need to know *why* information-processing functions in this way and *how exactly* influence depends on the recognition of reference groups.

Why are some kinds of extremity desirable? Clearly the definition of persuasiveness is a central unresolved issue for persuasive arguments theory. The parallel problem for social comparison theory is to explain why some kinds of extremity are desirable. Let us take a specimen social comparison explanation to illustrate.

A sample of people regard risk as socially desirable; so when they give their initial pretest response on a choice dilemma item they choose mostly relatively risky options. Discussion of the item in groups reveals that this preference for risk is shared. But why is the group not content with this agreement, why do they not now converge on the average of their pretest responses? Why do they polarize and become even riskier?

The social comparison theorist argues that they do so because they are competing among themselves to endorse the socially desirable option to the greatest extent or because the moderates discover that others are more extreme and need to catch up in the social desirability stakes by becoming riskier too. Groups, in other words, are not effective in changing opinions because they create pressure to agree on some uniform compromise position, but because they provide an environment where individuals can remedy any problems in self-image maintenance which arise because the degree of the desirable attribute (risk) they should present to others is not clear before discussion.

What does this assume? First and foremost it assumes that there is some social/cultural standard *outside the group context* which motivates changes in opinion. Group members are not content to combine their opinions around some average of their views or around a group-based norm because they are pulled along by some external criterion (risk is socially valued).

There is a number of empirical problems here (Wetherell, 1983), the most illuminating arising from the confederate or 'fake norm' studies noted above. This research demonstrates that if you take a subject who like the rest of the sample has a pretest tendency towards some option (say risk) and expose them to a group consensus advocating a cautious response, they will conform and shift to caution. They shift to much the same extent as if the consensus advocated risk. But why should they conform to a cautious consensus if there is a strong social value for risk? Perhaps because in this case implicit group pressure is created (Myers and Lamm, 1976, p. 615), but if this pressure operates in these kinds of cases might it not also be a motivation in groups which all share a pretest tendency to risk? That is, subjects may not be motivated by their recognition of an external social value but by their recognition that this is their discussion group's norm.

One further consideration suggests the importance of this point. It is vital to distinguish between divergence from the group which enhances self-esteem in a given context and plain deviance (i.e., being different in a disapproved, negatively valued direction). A person in a moderately risky group who takes an extremely risky position is diverging in a positively valued direction; this is apparently not a deviant act from the group's perspective. If he or she took an extremely cautious position, however, this almost certainly would be deviant and self-esteem could not be enhanced in the same way. Competition to become more extreme, therefore, is likely to depend not on cultural values *per se* but the norm evident in the particular group context.

It seems likely that certain kinds of extremity are not desirable generally but only because they become the tendency (norm) for the discussion group. If so, some account must be given of group norm formation and conformity processes in polarizing groups.

Social comparison and persuasive arguments models thus reach a similar impasse. The character of group interaction seems likely to be a dynamic contributor to influence determining what is seen as persuasive and what is valued, the problem notwithstanding of how pressure to uniformity alone might cause polarization, yet both theories tend to treat group discussion as a neutral environment responsible at most for some 'noise' or random effects. The crucial causal variables are seen as having their origin elsewhere, either in the information-processing strategies of the individual or in their desire to maintain and enhance self-esteem. These traits and states of the individual are presumed to exist prior to group interaction and persist relatively unchanged through discussion. Little attention is paid as a result to factors or psychological states which might emerge from the group process itself. At this point in the discussion, therefore, it seems apposite to ask the following question.

What part does group process play? Few studies have been conducted on this topic, but none the less it is clear that factors which disrupt or enhance the feeling of group belongingness do affect polarization. Forgas (1977) and Moscovici and Lecuyer (1972) have shown that features which interfere with the ease of group interaction (certain spacing and physical layouts, following procedural rules) inhibit polarization. On the other hand, a sense of common fate (Kogan and Carlson, 1969) and intragroup similarity (Moscovici and Zaleska, cited in Zaleska, 1978) promote opinion shifts. And Doise (1969), replicated by Skinner and Stephenson (1981), has demonstrated that the implicit introduction of a rival outgroup into considerations (students from one school of architecture were asked to ponder the likely opinions of students from another school before discussing their own views) increases polarization. It seems difficult to account for any of these findings in terms of the ratio of persuasive and novel arguments presented or social comparison.

Although further work needs to be done, it is not surprising that cohesiveness, group identification and other specifically group effects are implicated in polarization and in the extent and determination of group influence. These studies strongly suggest that polarization is a genuinely group-mediated process.

However, in contrast to this conclusion, polarization has been defined traditionally in the principal reviews (Lamm and Myers, 1978; Myers and Lamm, 1976) as a sample effect. That is, it has been seen as an outcome of the comparison of individuals' responses before and after discussion across the whole sample. There is no suggestion that polarization also occurs at the level of specific groups and is thus a group-based effect (so that if a group has an initial tendency we can expect it to strengthen this tendency). 'Sample' polarization and 'group' polarization are obviously likely to be related but Lamm and Myers specifically note that 'the prediscussion response means for particular groups do not predict variation among group shifts on a given item' (1978, p. 170).

This statement is based on a correlational study conducted by Teger and Pruitt (1967) with choice dilemmas. However, there would seem to be a number of problems with this research: principally, that it assumes tht the extent of risky shift rather than polarization or shift in line with initial group tendency is the appropriate measure (Wetherell, 1983). When this question was investigated by Fraser, Gouge and Billig (1971), it was found that 'a group . . . initially inclined toward one alternative (risky or cautious) was six times more likely, following discussion, to agree on a more polarized position than a less polarized one' (p. 21). This is an important finding for the attempt to develop a genuinely group-based theory of polarization, as it confirms that polarization will be bound up with the process occurring within particular groups. We can proceed on this assumption. But, ideally, more correlational work is needed to confirm this point.

What are the limits of polarization? The final problem concerns the boundaries of polarization – another key theoretical issue. For what range of situations is polarization predicted? Each theory defines these limits according to its own criteria but neither answers this important practical question very successfully.

Social comparison theory customarily distinguishes between items which are factual and invite an accuracy frame of reference (an orientation towards factual correctness) and items involving values which click into a rank order evaluation (where responses are differentially valued) such that people are concerned about their self-presentation *vis-à-vis* others (Baron Sanders, and Baron, 1975, cited in Lamm and Myers, 1978; Baron and Roper, 1976). Polarization has been assumed to be associated with the latter.

Although this seems a reasonable proposition in line with the general distinction in influence research between judgements of the physical versus the social environment, the evidence unfortunately suggests that polarization does not stop where factual judgement begins. As we have already indicated, several studies have shown that discussions of matters of obscure fact (e.g., how far Sodom on the Dead Sea is below sea level) will produce polarization (Doise, 1971b; Vidmar, 1974; Vinokur and Burnstein, 1978a). Group interaction seems to pull people towards extremity regardless of whether the item is factual or evaluative. This is a further indication that models of polarization cannot be based on externally defined social values.

These findings do not overly concern the persuasive arguments theorist, who would claim that polarization is predicted only when there are novel and persuasive arguments to share. It is immaterial whether the judgements are factual or evaluative. What is not clear, however, is why, with items of obscure fact, new persuasive material is more likely to emerge for the dominant pole or in line with the pretest trend? Some explication is required if the persuasive arguments interpretation is to convince.

Persuasive arguments theory has a more serious problem still. If polarization is fundamentally dependent on argument exchange, then it should also be the case that polarization would not eventuate in cases where there is not scope for argumentation. Contrary to this hypothesis, Myers (1977, cited in Lamm and Myers, 1978) has shown that polarization can be obtained for judgements of attractiveness of people on slides, while Baron and Roper (1976) demonstrated polarization for judgements of a visual illusion when a value was attached (judgements of a certain kind were described as indicating greater intelligence). Similarly, it is possible to think of cases of behavioural polarization like crowd disturbances which seem to proceed without argumentation.

Burnstein and Vinokur (1977) have maintained that argumentation is still involved in these cases: for example, subjects in Baron and Roper's study might have thought 'I am intelligent, intelligent people make large estimates, therefore . . . ' (p. 327). If this is accepted, however, concepts of novelty and persuasiveness become irretrievably ill-defined and blurred. Any kind of mental state would seem to count as a persuasive and novel argument.

Future research must address this issue of limits, especially if it is to move outside the laboratory into applied fields. Is polarization related to the type of item and evaluative context, is it a matter of informational input, or is there some other criterion? If, as seems likely, some other criterion is involved, what will differentiate polarizing from non-polarizing situations, and equally importantly, what is likely to happen to discussion groups over time?

A self-categorization theory of group polarization

Several major problems with existing explanations have now been identified. In essence these boil down to two points: incorporating group processes such as the development of group norms which define persuasiveness and distinguishing between situations where group influence produces convergent polarization versus convergence without polarization. It is our contention that the development of a self-categorization model (Turner and Oakes, 1986; Wetherell et al., 1985) can help solve these basic problems.

The self-categorization explanation of polarization will be familiar from chapter 4, where it was derived from the theory of referent informational influence and the wider perspective on group behaviour developed in this book. It can now be fleshed out in the context of past and present polarization research.

In contrast to other approaches the self-categorization model begins with the fact that people who come together in groups develop a perception of what they share in common and the features which distinguish them from other groups. Influence and persuasion are assumed to be intimately connected with this perception. So that, we claim, the informational value of a response or its 'persuasiveness' is *exactly equivalent* to the degree that it is perceived to be exemplary of some ingroup norm or consensus.

To a large extent what is seen as competent and appropriate behaviour or opinions to hold depends on the groups of which one is a member at any given time. Furthermore, the greater the consensus within a group, the more likely it is that the group's view will be seen to encapsulate some objectively correct feature of the world. People are open to influence or persuasion when they expect to agree with other people and they expect to agree if others are perceived as members of the same social category (i.e., ingroup as opposed to outgroup members) and thus as an appropriate reference group. Moreover, as the importance or salience of that group membership increases so will the expectation of agreement and probability of mutual influence.

This analysis of influence, unlike Burnstein and Vinokur's approach, gives real substance to the notion of a persuasive argument. The properties attributed to arguments can be directly related to the social context in which the material is produced. It is also consistent with the research demonstrating that group cohesiveness, identification and similar variables affect opinion shifts. Moreover, close attention to the processes involved in developing a self-categorization as a group member as well as ingroup norm formation circumvents the problems social comparison theorists face explaining why certain kinds of extremity are desirable as broad 'social values' when it seems clear that local group norms regulate opinion shifts.

Given the general principle that influence and susceptibility to persuasion depend upon the perceived similarity between self and others in terms of category membership, the next step in the self-categorization model is to specify where influence will be maximal or what will be the most persuasive opinion in a group. It is suggested tht group members will converge on the opinion which is most prototypical of the initial ingroup consensus.

To recapitulate the argument in chapters 3 and 4, prototypicality can be defined by the meta-contrast ratio, the ratio of the average difference perceived between ingroup and outgroup members over the average difference perceived between ingroup members. The prototypicality or representativeness of a group member (opinion, etc.) depends upon increasing differences from outgroup members and decreasing differences from members of the same category. The most prototypical member in this sense is predicted to be the most persuasive and group discussion and interaction will, all things being equal, produce conformity to their position.

It is worth reiterating that conformity to ingroup norms is not viewed pejoratively as a type of unreasonable yielding to majority pressure, whose natural opposite is individual integrity. Rather it is seen as a highly adaptive group process: the adherence or movement of group members towards shared norms and values, akin to Moscovici's (1976) description of 'normalization'.

One question remains: under what conditions does conformity produce convergence on the average position or initial group mean and when does it result in polarization of that mean? Both outcomes can be accounted for. It was argued in chapter 4 that prototypicality is tied to the dimension of comparison used for responses and the initial distribution of individuals' pregroup opinions on the comparative scale. (It is assumed that a seven-point attitude scale, for instance, sets up the frame of reference for social comparison, specifying the pool of possible opinions). As a simple example of this link we can take the following instance:

−3	−2	−1	0	+1	+2	+3
0	0	A	B	C	0	0

Here, for group members, A, B and C, B is the most prototypical individual, being most different from possible outgroup responses (−3, −2, +2, +3) and most similar to other ingroup members. In other words, convergence on the average, the group's pretest mean (assuming this is a group about to begin a discussion), would be anticipated, as a result of mutual influence.

As the distribution of individuals' responses becomes displaced from the midpoint of the scale, however, it is possible to demonstrate that members whose responses are already polarized (i.e., those whose responses are displaced from the mean in line with the initial tendency, at +2 say on a −3 to +3 scale where +1 is the group's pretest mean) become more prototypical. For example, take a group with the following distribution:

−3	−2	−1	0	+1	+2	+3
0	0	0	0	A	B	C

Here, the more extreme member, C, has become progressively more prototypical than the moderate A. It can be seen how polarization or enhancement of the pretest mean might be expected under these conditions (e.g., if the group comprised only A and C, so that C was the most prototypical member – see chapter 4 for a more detailed discussion). In essence, in these cases, members' perception of the group norm follows a classic categorization effect: intergroup or inter-category differences, defined by the response scale, are accentuated, as also is intra-category homogeneity (Tajfel and Wilkes, 1963; Taylor et al., 1978).

To summarize, the main points of the self-categorization theory of polarization are, first, that persuasion is dependent upon self-categorizations which create a common identity within a group. Secondly, polarization of opinions results because group members adjust their opinion in line with their image of the group position (conform) and more extreme, already polarized, *prototypical* responses determine this image. Finally, the prior condition for polarization to occur as a result of mutual influence is perception of the displacement of the initial group responses from the psychological midpoint of the appropriate reference scale.

This account of group influence achieves several goals. First, it resolves the problems with social comparison and persuasive arguments theories identified earlier, through tying persuasiveness to the context of group discussion and explaining why extremity becomes normative. Secondly, and perhaps most importantly, it allows for the satisfactory integration of two separate bodies of research, polarization studies and early work on convergence effects; providing the beginnings of an answer at the same time to the vexing question of the boundaries and limits on polarization. Integration became imperative once polarization was demonstrated for factual items, effectively breaking down previously workable distinctions between judgments of the social and physical world.

It is important to appreciate that the conditions for mutual influence described in self-categorization theory will often compete with other kinds of variables, both within the laboratory and without, and therefore may be less than optimal. Individuals are assumed to be most open to influence when they identify with a group and see themselves as similar to other members of that category; when, too, they are uncertain of their judgement, see consensus as important and take for granted that all are responding to the same stimulus. Conditions of this kind are very common and thus self-categorization theory has a wide generality.

The reverse of the above can be taken as minimizing the possibility of mutual influence and convergence. Contrasting group identifications of different strengths would be expected to undermine influence pressures. As a woman one might identify with other women but cease to identify as it became apparent that political views diverged. In some situations the global identity will be salient, in others more specific self-definitions. Similarly, considerable initial disagreement in a group, say among members of a court jury, raises the possibility of attributing differences in opinion to personal qualities (intelligence, rationality, degree of insight), thus disrupting the perception of category equivalence or interchangeability with respect to the evidence and the basis for mutual influence. As McLachan (1985) suggests, individuals in these cases may come to see themselves as minorities of one within the group. Ultimately, it is an empirical question whether the conditions described by self-categorization theory actually obtain and will therefore produce the outcomes of mutual influence (such as polarization and convergence).

A self-categorization model of polarization, in effect, reconciles social comparison and argumentation processes within a new framework. Polarization is seen as the result of an informational process of persuasion (although no sharp distinction is made between arguments and positions or members as the vehicles of such a process) and also as movement to more extreme, valued positions. Social comparison is recognized as fundamental, but in the form of a meta-comparison between intergroup and intragroup differences and any social differentiation that might occur is assumed to be in the direction of enhancing one's conformity to the prototypical ideal relative to fellow group members (cf. Codol, 1975; Myers and Kaplan, 1976). In many respects the important contribution of the present theory is to bring together the concepts of social value and informational influence rather than continuing the arbitrary divide between the two.

Despite the overlap with many aspects of social comparison and persuasive arguments models, a self-categorization explanation also results in a set of distinctive predictions which allow for empirical testing. These predictions can be summarized as follows:

1   Identification or perception of category equivalence is required for influence and polarization will increase as identification with the group increases. Identification can be manipulated through the variables which determine the salience of ingroup-outgroup differentiations.

2   Subjects working with a self-categorization which stresses common identity with the group should develop a more exaggerated perception of the group norm than non-involved subjects.

3   Polarization should be obtained for either factual or value-laden items. What will prove to be crucial is not the accuracy or evaluative frame of reference subjects adopt, but the relationship between the group's initial distribution of responses and the psychological midpoint of the scale. It should be possible to manipulate experimentally the perception of that displacement (presence and direction or absence) in groups and thus affect shifts.

4   There should be a relationship between a particular group's pretest mean and their consensus or posttest if polarization is a group-based phenomenon. Furthermore, *contra* persuasive arguments theory, groups who are more extreme initially (show greater displacement from the psychological midpoint) should be more likely to polarize than more moderate groups, all other things being equal. This is predicted on the basis that as displacement increases more extreme responses become more prototypical. Persuasive arguments theory predicts that more moderate groups are more likely to gain from the exchange of arguments.

No doubt as the theory develops other hypotheses which permit a contrast with traditional models of polarization will emerge. Research on this new approach is still in its early stages, yet the first and second predictions have been confirmed and aspects of the third and fourth. This programme of work and the results will be described in the next section.

Evidence for the self-categorization theory of polarization

In this account of the empirical evidence we will refer to published studies and work in progress (Wetherell et al., 1985), as well as to independent tests of self-categorization theory predictions (Mackie, 1986; Mackie and Cooper, 1984; McLachlan, 1985) and past polarization research where relevant.

Much of the work conducted to date has concerned the effects of identification and categorization upon opinion shifts. The first study we set up to investigate identification looked at the impact of different types of group contexts upon the persuasiveness of information and arguments (Wetherell et al., 1985, experiment 1). If subjects believe arguments come from an ingroup as opposed to an outgroup and from people who are similar rather than dissimilar to themselves, are they more likely to be persuaded?

All subjects were asked to listen to the *same* tape-recording of a group discussion. Some were told, however, that they would shortly be joining this group as a new member for a debate with another group and we knew from value scales completed earlier that they were very similar to the individuals in the group (ingroup similar condition); others were told that this was an ingroup but they were very dissimilar; yet others, that the tape-recorded group was the group they would be debating against in the next phase of the study but they were very similar (outgroup similar condition), and the remainder were told that this was a dissimilar outgroup. In fact subjects were assigned randomly to these four conditions. Their opinions about the items being discussed in the tape were measured in a pretest before they received any other instructions and after they had listened to the tape-recording. They were told that listening to the group was intended to familiarize them with these kinds of group discussions.

Because exactly the same tape was used in all cases it was possible to examine whether identical arguments were differentially influential according to perceptions of the group context. In self-categorization theory terms both perceived similarity and ingroup membership should provide a basis for identification and recognition of category equivalence, facilitating openness to influence; whereas Burnstein and

Vinokur would have difficulty explaining any difference in opinion shifts towards the group across the four conditions, as the informational properties of the arguments have remained constant.

The results unequivocally demonstrated that subjects are significantly more likely to be persuaded by the same arguments from an ingroup than an outgroup and from a similar than a dissimilar group, as measured, for instance, by relative shift scores. Relative shift scores take into account ceiling effects (the total amount of shift possible in a particular direction on a fixed attitude scale). We found, too, that the tape-recorded group was more persuasive when arguing for a position that was in the same direction as the subjects' mean pretest score or sample pretest mean, in contrast to cases where they argued in the opposite direction. Again, greater identification (perception of similarity, interchangeability) would be expected where there was initial agreement.

This pattern of results may not surprise many social psychologists but it is an important demonstration for polarization research, particularly in light of Burnstein's recent assertion that 'social influence can be explained in informational terms alone' (1982, p. 121). In this experiment movement to the group varied not with informational content but with the social psychological process of group identification.

Disputes between rival theories are rarely settled so easily, however. Burnstein could point to a study he conducted with Vinokur in 1978 (b) which apparently demonstrates that informational pressures have a more powerful effect than even dividing a group into opposing factions or subgroups. Awareness of subgroupings could be seen, *prima facie*, as a group context variable.

In the study in question Vinokur and Burnstein constructed six-person groups so that three members had pro-risk pretest opinions (one subgroup) and three pro-caution opinions (the other subgroup). Half the groups had their attention drawn to this difference of opinion through seating arrangements, etc., while the difference was not made salient for the other half. They found that subjects tended to converge, with both subgroups moving closer together after discussion, irrespective of whether the initial differences were made salient. Vinokur and Burnstein argue that this outcome could be predicted from the pattern of diffusion of novel persuasive arguments in the groups.

From a self-categorization point of view, surely increasing the salience of the subgroupings should have disrupted or inhibited mutual influence? This prediction follows from the theory and thus Vinokur and Burnstein's results appear disconfirmatory. However, there is a number of reasons why these findings cannot be taken face value, and which vitiate any such conclusion.

First, Vinokur and Burnstein instructed subjects to reach a consensus in their group as a whole, despite the subgroupings. It seems likely that this instruction would immediately set up a higher order imperative, demanding that a common identity be found for discussion, and leading to the redefinition of the middle ground as the prototypical group position. Added to which, the subgroup disagreements did not concern issues of importance to the subjects and, finally, the response scale used was of a continuous kind rather than a Likert-type which unambiguously splits opinions into different categories (pro versus anti).

Given these problems, it seemed sensible to replicate the study (Wetherell and Turner, in preparation a) and this experiment stands as our second investigation of identification effects. Following Vinokur and Burnstein's procedure, discussion groups were preselected so that each consisted of divided subgroups. Similarly, in one condition subjects' attention was drawn to the disagreement and they were told to expect 'a sharp division of opinion'. The subgroups were given labels, A and B, and seating arrangements were concordant with this; while in the other condition no mention was made of divisions.

Departing from Vinokur and Burnstein's method, subjects in our study discussed controversial issues of some interest to them, using a Likert-type scale which clearly separated pro and anti positions with a neutral midpoint in between. Furthermore, they were simply asked to discuss and exchange views 'going through all the pros and cons' and not instructed to reach a consensus within the group. Shifts in opinion were measured by comparing the pretest responses with a posttest completed by each individual separately after discussion.

Vinokur and Burnstein must once again predict convergence between the subgroups with no difference between conditions as, despite slight changes in the procedure, the probable diffusion of arguments remains the same. From the perspective of self-categorization theory, however, a significant difference between the two conditions would be anticipated. Although the subgroup division in this experiment is not a particularly strong manipulation (compared, say, to naturally occurring cases where subgroupings are associated with vested conflicting interests), it should be the case that when divisions are made salient, mutual influence within the group as a whole will be inhibited, assuming no strong pressures to reach agreement.

Indeed, we found that for three out of five items there was a significant interaction in the direction expected between condition (salient/non-salient) and degree of convergence between the subgroups after discussion, $F(1,16) = 7.54$, $p < .01$; $F = 8.45$, $p < .01$, $F = 43.46$,

$p < .000$ (using groups as the unit of analysis); the interactions for the fourth item approached significance, $F = 2.43$, $p < .14$, and was non-significant for the fifth item, $F = 0.18$. Subgroup convergence was considerably less likely when subjects' attention was explicitly drawn to the disagreement within the group.

This finding supports the conclusions from our first experiment and intimates that Vinokur and Burnstein's failure to find differences may be a result of their procedure rather than the power of informational pressures alone.

The results from the first two studies are commensurate with previous work, referred to earlier, demonstrating increased polarization with increased identification (Doise, 1969; Skinner and Stephenson, 1981) and the general evidence relating categorization to group processes (P. T. Allen and Stephenson, 1983; Boyanowsky and V. L. Allen, 1973; Tajfel, 1981a; Turner, 1985; Turner and Giles, 1981b; Wilder, 1981; Wilder and Cooper, 1981; Wilder and Shapiro, 1984).

Moreover, Mackie and Cooper (1984, experiment 1), adopting a slightly different procedure from that described in our first experiment, independently found that attitudes polarized in the direction advocated on the tape only in the ingroup conditions. Interestingly there was clear evidence that the movement to the ingroup norm represented private acceptance or genuine attitude change; that the ingroup norm had an 'informational' impact in other words.

One other study (Reid and Sumiga, 1984) along these lines should be noted, because it has produced rather mixed results. Reid and Sumiga found that representatives of student course groups tended to polarize less when they expected to engage in an intergroup rather than an intragroup debate on important issues, although there was some evidence that where representatives prepared for the debate in discussion teams, the anticipated intergroup debate produced more polarization on unimportant issues than did the expected intragroup debate. It seems possible that whereas the expected intragroup debate enhanced ingroup identification and led to polarization on the stereotypical attitudes defining ingroup identity, the 'intergroup' debate between student groups may in fact have made the higher level ingroup category of 'student' salient and redefined the relevant norms of behaviour to be presenting a competent, winnable case – the point of a debate being after all to persuade one's opponents (or at least the audience), which implies according to the present theory some attempt to identify 'common ground' for discussion.

Overall, the mounting evidence for the importance of group context in persuasion is making it more and more difficult to maintain a distinction between 'informational' criteria and social factors. Some account of the relationship between the two cannot be avoided.

So far we have stressed the implications of these identification or categorization studies for persuasive arguments theory, although they also raise problems for social comparison theorists. The third study we shall describe can be more directly related to social comparison models (Wetherell et al., 1985, experiment 2).

This experiment investigated the extent to which polarization depends upon the perception of group members' responses as stereo-typcial of or normative for an ingroup category. It is predicted that polarization will only occur to the degree that the dominant response tendency is perceived as a stereotypical group characteristic and therefore as socially normative (appropriate, correct, valued, etc.). A broad social value for risk, for example, the norm of some superordinate cultural identity of the type emphasized by socal comparison theorists, may well determine an individual's pretest response, but intragroup opinion shifts we hypothesize reflect the immediate normative context: social values are transformed into specific group norms through the combination of individuals' intitial pretest tendencies. Correspondingly, if the initial response tendencies are not perceptually combined in the group to form a shared consensual reaction or stereotypical ingroup norm, but remain as differing individual responses, they will exert no persuasive impact.

Subjects' perception of the dominant opinion as a shared group characteristic versus an unrelated individual characteristic was manipulated in the following way. First, they were told on the basis of false feedback from a fake decision-making test administered earlier in the experiment that they had a consistent decision-making style: either to go for risky or cautious options. Subjects randomly allocated to the stereotypical group characteristic condition were given this information in a context which stressed that these decision-making styles reflected differences between groups of people. When their own decision-making style was announced they were told to join Group X, 'risky decision-makers', on one side of the room or Group Y, 'cautious decision-makers', on the other side. That is, *decision-making style was consistently associated with an intergroup division*. This intergroup division and the shared, consensual nature of differences was maintained in the second phase of the experiment when subjects were divided within their broader groups into smaller, four-person groups to discuss a range of choice dilemma items and reach consensus.

In contrast to this, subjects randomly allocated to the individual characteristic condition were told that risky and cautious decision-making styles reflected personality differences between people and thus could determine whether they were *risky or cautious individuals*. Announcements of individual status were made in no particular order, with no explicit or implicit grouping. Then, as in the other condition, subjects were randomly assigned into discussion groups marked as containing four 'risky individuals' or four 'cautious individuals'.

The expectation was that in this latter condition risk and caution would be seen as idiosyncratic response biases rather than shared normative values and may even be perceived as deviance from the normal, usual reaction. Individual differences have been made salient as opposed to group differences which imply the presence of shared norms.

Self-categorization theory predicts that in the stereotypical group characteristic condition 'risky groups' will polarize to risk and 'cautious groups' to caution independently of the type of choice dilemma discussed, i.e., of whether the initial pretest tendency in the sample as a whole was towards risk or caution for a particular item. Subjects completed a pretest as the first task in the experiment and we could assess the effects of the experimental manipulations by comparing this pretest response with the consensus reached in discussion or with the individually completed posttest. In the individual characteristic condition it was anticipated shifts of this kind would be inhibited. In essence, we are assuming that influence and opinion change depend, not on people seeking to accentuate their individual differences from others, but on movement or conformity to what are perceived as the shared and common attributes of the group.

The results demonstrated the predicted effects. For both possible comparisons between pretest and posttest opinion and pretest and consensus, there was a significant interaction between subjects' condition (stereotypical group characteristic versus unrelated individual attribute) and the attribute (risky or cautious) they had been arbitrarily assigned, $F(1,92) = 7.18, p < .01$ for pretest/posttest, and $F(1, 20) = 5.43, p < .05$ for pretest/group consensus (with the group as the unit of anlaysis for this last comparison). In sum, 'risky groups' tended to shift to riskier opinions and 'cautious groups' to more cautious opinions in the stereotypical group characteristic condition, whereas in the individual trait condition 'risky individuals' shifted to caution while 'cautious individuals' demonstrated hardly any shift.

Other effects emerged from the analysis (see Wetherell et al., 1985) but this finding is the key one in terms of prior predictions. Opinion shift was clearly regulated by the extent to which subjects could perceive an attribute as stereotypical or normative as opposed to an individuating personality trait. This effect makes perfect sense if polarization represents movement towards the prototypical ingroup position since defining the shared characteristics of the group in advance (for risk or caution in this case) will ensure that arguments/positions/members in line with the stereotype attributed to the group will tend to be perceived as more representative of the group as a whole and hence more persuasive and valued. On the other hand, providing the same information but in a way which differentiates one individual from another and stresses inter-individual variety should tend to make it more difficult to identify with each other in terms of their common characteristics and also may lead to the perception that their individual tendency is a deviation from some higher level ingroup norm (e.g., 'rational' decision-making which is neither risky nor cautious). Arguments in line with an individual deviation from the wider cultural norm are by definition less consensual and so less persuasive and may tend to be negatively valued.

It is difficult to see how persuasive arguments theorists would account for the main findings of this study, but the results have a particular bearing on the social differentiation version of the social comparison analysis. This version argues that polarization occurs because individuals actively compete with each other to take up the most extreme, valued positions. Why, then, did 'risky individuals' show a general shift to caution when social comparison theorists argue that for many of the discussion items risk has a high positive value and supposedly conveys ability and competence (Jellison and Arkin, 1977)? The individualizing of risky or cautious attributes as personality traits should have no effect upon the general process of social differentiation or the rewarding of extremity which is assumed to determine opinion shifts. If 'risky groups' shift to risk, so should 'risky individuals'. The moral seems to be that, as we have argued, value varies according to the group or discussion context and thus this local context must be taken into account.

This last experiment and the previous two concerned the background conditions required for mutual influence and thus the perception of prototypicality. It also follows from self-categorization theory that subjects who perceive a common identity with a group and who are thus concerned to discover a representative group position through intergroup comparison should develop a more exaggerated perception of the group norm than non-involved subjects.

This hypothesis was investigated by Mackie and Cooper (1984, experiment 2). Subjects were instructed to listen to taped discussions attributed to their own group or to some group to which they were unrelated and estimate the consensual position of the group; they found that subjects' perceptions of their own group's norms were significantly more extreme than uninvolved subjects' perceptions and, once more, subjects were more influenced in the ingroup conditions.

In two later experiments Mackie (1986) found evidence that the formation and salience of ingroup-outgroup categorizations lead to the perceptual extremitization of the ingroup norm. In the first study subjects perceived relevant information attributed to speakers categorized as a group as representing a more extreme position on the issue than when the same information was attributed to non-categorized speakers, and polarized to adopt this more extreme position when the information was believed to come from their ingroup. In the second study the salience of group membership or an individual orientation was manipulated by instructions producing intergroup competition or not and, independently, intragroup (interpersonal) competition or not. As predicted from the self-categorization analysis and very much in line with the results of our experiment on 'risky groups' versus 'risky individuals', intergroup competition (enhancing the salience of ingroup versus outgroup membership) resulted in ingroup norms being perceived as more extreme and polarization due to conformity to these norms, but no extremitization occurred in the intragroup competition condition and here attitudes shifted to a more neutral position. Mackie concludes that her studies provide considerable support for the self-categorization theory of group polarization as conformity to extremitized ingroup norms.

Reid (1983) has also demonstrated that subjects tend to adopt more extreme positions in line with and relevant to their group identity after comparison with an outgroup than with ingroup members. Reid and Sumiga (1984) note that subjects instructed to list arguments in preparation for a debate generated twice as many arguments supporting as opposing ingroup attitudes, and rated the ingroup arguments as more convincing, particularly those related to the issue they expected to debate with a rival outgroup. Moreover, McLachlan (1985, 1986) has confirmed that participants hold quite a different view of the persuasiveness of arguments after discussion *per se*. In particular, they accentuate the difference in perceived relevance between arguments favouring their decision and those against. There can be little doubt that the perception and reception of an argument or position is not a constant property throughout review and discussion but varies flexibly according to identity considerations.

In the fourth study described here we chose, given the centrality of the prototypicality/opinion shift relationship to self-categorization theory, to conduct a detailed correlational analysis of our predictions for *specific group shifts* (Wetherell et al., 1985, experiment 3), i.e., to go to the heart of the process within the group, and model our theoretical predictions directly.

There are several different kinds of measures possible when individuals consider an issue and then discuss it to consensus in a group. First, there is the standard pretest mean (PRE) or record of the group members' prediscussion view and the posttest mean (POST) or mean of postdiscussion views. Opinion shift (S) is simply the difference between PRE and POST. Secondly, there are the measures identified by the self-categorization analysis of polarization, namely, the prototypical position (P), taken as the position in the group with the highest meta-contrast ratio as defined earlier, and D, the discrepancy (difference) between the pretest mean (PRE) and the most prototypical position (P).

If, as we claim, the most prototypical position is the most influential opinion in the group, and groups with the largest discrepancy between their pretest mean and prototype polarize the most, then we should find correlations between P and POST, D and S and more generally between PRE and S. This last correlation at the between-group within-item level would confirm that polarization is genuinely group-based as well as the sample effect it is normally taken to be. In addition, PRE might be expected to correlate with POST at the between-group within-item level, P with POST and PRE with D.

The data for this correlational test were collected from a standard polarization experiment. Thirty-one five-person groups were asked to discuss to consensus five controversial issues using Likert-type response scales. A pretest of individual opinion was administered before the discussion and individuals' posttest opinions collected subsequently. Groups were preselected on the basis of initial pretest opinions to maximize the spread of pretest or group means across the response scales; they were spread, that is, across pro and anti scale positions with all degrees of extremity to allow a reasonable variety of pretest means for the examination of the hypotheses.

We found that the overwhelming majority of all possible correlations between PRE, P, D and POST were significantly positive, indicating strongly that each group seems to be characterized by a definite normative tendency related to its initial consensus, e.g., PRE with POST, $rs =$ .81, .90, .66, .62 and .92, $ps < .001$ for each of the five items, PRE with P, $rs = .90, .85, .87, .89$ and .94, $ps < .001$. The data for P and POST are of particular importance for the hypothesis that group members tend to converge on the prototype, $rs = .71, .80, .59, .47$ and .90, $ps < .001$ or .01. Another finding of special theoretical interest was that, as expected, the displacement of the ingroup pretest mean from the scale midpoint (which can be measured simply by PRE) does predict within items the discrepancy (D) between the pretest mean and the ingroup prototype, rs = .38, .36, .61, .31 and .60, ps < .05 or .001.

Although correlational analysis is straightforward in these cases and the results are clearcut, analysis becomes problematic when S or shift scores are considered. First, there is the problem of ceiling effects. A group with a moderate pretest mean can shift a much greater distance on the response scale than one with a pretest mean which is already extreme. There is nowhere for them to shift to, so to speak, although theoretically more shift might be expected in this group than in the more moderate group with perhaps only a small discrepancy between their pretest mean and the most prototypical position.

There is also the general problem, noted earlier, of maximizing in a laboratory experiment the optimal conditions for mutual influence specified by self-categorization theory. Independently of the contribution of PRE, uncontrolled background variables may operate to reduce S.

The procedures taken to minimize ceiling effects are described in detail in Wetherell et al.. Suffice to say that through using *relative* rather than absolute shifts and averaging differentially obtained relative shift scores this difficulty can be combated to a degree. The final PRE/relative shift correlations for the items were .10, .21, .33, .56 and .45, ps of < .30, .13, .03, .001 and .01, respectively. There is some evidence, therefore, of a relationship between these two measures. This suggests that, contrary to Lamm and Myers's (1978) assertion, it is possible to predict variation among group shifts on a given item using pretest means. Important implications follow since polarization can be seen both as a sample phenomenon and a phenomenon which occurs at the specific group level, making it entirely reasonable to propose a group conformity explanation as well as the sample-based persuasive arguments and social comparison models. Furthermore, the correlation between D and S within items is itself positively related to the extent of obtained group polarization on that item, r = .87, p < .03 (N = 5 items). And across items, a near perfect correlation was found between a measure of the mean extremitized ingroup norm (the mean of D and P, which were highly correlated) per item and mean polarization (the mean of sample and group polarization, also highly correlated) per item, r = .96, p < .01 (N = 5).

As other correlational studies are completed, the mechanics of the process within groups should become yet clearer. Combined with this it should be possible to begin to manipulate group members' perception of the degree of displacement from the psychological midpoint of a response scale and thus directly affect their shifts. Work is beginning along these lines using classic factual judgement designs such as in the Sherif (1936) autokinetic effect study. This assumes, however, that polarization will prove to be related not to the type of item being discussed (factual or evaluative) but limited and determined by the relationship between a group's initial distribution of responses and the midpoint of the salient reference or response scale, combined with background group context conditions which will work to magnify or reduce influence pressures.

The final study reviewed here was concerned with this issue (Wetherell and Turner, in preparation b). It was noted earlier that there are several studies demonstrating polarization for factual items given an initial prediscussion tendency, and these are difficult to explain in terms of social comparison theory. Baron et al. (1975, cited in Lamm and Myers, 1978) maintain, however, that the frame of reference (in a somewhat different sense from that used in the self-categorization theory) the subjects adopt as well as the type of item determine shifts. If group members believe it is important to be accurate in their decision-making then social value considerations and being different from others in a valued direction become secondary motivations. Paradoxically, other social comparison theorists (Jellison and Arkin, 1977) seem to assert that, since polarization is associated with groups rewarding the presentation of ability, there might only be polarization for factual judgements if accuracy is stressed, because, if accuracy and rationality are not stressed, factual decisions become simply a matter of individual guesswork and not connected with ability.

It is a simple matter to test the importance of an accuracy frame of reference. Subjects in this last study were given items of obscure fact to discuss (e.g. estimate how many feet below sea level the town of Sodom is on the inland Dead Sea). Half were told that group decisions generally lead to more right answers than individual judgement alone and we expected groups to obtain correct responses. They were instructed to strive to work out the right answer and they would be informed if they succeeded (accuracy condition). The other half were told their decisions would be based on guesswork because the facts were obscure and they shouldn't feel under pressure to find the right answer in their group.

The results demonstrated moderate group polarization, $F(1,16) = 8.05$, $p < .01$, for a pretest-group consensus comparison, and no difference in the degree of opinion shift between conditions. This pattern fits neither version of social comparison theory but is consistent with the hypothesis that the crucial conditions for polarization lie in the systematic displacement of group pretest means from the midpoint of the scale (as was the case with the groups in this experiment). If a group was divided in opinion, i.e., without an initial normative tendency, then pressures to be accurate might lead to convergence, but in this experiment, with shared initial tendencies, shared prototypical positions would be more extreme, and hence the polarization regardless of item type.

Conclusion

In conclusion, it will obviously take time before any new theory can produce the same volume of relevant data as existing theories or accommodate theoretically all the empirical intricacies of such a long-established and self-avowedly complex field as polarization. Nevertheless, the studies reviewed here would seem to represent definite evidence for the distinctive predictions of self-categorization/referent informational influence theory – with respect to the importance of ingroup identification and the salience of ingroup-outgroup categorizations, that polarization follows from conformity to polarized norms, and that the polarization of norms is a function of the relationship between the ingroup's initial distribution of opinions and the social frame of reference as embodied in the presence of a rival outgroup or the response scale.

The wider significance of the polarization phenomenon for social psychology should not be ignored. The phenomenon is interesting in its own right but it is also vitally important as a key to the general processes of group influence and conformity. This recognition has been at the forefront of our attempt to develop a new theoretical perspective. The aim is that a self-categorization analysis, through a radical reconceptualization of the influence process, will succeed in unifying conformity and polarization effects – reinstating in this way the group concept as an explanatory social psychological process and fostering a distinctive group psychology.

8

Crowd Behaviour as Social Action

(Stephen Reicher)

Introduction

The study of the crowd is rooted in a contradiction. On the one hand, crowd phenomena are a challenge to social psychology. Studies of crowd events have revealed complex behavioural characteristics. Not only is the behaviour spontaneous and apparently without overt leadership, but it also displays clear patterns and limits. Moreover, these patterns have social meaning: they are intelligible as the application of ideological systems of understanding to particular circumstances in the real world. The challenge, then, is to explain how large numbers of people are able to act together, to act in ways that are socially meaningful, but to do so without any planning or formal co-ordination. It is, in a phrase, to explain the 'spontaneous sociality' of crowd action.

The challenge is especially significant in that in order to account for the manner in which the behaviour of the crowd member displays ideological form, one needs to specify the manner in which human cognition can be socially structured. In other words, the nature of crowd action demonstrates the need for a social psychology which places the individual in society and which relates conduct to context. Herein lies the contradiction. For the actual history of crowd psychology is one of distortion of the relationship between individual and society.

The early theories of the crowd abstracted the individual from society and behaviour from its social context. They took actions that were the product of particular forms of social conflict and represented them as generic aspects of the crowd. Thus, through a process of reification, crowd behaviour was changed from being an outcome of social process into an unchanging entity. What disagreement there was lay in deciding where to locate this entity: whether as the product of individual nature or as the manifestation of a disembodied collective mind. Either the social disappeared into the individual or the individual disappeared from the social. These tendencies are still pervasive in social psychology.

A large part of the motivation for the development of the self-categorization theory of the group and the social identity perspective in general has been dissatisfaction with the shortcomings of reified explanation. The aim has been to overcome the separation that has been wrought between the individual and society, and to find a way of relating psychological processes to the historical, cultural, political and economic determinants of behaviour. It is central to the concept of social identity that it is viewed as being at the same time a social construct and an individual cognitive construct. Hence, social identity processes are attempts to deal with the construction of a 'socially structured field within the individual' (Asch, cited in Brown and Turner, 1981).

It is because the self-categorization theory resocializes the concept of the individual that it can provide the basis for an explanation of crowd behaviour. This is not to say that the theory provides as yet a fully satisfactory explanation of the crowd, but it is to say that it is unique in social psychology in being able to set one off in the right direction. Other approaches are unable to account for the social form of crowd action precisely because they misconceptualize the individual/social relationship. The task therefore is to build upon self-categorization theory to develop a psychology of crowd action.

The purpose of this chapter is, first, to analyse the distortions of existing crowd theory and to explain how they came about, secondly, to show how this body of theory fails to address the complexities of crowd phenomena and to lay down the criteria for an adequate crowd psychology, and, thirdly, to propose such a psychology, based on the self-categorization theory, and to examine its adequacy through the use of experimental and field research.

The politics of crowd theory

The context of crowd psychology

Crowd psychology is a product of nineteenth-century thought. It was in a sense the systematized expression of the dominant fear of the propertied classes, the fear of the 'mob'. This sentiment is well expressed by the French statesman Thiers, who in a speech delivered on 24 May 1850 spoke of 'the name, one of the worst stigmatized in history, mark you, of mob. The vile mob which brought every republic down in ruin'

(Chevalier, 1973, p. 364). The fear of the mob represented a generalized concern about social order resulting from a fundamental transformation in social relations.

The process of industrialization had disrupted the ties of rural society. Authority had been personal and traditional, based on face-to-face contacts between parson, squire and labourer, but as the nineteenth-century progressed there was the formation of a mass urban proletariat and a physical separation between worker and owner. Working class life became unknown to the ruling classes. A genuine crisis of social control developed and bourgeois fears were exacerbated by ignorance. To the extent that the significance of any form of dissent was obscured, even the most minor act could be read as a prelude to catastrophe. In a state of permanent panic of revolutionary overthrow, all the fears of the ruling classes of Europe became condensed into one terrifying symbol: the crowd. These fears were particulary acute in France during the last quarter of the century.

In this context the nature of the crowd became a matter of acute public concern. It was not a matter to be left to academics but was debated in newspapers and society journals. Thus two biases came to pervade the debate: a political bias of overt hostility to crowd action, the aim being not to understand but to discredit the crowd and eliminate it as a threat, and a bias of perspective, the commentators never being participants, never being of the crowd but viewing it from outside, without an understanding of the beliefs and experience of those involved in protest. In consequence, their's was an attitude of genuine dismay; they could not see reasons for crowd action, it all seemed genuinely senseless.

These biases were built into early crowd psychologies, for the theorists were gentlemen scholars who shared the prejudices and perspectives of their class. They never studied crowds at first hand, since they assumed *a priori* that they were undesirable, destructive and senseless. They then used the tools of an emerging positivistic social science to 'explain' these alleged characteristics. Thus crowd psychology was born as a looking-glass science. Rather than theory being used to account for empirical phenomena, the enterprise started from ideological prejudices and used theory to give these substance. In this way political bias was woven into the fabric of crowd psychology and came to determine the basic assumptions of the science.

Gustave LeBon and the birth of crowd psychology

Of all the early crowd psychologists only one is still remembered today,

Gustave LeBon. That he is remembered is due in part to his work as a popularizer. Equally important in explaining his influence was his explicit ambition to use crowd psychology as a political tool. He was above all concerned to employ his ideas in combating working class activism, and confessed himself proudest of his anti-socialist writings. LeBon's success is measured in the appreciation of Goebbels and Mussolini who declared that LeBon's ideas had been instrumental in the construction of an Italian fascist state.

LeBon's major work was *The Crowd: A Study of the Popular Mind*, first published in 1895. Gordon Allport has described it as the most widely read psychology book of all time. LeBon's basic characterization of the crowd is as follows. When people assemble in a mass they become anonymous, which leads to a loss of the sense of self and of personal responsibility. Instead, behaviour comes to be dominated by a collective racial unconscious. Since this unconscious represents a primitive state of evolution in which intellect is absent and atavistic emotions predominate, so behaviour lacks the attributes of 'civilization'. LeBon sums up the characteristics of such behaviour in a single flourish: 'Several of the special characteristics of crowds such as impulsivity, irritability, incapacity to reason, absence of judgement or critical spirit, exaggeration of emotions and more besides are also observed amidst lower forms of evolution such as the savage and the child' (1895, p. 23).

While the operation of the racial unconscious was at its clearest in the crowd, LeBon did not believe this to be the only time it was in evidence. Indeed, he asserted that all forms of mass assembly from juries to parliamentary assemblies exhibited its operation to some extent. Thus a distinction was drawn between the rationality of the social isolate and the idiocy of social being. It is a sentiment taken to extremes by Tarde who asserted that 'Society is imitation and imitation is a form of somnambulism' (1901, p. 95).

LeBon's crowd psychology may be read as a sustained attack upon collective protest. First, it systematically excludes the role of authority in crowd events. This is true both of the general social background which provokes protest as well as the more immediate role of army or police during specific events. In fact, historical research from the nineteenth century, as well as the twentieth, shows nearly all confrontation to be generated by the intervention of official forces (Feagin and Hahn, 1973; Tilly, Tilly and Tilly, 1975). Moreover, statistical evidence indicates that the great majority of acts of violence are perpetrated by such forces. Feagin and Hahn (1973) in their analysis of the American urban protests of the 1960s show that 89 per cent of those who died were civilians. However, in all the pages of crowd psychology authority, the outgroup, disappears. All that appears is the crowd, like some psychopathic jack-in-the-box. It suddenly and mysteriously emerges, goes through its automatic and uniformly vicious motions and then equally mysteriously disappears.

This leads on to the second point. For, by occluding the context of crowd action, this action is inevitably pathologized. If the outgroup is ignored, violence cannot be understood as arising from a process of intergroup conflict. Instead it is attributed to the crowd itself. Thus the forms of nineteenth-century class struggle are translated into generic characteristics of the crowd: the crowd is violent, it is destructive, it is pathological. The ideological consequences of this are that, on the one hand, it sanctions a refusal to heed the demands articulated through protest and, on the other, it legitimates the repression of protest. In the words of Lewis Carroll, 'if there is no meaning in it, that saves a world of trouble you know, as we needn't try to find any'.

Thirdly, LeBon does not limit his assertion of mental inferiority to the popular masses in protest but extends it to the popular masses in general. All collective life displays· some level of pathology. Thus a general distinction is drawn between the individuality of an isolated person, which alone can lead to rational or planned behaviour, and its antithesis, which is social being.

This separation of the individual and the social lies at the core of LeBon's theory. It is the inevitable result of attempting to deny the social rationale of crowd behaviour and it leads to distortions at both a theoretical and empirical level. Theoretically, the consequence is a reified psychology, for if crowd action cannot be seen as intelligent adaptation to a particular context, it must be treated as the reflection of a predetermined psychic structure. Empirically, one is led to assert that crowd behaviour is always the same, irrespective of situation. Thus LeBon sees the crowd as reflecting the 'racial unconscious', a reified entity located outside the individual, resulting in behaviour which is 'only powerful for destruction'.

It is important to distinguish between the particular form taken by LeBon's crowd psychology and the basic errors underlying it. Many attacks have been made upon the specifics by critics who have then gone on to elaborate new forms of desocialized and reified theory. Perhaps the best example of this comes from the work of Floyd Allport.

Allport was fiercely critical of the notion of a 'racial unconscious' or 'group mind' and denounced it as a purely metaphysical notion. Thought, he argued, cannot be separated from the individual thinker and 'there is no psychology of groups which is not essentially and entirely a psychology of individuals' (Allport, 1924, p. 4). From this critique Allport went on to argue that similarities of crowd behaviour reflect not a collective consciousness but the similarities in mental constitution of crowd members. Rather than obscuring individuality the crowd context accentuates it. These ideas are summed up in a famous aphorism: 'the individual in the crowd behaves just as he would alone only more so' (1924, p. 295).

There are two possible interpretations of these words. Modern social psychology has derived the notion that the company of others leads to the accentuation of idiosyncratic individual response profiles, i.e., the concept of 'social facilitation'. However, Allport also believed that the level of inter-stimulation in the crowd leads to the eclipse of all learnt responses and reveals a biological universal, the reflex of struggle. This is the urge to destroy anything that stops one satisfying one's basic needs, for food, for sex, for family love. Normally this urge is socialized so as to discourage the harming of others; yet as learnt socialization is overcome, the basic unsocialized drive comes to the fore and the 'drive to kill or destroy now spends itself in unimpeded fury' (Allport, 1924, p. 312).

It is evident from this that Allport shares the same basic premises as LeBon. Both refuse the possibility that individual cognition may be subject to social determination in the crowd; both see crowd behaviour as the manifestation of an atavistic universal; both see this behaviour as inevitably negative and destructive. The only difference is that, whereas LeBon sees this universal as in contradiction to and located outside the individual, Allport sees it as the underlying essence of individuality and as located firmly within individual nature. Despite this disagreement, both approaches share similar problems. These become clear when one examines Allport's treatment of a 'typical case'.

Allport writes of an incident in which striking miners stormed their pit, which was being kept open by non-union labour. These 'scabs' were captured and forced to march towards the local town. Suddenly they were told to run and, as they fled, they were shot down by the strikers. This, Allport argues, displays the asocial excess which results from the expression of an unmodified struggle reflex. Because the strike-breakers stood in the way of union victory and hence money for food and family, they were automatically slaughtered as excitement escalated to a certain pitch.

A fuller account of the event reveals a different story. The strike occurred in Williamson County, Illinois, in 1922. It demanded the improvement of conditions officially described as 'worse than the slaves before the civil war'. After eight weeks the company imported labour to reopen the pit. When strikers tried to talk to these men, pit guards shot and killed five of them. Shortly afterwards another striker was shot while half a mile away from the pit. At this point the men organized a march on the mine. They proceeded in skirmish lines under the discipline of war veterans. A plane circled overhead dropping dynamite on the pit. As they advanced, they came under concerted machine-gun fire from pit guards but nevertheless the mine was taken and only afterwards did the massacre occur. Local juries later refused to convict anyone for what had occurred.

As opposed to the massacre being a reflex action it is only explicable as the end result of a history of conflict between management and union. Williamson County was part of a strike wave that had been almost continuous since 1919. For over two years strikers had rejected armed violence. Only after arms had been used against them, including the use of tanks and an airborne squadron, did strikers accept the legitimacy of responding with arms – a conception reflected in the behaviour of the local jurors. Thus crowd behaviour changed over time, developing as a function of new conceptions that arose out of the conflict itself. Far from being typical, the massacre was only possible at the end of this process. It was, in fact, a unique event.

This analysis of the Williamson strike reveals a crucial aspect of the crowd. Not only is behaviour part of a developing intergroup process but also at any one time it expresses the collective understanding which crowd members have of what is proper and what is possible in their social world. A series of detailed studies of crowd events shows that they are not random but possess a clear pattern (e.g., Davis, 1978; Reddy, 1977; Thompson, 1971). Indeed, even an author of the official analysis of the American urban unrest of the 1960s concluded later that 'restraint and selectivity were among the most crucial features of the riots' (Fogelson, 1971). These patterns, which to the outsider may seem senseless, gain meaning when seen in the light of the ideological under-standings of the participants. This is well illustrated by Smith's (1980) account of the Cambrian Combine coal strike of 1910–11 in Wales.

The success of this dispute depended, as before, on stopping the use of strike-breaking labour. This was achieved in all but one pit, the Glamorgan colliery near Tonypandy. The police defended this pit in force against local pickets. Glamorgan had been chosen as the 'citadel of the coal owners' assertion . . . of the rights of property ownership'. On the evening of 7 November 1910 a large crowd of pickets gathered outside the pit. The police chose to charge and disperse them, after which the troops were called in. Shortly afterwards there was a 'riot' in Tonypandy: the returning picketers proceeded in mass through the streets and a number of shops were attacked and ransacked.

Contemporary press reports described the events as the senseless acts of a frustrated mob on the rampage. Yet a close investigation shows that shops were not attacked haphazardly. Although the event was spontaneous and unorganized, only those traders who were seen to collude with the mine owners in oppressing the workforce and in undermining the strike had their premises attacked.

The link between the picket and the riot can be understood in terms of a conflict between two definitions of community. For the owners it meant an order based on deference to authority and respect for property rights. For the miners it meant a level of communal care and welfare. Where the ownership of property was used against such basic rights, where coal owners locked the men out and traders refused credit so as jointly to starve the strikers into submission, so strikers expressed in their actions a rejection of the right to property.

The importance of such analyses lies in the question they set for psychological explanation, i.e., how can ideological understanding come spontaneously to be expressed in the behaviour of crowd members? The point about this question is that it demands an understanding of how social beliefs influence the operation of individual minds. Yet this is precisely what the reified psychologies of LeBon and Allport exclude. Both divide individuals from their social context. Crowd behaviour is seen as either the expression of a disembodied group mind or an asocial individual nature. Therefore both are forced to deny that crowd action is a meaningful reaction to specific contexts. An entirely new approach to the crowd is needed, one which starts from a fully socialized concept of the individual.

Between the 1920s and 1980s there have of course been many developments in crowd theory. However, the fundamental premises of the earlier work have not only been left largely unchallenged, but also form the basis for these developments. What has occurred is more a shift of scope than of perspective. Modern researchers have eschewed general theory and instead subjected particular hypotheses, derived from classical writings, to experimental test. The most direct example of this is found in de-individuation research. As Cannavale, one of the original de-individuation theorists, admits, the notion is a direct translation of the LeBonian concept of 'submergence': that, as people become anonymous, personal control is lost and behaviour becomes atavistic (Cannavale, Scarr and Pepitone, 1970).

Derived from Allport's work (amongst others) is a body of research on the relationship between frustration and aggression, the original strict formulation that frustration is necessary and sufficient for aggression being progressively relaxed in the face of repeated empirical disconfirmations. There are other approaches in the individualistic tradition such as social facilitation research and the rational choice model championed by Brown (1965). But for all their refinements and qualifications, they retain the disjunction between social and individual levels of explanation and are therefore incapable of explaining the social form of crowd action.

The only attempt at a genuinely new model of the crowd is to be found in the 'emergent norm theory' of R. H. Turner and Killian (1972). They propose that crowd behaviour is guided by social norms which are constructed during a period of 'milling' which precedes action. Norms are derived from the behaviour of prominent individuals in a process that is termed 'keynoting'. In one sense this model is a qualitative advance on previous work. Turner and Killian and other advocates of the theory stress the way in which crowd events have a pattern which reflects normative structure and that they are not generically mindless nor destructive. However, the model of norm construction they employ is inadequate for their aim of explaining the social form of action.

The model is an adaptation of mainstream small group theory; group norms emerge from interpersonal interactions. But if norms are subsequent to interpersonal events, then they can only be limited by the nature of the individuals involved. The social, therefore, is seen ultimately as arising from individuality (see chapters 2 and 4) and thus there is no basis for explaining the ideological coherence of group norms. Turner and Killian have established the need to account for the sociality of crowd action, yet the lack of a fully socialized psychology as part of that account remains as acute as ever.

Applying the self-categorization theory to crowd behaviour

The problems arising from the division of individual and social were not limited to the domain of crowd psychology, but came to dominate the entire field of social psychology. In fact it is possible to trace a causal link, for early social psychology was dominated by discussion of the crowd, both in Europe and the United States. However, while the group mind tradition still has some influence on contemporary thought, particularly within de-individuation research (see Reicher, 1984b), it has been the individualistic approach deriving from Allport that has come to dominate the mainstream of social psychology.

The essence of psychological individualism consists in analysing behaviour as the interaction between distinct individuals and in terms of their respective and unique individuality. In this way the contextual and cultural specificity of behaviour is ignored and the patterns of a particular society tend to become the basis for general models of behaviour. What has become known as the European school of social psychology (Tajfel, 1984) originated in a critique of such a desocialized view of the individual (e.g., Moscovici, 1972; Tajfel, 1972b). In this sense, the European school and the earlier interactionist perspective in social psychology (see chapter 1) are heirs to a long tradition which includes amongst others the views of Marxists, Durkheimians and Symbolic Interactionists. For all their critical power, however, none of the latter are at a level where they can specify the actual processes through which the social individual emerges, nor can they ever predict the outcome of such processes. What Charles Morris says in his introduction to *Mind, Self and Society* is as true of Symbolic Interactionism as of the others: 'The magic hat of the social, out of which mind and the self were to be drawn, was in part loaded in advance: and for the rest there was merely a pious announcement that the trick could be done, while the performance itself never took place' (Mead, 1934, p. xiv).

In contrast to this, the social identity theory of the group, while based upon a critical theoretical tradition, aims to specify the precise manner in which human cognition is socially structured. The very concept of social identity encapsulates this aspiration (see Turner and Oakes, 1986), for while such an identity is part of an individual's cognitive apparatus, it is at one and the same time defined in a manner that is social and independent of the individual. To define oneself as a 'socialist', for example, is to say something fundamental about what one is as an individual; yet the meaning of 'socialism' is a social product that is irreducible to any one given person. Thus the concept avoids either defining a social mind independent of the individual or an individuality independent of society: it is capable of addressing the problem of social individuality.

In some ways social identity research has become more social as it has developed. The early work concentrated on general processes of intergroup differentiation and conflict (Tajfel, 1974, 1978; Tajfel and Turner, 1979; Turner, 1975). It was concerned to show that defining oneself in terms of membership of a social category had certain inevitable consequences for one's relations with members of other groups. But while showing that group processes are irreducible to attributes of individuality, the research focused on generic consequences of social identification and did not examine the nature of social identity as a form of self-perception, as the basis of shared group membership and the mechanism of producing its higher order properties, nor how the specific ideological content of a particular identity can come to influence behaviour. It is in raising and proposing solutions to the latter issues that the self-categorization theory makes its distinctive contribution.

The self-categorization theory proposes that self-stereotyping in terms of a social category gives rise to a process of social influence, which has been termed 'referent informational influence' (chapter 4). This process is especially relevant to the problem of how the ideological content of an identity is translated into collective behaviour. One way of conceptualizing the process is as follows (Turner, 1982): (1) the individual defines him- of herself as member of a distinct social category, (2) the individual learns or forms the stereotypical norms of the category (in the language of chapter 4, they become aware of social and behavioural dimensions stereotypically correlated with their ingroup self-category, of the prototypical and hence normative actions and attributes within the specific social context), (3) under conditions, therefore, where that ingroup category becomes salient and the individual perceives him- or herself as interchangeable in relevant respects with other ingroup members, they will tend to assign these norms to themselves, employing the attributes of their social identity to define appropriate conduct for them in the context. Thus, as a category membership becomes salient, so the individual conforms to those attributes which define the category. The consequence is that the content of group members' behaviour is dictated by the definition of a social category, which itself is a social and ideological product. In this way referent informational influence represents a specific process through which the behaviour of individuals in a collective context acquires ideologically significant forms: in other words, it meets the fundamental criterion for a theory of crowd behaviour.

Nevertheless, the crowd cannot be simply equated with other groups. A major reason for concern with the crowd has been because it seemed to differ from other social groups. Crowd events do not unfold as part of a routine. They are characteristically marked by a high degree of novelty and ambiguity. Therefore, where the self-categorization theory suggests that group members conform to the stereotypical norms associated with their category, the problem in the crowd is that it is often unclear which norms are relevant or whether indeed there are identity-based norms for the specific situation.

The difficulties are compounded by the absence of formal decision-making processes. In the middle of a crowd event there is not opportunity to discuss and democratically decide on norms of action. Nor is there evidence of an alternative hierarchical structure in which orders are given by predetermined leaders. While it is frequently asserted that crowds are manipulated by conscious agitators, historical research has been singularly unsuccessful in unearthing these shadowy figures. Even where clear attempts at direction have been made, the 'leaders' have often ended up being forced to follow rather than determine collective decisions (cf. Trotsky, 1977). The problem, then, is: if social identity is the basis for group behaviour, what does one do in unprecedented situations for which there are apparently no norms available and no obvious means of creating new norms? It is this question of identity construction, it can be argued, which lies at the heart of crowd psychology.

The answer provided by self-categorization theory is in terms of the 'inductive aspect of categorization' (Turner, 1982). Tajfel (1972a) defines the deductive aspect of categorization as the assignment of attributes of the category as a whole to individuals on the basis of their membership in the category (as in stereotyping) and the inductive aspect as the identification of the individual as a member of the category. For Turner (1982), however, induction is the process of inferring the characteristics of the category as a whole from the attributes of individual members. As we have seen (chapters 3, 4, 6 and 7), the basic hypothesis is that features of individual members which correlate with a given ingroup-outgroup categorization (i.e., features in terms of which social comparisons tend to maximize the meta-contrast between intragroup and intergroup differences) in a direction consistent with the social meaning of the category tend to be perceived as stereotypical of and hence normative for the ingroup. To the degree that any individual is perceived as being a group member, therefore, his or her behaviour provides information relevant to defining the prototypical/normative attributes of group membership. Moreover, to the degree that any individual is perceived as being especially exemplary or representative of the group (e.g., having been designated leader, carrying a banner or some other symbol of membership, being in any way socially prominent), then his or her actions are likely to play a disproportionate role in defining what is appropriate behaviour. In sense, what is proposed is a kind of self-fulfilling process in the formation of identity: since being a group member implies behaviour stereotypical of the group, the stereotype will tend to be inferred and created from that behaviour.

Although this process is meant as a general characteristic of groups, there are two reasons why it is of special significance in the crowd. First, since there are often no pre-established situation-specific norms of relevance and no institutionalized means of deliberation, induction will often be the sole means of determining normative behaviour – crowd norms thus tend to be almost wholly 'emergent' or 'spontaneous'.

Secondly, due to the absence of group structure in the crowd, the notion of an 'exemplary member' will not be restricted to a few chosen representatives, but will indeed refer to anyone who can be unambiguously defined as a group member.

As an illustration of how induction works, consider the following case. A group of individuals is involved in an anti-fascist demonstration which suddenly comes upon a facist rally. The problem that confronts them is 'what does one do, as an anti-fascist, in this situation?'. Suppose, then, that a person who is seen to be an ingroup member – perhaps by a badge that is worn, or a slogan shouted – picks up a stone and throws it toward the rally. That act, or rather the idea of breaking up the rally which it represents, may become a criterial attribute of the crowd. Hence a hail of stones, bricks and slogans may now descend on the fascist gathering.

This example makes the further important point that identity construction in the crowd does not occur in a void. Individuals are not involved in creating a completely new identity but rather in determining the situational significance of an existing category. Consequently there will be limits to the process of norm creation, the constraints being determined by the historical and ideological continuity that the category represents. For example, the physical disruption of an anti-fascist rally may become a stereotypical attribute for a crowd of anti-fascists, but racist provocation could not. The entire process of identity construction can be summarized as follows: there is an immediate identification with a superordinate category which defines a field of possible identities; crowd members must then construct a specific situational identity which determines appropriate behavioural norms and the means by which they do this is the inductive aspect of self-categorization.

This analysis makes two basic assumptions. The first is that crowd members act in terms of a common social identity. Given that the categorization and influence processes described above depend upon social identification, accounting for the ideological coherence of crowd action through these processes requires that all participants share the same identity and that it be highly salient. This assumption is in direct opposition to one of the classic propositions of crowd psychology that the conditions prevailing in the crowd lead to a loss of identity. It will be recalled that LeBon argued that gathering in a crowd leads to anonymity, lack of identifiability and an occlusion of any sense of self. In contrast, what is being argued here is that the 'physical' aspects of the crowd – in which the boundary between ingroup and outgroup and hence the individual's group location is made very clear – act so as to make membership of social categories obvious. Therefore it is not that identity is destroyed in the crowd but rather that it is refocused upon a common category membership.

The second assumption is that the content of crowd behaviour will be limited by the nature of the relevant social category. Social influence will only occur for communications which are consonant with the attributes which define that category. Once again, this contradicts classical notions of the crowd. In the past it has been assumed that crowd action is generically destructive and that there are no limits to that destruction. Here it is proposed not only that crowds may be both destructive and creative, but that the possible forms that either may take will be circumscribed by social identity.

Empirical studies of the crowd

The methodological approach

There is a double problem to be faced in validating the model of the previous section. The first consists in establishing the plausibility of the basic identity processes, the second in showing that these processes actually apply in the crowd context. These two problems raise different methodological questions. On the one hand crowd events are almost impervious to controlled analysis. They are by nature spontaneous and unpredictable and therefore inherently unsuitable for examining theoretical processes. Indeed Milgram and Toch (1969) identify these difficulties as one of the major factors accounting for the decline of crowd psychology after the 1920s. In contrast, the ability to impose controlled manipulation of variables makes of the laboratory an ideal context within which to examine the validity of specific detailed processes.

On the other hand, for all that one may be able to examine the operation of particular processes in the laboratory, this gives no indication as to whether these processes actually operate in the crowd. For instance, one may establish that under conditions where identity is salient, only those messages consonant with the attributes defining that identity are influential, but such experiments cannot say whether real crowd members act in terms of social identifications nor whether the form of crowd behaviour can be explained in terms of the nature of such identifications.

As a consequence, neither laboratory experimentation nor field research alone are capable of producing an adequate psychology of the crowd. Instead of counterposing the two methods and attempting to establish the superiority of one over the other, they should be seen as complementary (see Turner, 1981a). Each is appropriate to a different phase of a total research process. Three such phases may be identified. The first consists of an examination of the crowd in history in order to determine the nature of the behavioural phenomena which require explanation. The second consists of an experimental elaboration of the identity processes which form the basis for an explanation of crowd phenomena. The third phase involves a detailed examination of an actual crowd event in order to determine whether the social identity model is able to explain the nature of events. These three phases are not meant to be exhaustive; further elaborations of the present model will require renewed movement between the laboratory and the field.

The experimental studies

The effects of identifiability. The first aim of the experimental work was to examine the effects of those conditions associated with the crowd context upon behaviour. This question has been one of the principal concerns of crowd psychology ever since its inception. Indeed LeBon's work is based upon assumptions as to the psychological consequences of physical involvement with a mass of others. He was interested in the effects of immersion in a group and in particular the consequences that arise once individual crowd members are no longer distinguishable. These concerns are directly reflected in the recent experimental research on de-individuation (Diener, 1980; Festinger, Pepitone and Newcomb, 1952; Zimbardo, 1969). The classic and the modern work share in common two main assumptions.

The first assumption is that, as attention is drawn away from the self due to group immersion and anonymity, so the standards that normally control behaviour are removed. This contention is based on the second assumption: an individualistic model of the self. The self is seen as a unique property of the individual and, therefore, if attention is removed from self-as-individual, the only alternative is no self and thus no basis for behavioural standards.

The concept of social identity produces a radical break with the de-individuation tradition. It introduces the possibility that conditions which remove attention from personal aspects of the self refocus it upon social aspects of the self and hence render salient social bases of behavioural control. It therefore becomes imperative to examine more closely the way in which 'de-individuating' conditions manipulate the salience of different identities.

The theoretical blindness of de-individuation research to social dimensions of identity is reflected on a methodological level in an insensitivity to the social context in which identifiability is manipulated. This has led to two distinct ways of operationalizing de-individuation. In some cases it has meant merging the individual into a group such that individual and group are indistinguishable. In others it has meant visual anonymity produced through clothing or low lighting. However, 'de-individuation as immersion' and 'de-individuation as anonymity' may be expected to have fundamentally different effects on the salience of social identity.

The effects of immersion should be straightforward. As individuals are made part of a group and their behaviour becomes significant only as part of a collective response, so the salience of the relevant social identification and hence conformity to group norms will increase. The predicted effects of anonymity are more complex and dependent on context. Anonymity in an intergroup situation will decrease visual intragroup differences and increase visual intergroup differences. The consequence is an accentuation of the group boundary and therefore increased salience of group identity and identity-based behaviours. Conversely, where individuals are not in groups but intermingled, to make them anonymous would be to destroy any possibility of distinguishing ingroup and outgroup members. In this case the consequence would be to destroy any vestigial group boundary, to decrease salience of group identity and adherence to group norms.

A first experiment (Reicher, 1984b) was designed to test these predictions. Students from Science and Social Science faculties were initially shown a film. This presented arguments for and against vivisection and then showed the results of a supposed survey on the positions of various groups towards this topic. Social scientists were represented as being strongly anti-vivisection and scientists as being strongly pro-vivisection. The students were then referred to and identified either as group members or as individuals. In both group and individual conditions participants were either left visually identifiable in their own dress or else made anonymous. This was done by dressing them in baggy overalls and a cloth mask covering the whole head. All the participants completed three dependent measures. The first was an 'attitudes to vivisection' scale, the second presented four behavioural dilemmas in which one had to indicate willingness to help or hinder vivisectionists or anti-vivisectionists respectively. Finally there was a 'behaviour projection' scale which required one to divide resources between projects either involving or not involving vivisection. When the measures were completed everyone was brought together and debriefed.

Based upon the general hypotheses the predicted results were as follows: given a pro-vivisection norm for scientists and an anti-vivisection norm for social scientists, then, under group conditions, pro-vivisection behaviour will increase for scientists and decrease for social scientists. For scientists, anonymity will further increase pro-vivisection behaviour in group conditions, while in individual conditions it will further decrease pro-vivisection behaviour. For social scientists, the opposite will occur: anonymity in groups will decrease pro-vivisection responses and anonymity in individual conditions will increase pro-vivisection responses.

For the group manipulation the results on all three measures gave strong support for the predictions: as individual response was merged into group response, so individuals came to act in terms of the group norm. Scientists became considerably more pro-vivisection and social scientists increased their opposition to vivisection. The results of anonymity were much less straightforward. There was only one weak effect of anonymity, which was on the attitude measure. Moreover, while this was in the expected direction, it only applied to the scientists. This absence of anonymity effects is principally attributable to the strength of the group effects: group conditions were so effective in enhancing and individual conditions in attenuating the salience of social identity that the extra contribution of anonymity was negligible. Nevertheless, the consequences of anonymity give no support to the traditional de-individuation position and, where apparent, are explicable only in terms of the social identity theory.

Overall, then, the results indicate that conditions associated with the crowd predispose the expression of social identity-based behaviours. In particular it is clear that 'de-individuation as immersion' does not deregulate behaviour but rather brings into play strong social determinants of behaviour. However, there is a problem in extrapolating from these results to actual crowd behaviour. If, as has been argued, crowd events typically involve intergroup confrontations, then behaviour will be affected by the power of sanctions which the outgroup has over the ingroup. Such power relations are absent from the first study but where they operate one might expect anonymity to acquire a renewed significance. To be specific, ingroup members will be more likely to do things likely to invoke the sanction of the outgroup when they cannot be identified by the outgroup.

This argument may seem a return to LeBon's account of anonymity leading to an indiscriminate release of destructive behaviour, but there is a crucial difference. Behaviour will also be limited by ingroup norms. The argument depends on a distinction between antecedent processes and usable power to translate these processes into action, i.e., the crowd context may predispose individuals to act in terms of social identity but they will only actually do so where fear of sanctions is overcome. The important point is that the immunity conferred by anonymity will only facilitate the expression of behaviours that are consonant with the ingroup's social identity.

It is therefore necessary to distinguish between the intra- and the intergroup consequences of immersion and anonymity. The first study showed that within the group both factors work through manipulating the salience of social identity, although anonymity is of limited importance. On the intergroup level, where power relations are involved, both factors will be of importance in neutralizing outgroup sanctions. In particular, anonymity will make it impossible for the outgroup to identify individuals participating in the action. As a consequence immersion and anonymity will facilitate the expression of social identity-based behaviours proscribed by the outgroup. A second study was designed to test these predictions.

Participants were divided into groups of supporters and antagonists of the 'Campaign for Nuclear Disarmament' (CND). They were then shown a videotaped debate on the motion 'Britain should unilaterally discard all its nuclear weapons', which had two proposers and two opposers. At seven intervals during the debate participants were asked to evaluate how powerfully the arguments were expressed by either side. This was done by dividing points between the pro- and anti-CND positions. At the end of the debate a final overall evaluation was made, after which everybody completed an eight-item 'attitudes to nuclear disarmament' scale.

Both the pro- and anti-CND groups were divided into 'ingroup visible' and 'outgroup visible' conditions. In the former, each group sat around a separate table with a screen dividing them. They were told that at the end of the study members would read their evaluation points scores (the numbers of points awarded to pro- and anti-CND at each of the seven intervals while watching the debate) to an ingroup member who would collate them and hand to the outgroup the totalled scores for pro- and anti-CND for each of the seven choices. The outgroup would then decide how to partition these points totals for the ingroup amongst the ingroup members. Thus they were told that only ingroup members would know how individuals had responded and that when the outgroup came to distribute points amongst them it would have no means of penalizing those who showed extreme ingroup bias.

In the outgroup visible conditions each group sat in a 'V' formation, the two 'V's facing each other so that each group could see the other.

They were told that at the end of the study group members would read their evaluation points scores to a member of the outgroup, who would collate them; the outgroup would then decide how to partition the points totals for the ingroup amongst ingroup members. Thus they were led to believe that outgroup members would be able to scrutinize the reponses of each individual and would have the means of discriminating against those who were highly biased in favour of the ingroup. In fact the experiment was terminated and a debriefing session took place as soon as the attitude scale had been completed.

The predictions were that, for the evaluation of the debate, members would show ingroup bias by allocating more points to their own group than the other, but less bias would be shown when participants believed their responses would be visible to the outgroup. For the attitude scale, supporters of CND would be more favourable to unilateral disarmament than antagonists, but, assuming that attitudes are neither proscribed by nor discriminate against the outgroup, there should be no effects of visibility.

The overall results gave strong support to these predictions. Interestingly, however, there was a visibility effect for the one attitude item which at the time of the study (autumn 1982) addressed actions considered illegitimate by both sides. Direct action tactics were considered illegal by opponents of CND, whilst the measures used against such tactics were considered illegitimate by CND supporters. Consequently, this unexpected result further supports the contention that lack of visibility in an intergroup context only facilitates behaviours that are prescribed by ingroup identity and proscribed by the outgroup.

In conclusion, the two studies together suggest that the effects upon identifiability which are associated with being part of a crowd act so as to overdetermine the expression of social identity. Not only is such identity made salient but also the neutralization of outgroup power allows the expression of identity-based behaviours in a way that may be impossible in everyday life. This implies, in complete contradiction to the traditional image of the anarchic mob, that crowd action represents one of the clearest contexts in which to discover the social bases of behaviour.

The limits of social influence. Having demonstrated the relationship between crowd conditions and social identification, the second aim of the experimental research was to examine the consequences of social identification for the process of social influence. The self-categorization theory gives rise to two hypotheses: first, that processes of collective influence depend upon the salience of group identity and, secondly, that, given that the consequence of salience is conformity to the ingroup stereotype, only messages which define or make available norms which are consonant with that stereotype will be influential. The third study tested these hypotheses.

The experiment involved social science students who initially watched a videotape which purported to show the results of a survey into attitudes to the punishment of sexual offenders. As well as presenting arguments for and against heavy punishment the tape showed the positions of various groups. Social scientists were shown as having a strong norm towards high punishment. Participants then either had their social identity made salient by referring to and identifying them only in terms of their group membership or else social identity was made non-salient by referring to them as individuals and identifying them through a unique individual code.

There were two dependent measures. The first presented a set of eight dilemmas based upon vignettes of sexual harrassment or assault in which participants were asked to indicate what sort of punishment the offender should receive. However, before responding to each dilemma they were presented with a tape-recorded message which was purportedly that of a previous respondent. There were two conditions. In one, all the messages argued for leniency, while in the other the messages all stressed the need for punishment. After completing their responses the participants filled in an 'attitudes to punishment of sexual offenders' scale. Finally they were brought together and debriefed.

It was predicted that participants would give more punitive responses when their social science identity was made salient, but that the effects of the message manipulation would depend upon salience. When social science identity is not salient, responses will be influenced by message content. Participants will be more punitive when the message is punitive than when it is lenient. It can be presumed here that the effect of messege content is mediated by its appeal to existing higher order norms. When social science identity is salient, there will be no message effect, since the messages that are not congruent with that identity will have no effect upon responses and those that are will merely duplicate the effect of the salient ingroup norm.

Results on both the dilemmas and the attitude scale bear out these predictions. The number of jail sentences as opposed to lesser measures indicated as the appropriate punishment undergoes an overall increase where identity as a social scientist is made salient. The messages only affect the number of sentences when identity is not salient. Exactly the same pattern applies for the attitude scale. This indicates that the nature of the influence process is a function of the state of identification.

Where a specific identity is not salient, responses may be influenced against its norms. However, when that identity is salient, not only does behaviour conform to the ingroup stereotype but also the sole source of influence is likely to be in messages which clarify the content of that stereotype.

Two things should be noted about this argument. First, it suggests that far from being more liable to casual influence, collective behaviour introduces very strict limits upon the influence process. Secondly, it implies that the nature of those limits and therefore the range of possible collective actions will be determined by the content of the salient social identification.

The experimental studies in combination provide support for the self-categorization theory of crowd behaviour. They show that the conditions associated with crowds make social identity salient and that under these conditions behaviour both conforms to and is limited by the ingroup stereotype. It remains to show that these processes apply to actual crowd events and that the behaviour in such an event can be understood in terms of the social identity of the participants.

The field study

The field research (Reicher, 1984a) consists of an analysis of the disturbances which occurred in the St Pauls area of Bristol, England, on 2 April 1980. This analysis is based on a series of resources. First, a collection was made of all media sources; secondly, various official and semi-official reports were collected; thirdly, a series of photographs was amassed; finally, a number of interviews were conducted. Interviewees included several 'elite individuals' such as local councillors, police chiefs, clergy and 'community leaders' as well as about 30 individuals who participated in the events.

The account that follows was constructed out of these various sources; where events were corroborated by independent sources, they are not given. Only when unique information is supplied is the source identified. Interviewees are identified using the following code: race (W = white, B = black), sex (M = Male, F = Female) and approximate age. Thus WM25 indicates a 25-year-old white male.

The events of 2 April fall into two distinct phases. The first started with the police raid on the Black and White café and ended when the police left the St Pauls area. The second covers the period in which uniformed police were absent from the area, before re-entering with reinforcements. There are major differences between the two phases and they will be analysed separately.

The first phase of the 'St Pauls riot'. What became known as the St Pauls riot was in fact a complex series of events following a drugs and illegal drinking raid on the Black and White café in Grosvenor Road. There were three separate bouts of violence. The first occurred as the police were taking away Bertram Wilkes, owner of the café, who had been arrested. They were stoned by a large crowd gathered opposite the café. There was then a period of calm as the police loaded crates of drink, found in the café, into a van. The second bout of violence began as the van drove away and was so intense that police were forced to flee and regroup with reinforcements, before marching back to relieve some of their colleagues beleaguered inside the café. Only after prolonged conflict during which several police cars were burnt out were the police able to regain control.

The final and most violent phase began when a pick-up van came to take away the gutted cars and the police drew up in formation, intending to march down Grosvenor Road and clear the streets. As they started to do so the stoning began and the police were broken up into two groups. For half an hour between 6.45 and 7.15 p.m. two lots of 200 to 300 youths faced a total of some 60 police, one lot on City Road, the other on the green opposite Lloyds Bank. Finally all the police were forced back on to City Road, where they tried to regroup with riot shields. But they were still outnumbered and surrounded and were slowly forced down the road and out of St Pauls. By 7.30 p.m. they were back in Trinity Road police station.

Out of the officers involved 49 suffered some form of injury. Twenty-one police vehicles were damaged, eight by fire, of which six were gutted. Yet apart from photographers, of whom it was feared with some justification that their pictures might facilitate police identification, the police were the only target of collective attack. The crowd assaulted no private individuals nor attacked any private property. Indeed the event occurred against a backdrop of remarkable normality; cars drove through the area, people shopped, families watched and chatted.

This is not a claim that only the police were hurt. Several people were hit and windows broken by stray bricks. More importantly, one must distinguish between individual and collective actions. There is an important difference between isolated acts and those which become generalized and serve as the basis for collective norms. One person may throw a stone at a target but, unless others join in, it cannot be considered as collective behaviour. In determining the difference between acts which generalize and those which do not one can derive the boundaries of normative action. Thus the stoning of the police was

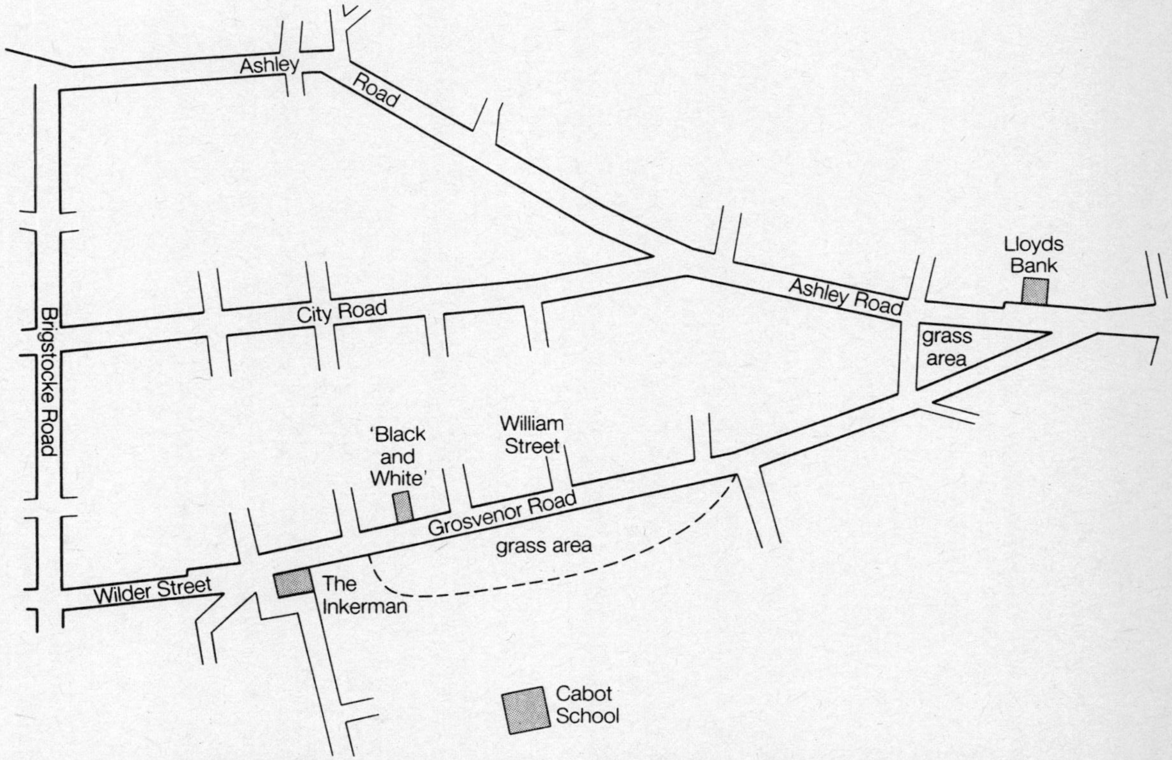
Ashley
Road
Brigstocke Road
City Road
Ashley Road
Lloyds
Bank
grass
area
'Black
and
White'
William
Street
Grosvenor Road
grass area
Wilder Street
The
Inkerman
Cabot
School

Figure 8.1 *Plan of St Pauls (from Reicher, S.D. (1984) The St Pauls Riot: An explanation of the limits of crowd action in terms of a social identity model.* European Journal of Social Psychology, 14, 1–21. *Reprinted by permission of John Wiley and Sons, Ltd.)*

described as follows: 'all hell was let loose after the first brick went in' (WM30), or else 'a few bricks went in and then people closed in the road and everybody started doing it' (WM17). However, the response to other targets was very different: 'a bus . . . got one window smashed . . . everyone went "ugh", "idiots"' (WF25). In some cases there seems to have been a prosocial norm. When the fire service came to put out a burning police car people helped unroll the hoses.

Apart from definite limits to the targets for attack there were also geographical limits to the events. Only the police in St Pauls came under attack and when they left the area they were not pursued. Asked why, one participant replied: 'it was just an assumption by everyone in the crowd – get [the police] out' (WM17). This quotation shows two things. First of all, within what was described as 'riot fury' (*The Sun* newspaper, 3 April 1980), there was a clear pattern to the events with strict limits to what was deemed legitimate behaviour. Secondly, that pattern was the result of neither preplanning nor overt leadership. Participants consistently describe their behaviour as spontaneous and when asked who initiated particular episodes would make responses such as 'anyone, everybody down there' (WF25). The possibility remains that there were conscious agitators of whom people were unaware, but this still begs the question of why particular acts became normative while others did not. It remains necessary to explain how the events displayed clear social form without the benefit of any consensual direction.

Despite the lack of leadership many participants expressed a sense of purpose. The specific purpose was 'getting [the police] out of St Pauls' (WM17); more generally it was resistance to outside control, of which the police were a symbol. When Desmond Pierre of the St Pauls Defence Committee was asked about its purpose, he replied: 'We are defending ourselves on a lot of issues, but the main one is just the right to lead a free life.' From this perspective the events are immediately comprehensible.

There are two important points about this sense of purpose. It is *collective*. Participants talk of themselves not as individuals but as part of a social group. This collective sense of self is apparent throughout participants' accounts. It pervades the way they talked of who was involved: 'it was St Pauls, you know . . . this was just St Pauls'. It affects the way they talked about the consequences: 'we feel great, we feel confident it was a victory' (BM age unknown); the social self-definition also affected how people related to each other. While the police suffered ferocious attack, and outsiders experienced intense fear (one woman declaring 'I thought I was going to be killed'), the relationship to those seen as part of the ingroup was entirely different. According to one participant 'it was really joyful, that's what they all leave out, the joy' (WM30). Once again the nature of the ingroup is precisely specified: 'you were grinning at everybody because everyone was from St Pauls' (WM17). The participants regarded themselves, their actions and the events as a whole in terms of their membership of the St Pauls community.

Secondly, the sense of purpose reveals something of the meaning of the St Pauls identity. Apart from the obvious geographical element, the central themes are those of a desire for control constantly thwarted by the domination and oppression of external agents, with specific reference to the police. Several respondents likened being from St Pauls to suffering racial oppression – as one resident observed of the crowd, 'politically they were all black' (WF28). This is not to say that the 'St Pauls community' or the participants were all black, but rather that their identity is defined in terms of black experience.

In light of this identification and bearing in mind the significance of the Black and White café itself, the events of the first phase become explicable. The Black and White café was the only public establishment owned and run by a local resident. It therefore not only had symbolic value but was a crucial resource for the self-organization of the community. In raiding the café and being seen to threaten its closure, the police were seen as making an open attack on the community's right to exist. The point is important for it undermines the notion that almost any 'spark' may initiate a riot. Far from this being so, each of the events that precipitated violence – arresting Wilkes, removing the stock, attempting to clear the streets – was a highly significant act from the perspective of group identity. They each validated the notion of the police as an agency undermining the autonomy of the community and, in so far as this identity provided a means of making sense of the actions (see chapter 6), they made it highly salient.

What is more, the content of events was entirely consonant with the principal dimensions of the St Pauls identity. Behaviour was limited to removing what was seen as an alien and illegitimate police presence. Thus violence directed against the police became normative while action against other targets did not. Similarly, violence was only acceptable within the St Pauls area, not a stone was thrown outside its geographical boundaries.

The close relationship between the content of the St Pauls identity and the events of the first phase provides strong support for the notion that social identity processes underly crowd behaviour. Also, the account of the manner in which particular actions became normative is consistent with the explanation of norm formation in the crowd in terms of the inductive aspect of categorization. At periods of uncertainty any action as long as it was performed by a group member and translated group identity into action was liable to become normative. Finally, the level of violence directed at the police was only possible because being outnumbered they had no way of arresting their assailants. Yet once again it should be stressed that however unprecedented or extreme the behaviours facilitated by this immunity, the power of the crowd did not lead to wanton destruction. It only facilitated actions that fell within the limits prescribed by the relevant social identity.

The second phase of the 'St Pauls riot'. As soon as the police had left the St Pauls area, members of the crowd began to take charge of traffic control. The only vehicles that were denied entry were police cars or those suspected of carrying plainclothes police. Otherwise the only impediment to traffic was a small and largely symbolic barricade built and set alight on City Road at the boundary of St Pauls.

Over the next four hours a series of attacks on property was made. It is difficult to establish exact timings or a clear sequence to events. It seems that the first attacks, situated around the junction of Grosvenor Road and Wilder Street, began at around 7.45 p.m. and that by 11.15 p.m. when the police had surrounded the area they had largely finished. Before discussing the events it is necessary to point to a difficulty in the analysis. Given that many attacks were occurring simultaneously and mostly under cover of nightfall it is frequently impossible to tell whether they were collective or individual acts. The damage record alone is an unreliable guide to collective intentions, for some of the damage may have been done by outsiders and, if witnessed, might have incurred collective disapproval. In fact, several local shops were broken into but were then defended collectively and further attacks were stopped.

Despite these difficulties, some patterns can be discerned. All the attacks were limited to the St Pauls area and there was no damage to private homes. Despite the fact that homes and shops are interspersed throughout St Pauls, it was impossible to spot even one broken window. Also there was a difference between shops owned by local residents and those owned by outsiders. The majority of the former were either left alone or actively defended. In some cases this defence was organized, as in the case of a group of Rastafarians (a black sect) outside the Roots record shop or the local priest who ensured that the local chemist was not looted. In other cases it was spontaneous: 'one white lad threw a bottle at the Kashmir. He was stopped by several people and told he was not to do it' (WM35).

In fact out of 16 locally owned shops (excluding service establishments) only four suffered any damage and for three of these there were special circumstances. One was collectively defended after individuals were seen inside it, another caught fire through being next to the bank and its owner came out to berate the crowd, and in the third case there seems to have been the settling of an old score. In contrast, all eight shops owned by outsiders were damaged, seven of them being extensively looted. Moreover, the looting seems to have been collective. In the case of Overbury's, a bicycle shop, 'they were forming a chain and passing out bikes and things . . . there were all sorts of people there, black and white. There were young and old' (WM25).

Of the shops which were attacked, four, all owned by outsiders, had stock vandalized as well as looted. These were Frank Voisey, a car showroom, Fowlers, a motorcycle shop, Barrowcrofts, an electrical goods shop, and Overbury's. In the last case bicycles were initially taken from the shop and laid in the road for cars to run over before the looting began. It is noticeable that in each case the shops took advantage of low costs in the area in order to run large showrooms selling expensive goods. Due to local poverty (one index shows 60 per cent of St Pauls children being eligible for free school meals, as against a county average of 21 per cent), these goods were mostly out of reach of the population and the shops were only used by outsiders.

Finally, a series of buildings was directly attacked rather than the damage being a side effect of looting. If one excludes those properties which suffered fire damage due to flames spreading from adjacent premises, there were four of these. They are the Department of Health and Social Services in Wilder Street, which was badly stoned, Washbrooks Stationers opposite the Inkerman pub, which suffered £65,000 fire damage, Lloyds Bank, which was destroyed by fire, and the Post Office near Lloyds, which was also severely damaged by fire. Washbrooks was the first to be set on fire and the flames threatened to spread to nearby homes. However, the fire service was initially denied access to St Pauls. When fire engines later tried to put out the blaze at Lloyds, they were fiercely stoned and as fire officers went into the burning bank their air supply was interfered with – a potentially lethal act.

Each of the attacks on buildings was carried out collectively. This is clearest in the case of Lloyds Bank: 'somebody suddenly shouted out "bank" and, once one went in, there was a shower of large stones, bricks . . . it was quite a spontaneous reaction' (WM35). The reason why these targets were chosen was made equally clear: 'we got the bank; that's where the moneymen live. That's Margaret Thatcher's government' (BM23). In fact all four buildings represent major financial institutions for local residents. Apart from the bank, the DHSS is where all forms of welfare benefit are claimed, (estimates of unemployment alone account for 30–70 per cent of adult residents), the Post Office is where 'giro' cheques (a form of government and other payment) can be redeemed and Washbrooks was housed in the same building as a local rent office.

These institutions have a dual significance: they symbolize the exclusion of an impoverished community from spheres of capital and state and they are the practical means through which the latter exert control over the community. The process of applying for benefit, claiming benefit and even cashing giro cheques, for example, subjects the individual to constant humiliation and investigation as well as publicly marking their poverty and wagelessness. It also operates a double bind, for as well as stressing exclusion the process demands at least overtly a conventional orientation to waged society. One must be seen to be available for and willing to work in order to claim. Thus, simultaneously, one is denied the benefits of a materialistic society and denied the possibility of elaborating an alternative. Poverty and domination are inextricably intertwined: the fusion of 'the moneymen' and 'Margaret Thatcher's government' is not fanciful but a central experience of St Pauls people. Any attempt to overcome material or cultural subordination must confront these institutions.

Therefore, far from being random, the targets and the nature of the attack upon them are highly meaningful. This is not to deny that a prominent motive in what happened was simple material gain: as one participant observed, 'kids want bicycles, things like sweets and groceries. People had never had it so good' (WM25). Yet this is not a sufficient explanation, for it tells nothing about the pattern of events.

In contrast to some opinions, the community did not attack itself; participants were quite clear about this: 'little corner shops did not get done because they are struggling like most of the people in St Pauls' (WM17), or more graphically: 'you don't shit on your own doorstep' (BM age unknown). The attacks that were made express a social understanding of the relationship between target and community. Where outsiders' shops were seen simply as profiting from locals, they were looted. The principle was 'I paid for this yesterday, it is mine now' (BF quoted by WM35). Where shops took advantage of St Pauls to sell goods beyond the range of residents, the goods themselves, symbols of a consumer society and a permanent mockery to indigenous poverty, were attacked. Where institutions were seen as imposing control over the community, the attempt was made to destroy the institution as a whole.

Despite the great subtlety of these events, participants stressed that 'there was no obvious leadership in the sense that "this is next on the list, we'll break into here" (WM30). As in the first phase, what happened seems to have been neither planned nor directed and, again, people's accounts and their behaviour point to their participation as members of the 'St Pauls community'. Once more there is a clear relationship between the content of this identification and the nature of events. Apart from the geographical element, the dimension of control is central, for the events can be seen as reactions against a set of institutions which bind the community into a position of powerlessness and poverty.

Being able 'to lead a free life' means as much an assault on the economic and political basis of domination as upon the police. So, in the same way as attacking the police, the looting, damage and arson were attacks on outside agencies of social control. The differences in the nature of the attack reflect differences in the understanding of the manner in which the different targets exerted control over the community. The reason why no direction was needed was that the legitimacy and therefore the generalizability of particular behaviours was determined by their relationship to this understanding, which itself was a common social conception of the way the St Pauls community related to other social agents.

The final point relates to the importance of power. The events of the second stage could not have occurred without the absence of the police and the cover of darkness. Participants candidly admit that there was a feeling of 'wait until it gets dark'. Yet the inability to be apprehended or identified was only used in order to manifest a socially defined and shared set of grievances. What was unprecedented was not so much the feeling of antagonism as an ability to express this antagonism in unmitigated form. The evidence indicates that crowd events are uniquely social; they allow a glimpse of people's social understanding of themselves and their social world that is hidden amongst the concerns of everyday life.

Conclusion

The empirical evidence demonstrates that the self-categorization theory is of use in explaining crowd behaviour. The experimental studies illustrate the explanatory viability and significance of social identity processes for social influence, and the field study shows that the theory is capable of accounting for the characteristics of an actual crowd event. In particular and in contrast to foregoing crowd psychologies, it is capable of explaining the central paradox of the crowd: how behaviour manages to be a complex and meaningful reaction to unprecedented circumstances without overt direction. Moreover, the ability of social identity processes to account for the spontaneous sociality of the crowd is made possible by the irreducible sociality of the concept itself. The concept acknowledges the social form of collective behaviour without seeing it as a construct out of purely intra- or inter-individual events because the social dimension is made neither separate from nor secondary to individual aspects of human cognition.

It is claimed, therefore, that the social identity theory of the group provides an adequate basis for developing a social psychological explanation of crowd behaviour. It is not suggested, however, that the explanation presented has yet been proved, nor that the processes of referent informational influence and in particular norm formation through the inductive aspect of categorization explain the specific content and the concrete historical development of crowd action.

One of the crucial aspects of the St Pauls 'riot' was the change that occurred as it developed. While it is true that it is possible to explain both phases using a broad notion of 'control' and that on the general level there is a definite continuity between them, there are also important differences. On a mundane level there is the difference in reaction to the fire service. At first they are welcomed and helped; later on they are barred and their lives put under threat, and this is a reflection of an underlying change. What started as a defensive reaction to a particular event develops into an offensive attempt to redefine the relationship between the community and a whole series of agents. Where the first phase was a matter of getting rid of the police, the second was a matter of taking control of the streets and determining who and what could take place upon them. Nobody, not even the fire service, had the right to come in uninvited. Moreover, it is clear that the participants felt that their relationships to outside agents had been changed as a result of the events. As one black youth said of the police: 'they will never again treat us with contempt . . . they will respect us now'.

As argued in the introduction, one aim of social identity research has been to counter the traditional tendency of psychology to reify behaviour. An aspect of this is the stress on the interaction between the social and psychological determinants of behaviour. There is a second and equally important aspect. By abstracting behaviours from their social context and universalizing the products of a given moment in history, crowd psychology has tended to exclude the possibility of social change. Social identity research, on the other hand, began with a clear commitment to produce a social psychology of social change. Tajfel (1974), for example, stated that 'social identity is understood here as an intervening causal mechanism in situations of social change'. The current explanation of the crowd, however, remains relatively static. It allows for change and development in that identity-based behaviours do not represent the imposition of a set of of predetermined attributes, but follow from the construction of a relatively autonomous 'situational identity' – within the limits of the relevant superordinate identity the latter may assume myriad forms and change rapidly. Indeed, salient self-categories at whatever level of abstraction, and the defining norms which accompany them, are not static or constant phenomena, but relative and fluid, varying with the specific social context that provides the frame of reference and the social relations perceived between people. But there is little systematic attempt to exploit this side of the theory; for example, extra-psychological factors in the induction of norms or changes of superordinate identity to do with political and economic realities and their ideological interpretation are treated almost as random events.

The key issue is raised of how one can combine in one theory the fact that social identity determines the form of social behaviour and is at the same time changed through that behaviour. This is an aspect of the question of how the individual (or psychology) can be at one and the same time the cause and the consequence of society. To understand the contribution of the self-categorization theory to this question, the role of social identity in social psychological interaction must be understood (see chapter 9): that social identity refers both to the attributes of a given self and is also by the very nature of its construction a model of social relations and that identity and social relations exist as reciprocally determining preconditions. This is illustrated in the way the concept was used to account for the events of St Pauls.

The St Pauls identity principally denoted a collective conception of the place of the community in its social world. This breaks down into two elements. First, a model of the nature of various social agencies. Secondly, the implications of this for the behaviour of the community: both how agencies impinge on community and how community can act upon these agencies. It is hardly surprising that there is an intimate connection between one's concept of self and one's understanding of the social world. On the one hand, a concept of one's place in the world will depend on how the world is organized (in a world structured by class it will be one's class that is of relevance; in a world structured by nation, nationality comes to the fore). On the other hand, one's behaviours will be constrained by the nature of the social relations in which one is enmeshed. Thus many of the stereotypical characteristics of subordinated groups – slyness, dishonesty, expressivity – represent inevitable strategies in dealing with a powerful adversary whom it is impossible to confront directly. Moreover, to take the case of the black movement in America, the change in these supposed attributes was integrally connected to a reconceptualization of the power relation between black and white stemming in part from liberation in Africa.

It is important, therefore, to have a dynamic view of identity, to see it not only as a determinant and reflection of what is but also as a model of what is possible within a particular set of social relations, in other words, as a theory of action in the social world. Changes in the nature of social relations will alter the ability of subjects to act and changes in subjects' actions will alter social relations. Social identity relates behaviour to its social context and explains its social form, but it does not imply the endless reproduction of society as it is; this would be to lapse into a new form of reification. It also provides a social psychological starting point in the analysis of social change.

9

Conclusion

This book began with the question of how individuals formed a psychological group and what effects group membership had on behaviour. Immediately, two larger questions appeared: does group formation represent any kind of distinctive psychological process, are individuals in any sense psychologically transformed in the creation of a group or is it merely a change in the content but not the underlying mechanisms of behaviour, and how is it possible for social psychology, part of the science of individual mental processes, to explain the higher order social properties of group behaviour in terms of the characteristics of the individual without being individualistic? We have proposed the following answers.

First, that, in general terms, individuals form a psychological group in so far as they develop a shared social categorization of themselves in contrast to others, which, in a given situation, becomes the basis of their attitudes and behaviour. This hypothesis has been elaborated in some detail and we have gone to some pains to explain how it differs from prevailing ideas and to indicate distinctive, testable predictions. We have also tried to show how it can provide better and simpler explanations of certain phenomena than the interdependence theory. There are, naturally, unresolved issues, or questions which at some point must be answered but which have been insufficiently addressed or not addressed at all. For example, is the fact of role differentiations within a group inconsistent with our analysis? The short answer is no: social roles are social norms specifying appropriate behaviour by all group members who find themselves in or are assigned to a given social position or function – they are usually, formally or informally, organizational norms. Thus intragroup differences between people based on role behaviour are not in the first instance *personal* differentiations (they do not define what is different about a person but what *every* member would do in the same position). On the contrary, it is only the interchangeability of group members (see Deutsch, 1949a, 1949b), the fact that others' actions can substitute for one's own, which makes an intragroup division of labour and the idea of a role which all are expected to enact in much the same way possible. Social roles do not belong merely to the role-occupants; they are shared norms of behaviour belonging to the whole group and may be seen as a development in the complexity of social identity (e.g., to define oneself as a Catholic is in part to define oneself in terms of and accept the institutional structure of that church). A new theory must needs take time to develop its point of view with respect to such questions. In this sense, the present theory is an interim statement, with capacity for elaboration, qualification and revision as research proceeds.

Secondly, it has been argued that group formation is a distinctive social-psychological process. The importance of the social categorization of the self is that it represents self-categorization at a higher, more inclusive level of abstraction than the personal self and thus functions to depersonalize individual self-perception and behaviour. The individual can internalize and take on the character of the social whole – not just in behaviour but in respect of their psychology, their self-identity. It has been suggested that collective processes are an adaptive achievement made possible by the capacity of the human self to vary in this way. This idea is anticipated in the analyses of McDougall and Asch, for example. A merit of the present theory is to systematize it in terms of causal psychological processes. It should be obvious from all that has gone before that 'depersonalization' is not a loss of identity, but its transformation. A term with more positive connotations might have been preferable, but the only alternatives have more disadvantages.

Thirdly, the self-categorization theory is presented as an illustration that social psychology need not be an individualistic science. It is an 'interactionist' theory (not to be confused with the idea of the person x situation interaction in personality research – although it is interactionist in this sense too). The idea of social psychological interaction was introduced in chapter 1. It is suggested that it provides the metatheoretical solution to the problem of the relationship of the individual to the group (until such time as theory and data catch up). It will be useful in concluding to try to state more exactly what we mean by social psychological interaction (and it is not an easy task) and relate the theory directly to it. This will provide a broader social scientific and historical context for understanding the proposed theory.

The idea of social psychological interaction comprises several related notions that can be stated as follows. Individuals in their multiplicity cannot be opposed to or in reality distinguished from society: individuals are society and society is the natural form of being of human individuals. The fallacy that the individual may be opposed to society arises from a legitimate but different contrast between a particular individual and others, resulting in the idea of uniqueness or individuality, but individuality itself is a social property of the individual and the terms of such a contrast are both within society. There is no such thing as the pre-social, asocial, purely biological, 'as if isolated' individual except as an analytic, fictional abstraction.

There is, in fact, a continuous reciprocal interaction and functional interdependence between the psychological processes of individuals and their activity, relations and products as society. Individuals in or as society are *psychologically creative* in that their social activity produces, makes possible, and transforms the distinctively human form of the individual mind, just as the individual mind is *socially creative* in that psychological processes make possible and mediate the distinctively human form of social behaviour. In this sense, mind and society, individual and group, are mutual preconditions, simultaneous emergent properties (i.e., higher order, distinctive, irreducible) of each other. Such a functional interaction holds both phylogenetically and ontogenetically.

Social psychological and social scientific explanations of social behaviour, therefore, do not represent different levels of phenomena in the sense that one is more or less 'basic' than the other, that one can be reduced to the other: their phenomena are interactive aspects of the same human process. Social psychological processes are or pertain to the psychological or subjective aspects of society. The task of social psychology as part of psychology (the science of individual mental processes) is *not to provide social explanations* of behaviour (this can be left to sociology, politics, etc.), *nor to provide 'psychological explanations' of*, i.e., *'psychologize'*, social behaviour, but *to explain the psychological aspects of society* (what McDougall, 1921, meant by but tactically misnamed the 'group mind'). This means understanding the structures and processes whereby society is psychologically represented in and mediated by individual minds. Individual minds are not individualistic in the ideological sense of being defined by some presocial psychological dynamic but are socially structured - society is in the individual as much as individuals are in society. Thus, the 'nothing but' stance of individualism, that society contains nothing but individuals, is refuted and stood on its head by the argument that individuals are more than we had ever supposed, parts which can (psychologically) contain the whole (see Asch, 1952, p. 257).

The last point that needs to be made is to assert the importance of socially mediated cognition in determining distinctively human social behaviour. The key product of social psychological interaction is socially mediated cognition, phenomenologically experienced as the perception of a shared, public, objective world (see chapter 4). Human social interaction is based upon psychological representations of the interaction, interactors and setting shared by the interactors. We act in an intersubjective world of shared social meanings.

The main ideas of the self-categorization theory – that there are different levels of abstraction of self-categorization and that group phenomena reflect self-perception and action in terms of the shared social categorical self – embody these notions. Thus, the theory recognizes in terms of the different levels of self-perception that human individuals are subjectively and in action both individual persons and society. The social categorical self or social identity is in form (the level of abstraction) and content (the defining stereotypical attributes) and social extent (the sociological or situational limits within which it is shared by people) precisely individuals in their societal aspect, and depersonalization is the process whereby people cease to be unique individuals and become *subjectively* the exemplars or representatives of society or some part of it, the living, self-aware embodiments of the historical, cultural and politico-ideological forces and movements which formed them. Indeed, psychologically speaking, they do not 'represent', they 'are'; they become self-conscious society, as McDougall would have put it. The personal self, too, reflecting one's individuality is assumed to be socially mediated, being based on intra-group comparisons and differentiations in terms of one's higher order group memberships.

Also, the social categorical self is a channel for social psychological interaction and a mechanism for the mutual emergence of irreducible social and psychological forms. The psychological process of the increase in the level of abstraction of self-categorization (and depersonalization) makes possible and induces social uniformities of action and attitudes as one responds in terms more of the stereotypical identity defining one's shared ingroup membership than one's distinctive personality. The *social form* of group action, its social unity and coherence, derives from the shared subjectivity of the identical ingroup self and the processes of social influence, consensual validation, norm formation and the like that follow from the psychological interchangeability of self and others. The psychological process of depersonalization is socially creative in making possible social processes of influence, unification, attraction and co-operation that would otherwise be unavailable. The impact of psychological principles on the emergent social form of behaviour is demonstrated in the polarization of social norms as a function of the cognitive meta-contrasts which define the prototypical characteristics of (social) categories.

Reciprocally, the group relations produced by social identity are psychologically creative in being the preconditions for the emergence of the social level of abstraction in the categorization of self and others and the specific behavioural and normative content of social categories. The individual psychological processes of comparison and categorization can only produce the social psychological process of depersonalization because of the objective social reality of sociological identity between people and the collective form of their life. Ingroup-outgroup categorizations more or less directly reflect social relations, the perceived social similarities and differences between people on the dimensions and in terms of the values deemed as relevant and important by society, and they become salient in perception as explanatory cognitive representations of the social invariances, regularities, or 'dispositions' of individual behaviour (chapter 6). The very fact of a continuum of self-perception varying from personal to ingroup self-categories is made possible by and reflects the distinctive capacity of human social behaviour to vary *objectively* in the level of abstraction or degree of inclusiveness of the behaving unit: *that we can and do act as both social groups and distinct individual persons.* The shared, consensual nature of particular ingroup categories, which we have taken for granted throughout, also indicates that they are products of social reality and influence.

Social identity is, therefore, a 'socially structured field' within the individual mind, an important element of the psychological or subjective processes of society. It is a mechanism whereby society forms the psychology of its members to pursue its goals and conflicts as for example 'citizens', 'Americans', 'Irish republicans', 'conservatives', 'socialists', or 'Catholics'. Its functioning provides group members with a shared psychological field, shared cognitive representations of themselves, their own identity, and the objective world in the form of shared social norms of fact and value and hence makes meaningful the simplest communications and emotions of a public, intersubjective life (see Asch, 1952; Farr and Moscovici, 1984).

Asch (1952) has pointed out that the essential ability of human beings which explains social psychological interaction is that they are parts (individuals) which can contain or recapitulate (psychologically) the whole (the group) and hence can regulate and co-ordinate their behaviour in terms of the idea of the whole to bring the whole into objective existence. The social identity concept is a specification of that 'psychological representation of the whole' and the self-categorization theory offers a detailed predictive explanation of how, psychologically, the whole is brought into existence and of how, therefore, individual psychological processes can produce more than just individual behaviour. Whatever the metatheoretical perspective, however, if the theory can contribute to renewed awareness of and interest in the group as a social psychological process, it will have proved its value.

References

Albert, R. S. (1953) Comments on the scientific function of the concept of cohesiveness. *American Journal of Sociology*, 59, 231–4.

Alexander, C. N., Zucker, L. G. and Brody, C. L. (1970) Experimental expectations and autokinetic experiences: consistency theories and judgemental convergence. *Sociometry*, 108–22.

Allen, P. T. and Stephenson, G. M. (1983) Intergroup understanding and size of organization. *British Journal of Industrial Relations*, 21, 312–29.

Allen, V. L. (1965) Situational factors in conformity. In L. Berkowitz (ed.), *Advances in Experimental Social Psychology*. New York: Academic Press, vol. 2, 133–75.

Allen, V. L. (1975) Social support for nonconformity. In L. Berkowitz (ed.), *Advances in Experimental Social Psychology*. New York: Academic Press, vol. 8, 2–43.

Allen, V. L. and Wilder, D. A. (1975) Categorization, belief similarity and group discrimination. *Journal of Personality and Social Psychology*, 32, 971–7.

Allen, V. L. and Wilder, D. A. (1977) Social comparison, self-evaluation, and conformity to the group. In J. M. Suls and R. L. Miller (eds), *Social comparison processes*. Washington DC: Hemisphere.

Allport, F. H. (1924) *Social psychology*. New York: Houghton, Mifflin.

Allport, F. H. (1962) A structuronomic conception of behaviour: Individual and collective. *Journal of Abnormal and Social Psychology*, 64, 3–30.

Anderson, N. H. and Graesser, C. G. (1976) An information integration analysis of attitude change in group discussion. *Journal of Personality and Social Psychology*, 34, 210–22.

Asch, S. E. (1952) *Social psychology*. Englewood Cliffs, NJ: Prentice-Hall.

Asch, S. E. (1956) Studies of independence and conformity: A minority of one against a unanimous majority. *Psychological Monographs: General and Applied*, 70, 1–70. Whole no. 416.

Ashmore, R. C. and DelBoca, F. K. (1981) Conceptual approaches to stereotypes and stereotyping. In D. L. Hamilton (ed.), *Cognitive processes in stereotyping and intergroup behaviour*. Hillsdale, NJ: Erlbaum.

Back, K. W. (1951). Influence through social communication. *Journal of Abnormal and Social Psychology*. 46, 9–23.

Bales, R. F. (1950): *Interaction process analysis: A method for the study of small groups*. Reading, Mass.: Addison-Wesley.

Baron, R. S., Dion, K. L., Baron, P. H. and Miller, N. (1971) Group consensus and cultural values as determinants of risk-taking. *Journal of Personality and Social Psychology*, 20, 446–55.

Baron, R. S., Monson, T. C. and Baron, P. H. (1973) Conformity pressure as a determinant of risk-taking. Replication and extension. *Journal of Personality and Social Psychology*, 28, 406–13.

Baron, R. S. and Roper, G. (1976) Reaffirmation of social comparison views of choice shifts: Averaging and extremitization in an autokinetic situation. *Journal of Personality and Social Psychology*, 35, 521–30.

Baron, R. S., Sanders, G. S. and Baron, P. H. (1975) *Social comparison reconceptualized: Implications for choice shifts, averaging effects and social facilitation*. Unpublished paper, University of Iowa.

Bem, S. L. (1974) The measurement of psychological androgyny. *Journal of Consulting and Clinical Psychology*, 42, 155–62.

Berkowitz, L. (1954) Group standards, cohesiveness, and productivity. *Human Relations*, 7, 509–19.

Berkowitz, L. and Walster, E. (1976) Equity theory: Towards a general theory of social interaction. In L. Berkowitz (ed.), *Advances in Experimental Social Psychology*. New York: Academic Press, vol. 9.

Billig, M. G. (1976) *Social psychology and intergroup relations*. London: Academic Press.

Billig, M. G. and Tajfel, H. (1973) Social categorization and similarity in intergroup behaviour. *European Journal of Social Psychology*, 3, 27–52.

Blake, R. R. and Mouton, J. S. (1961) Reactions to intergroup competition under win-lose conditions. *Management Science*, 7, 420–35.

Blascovich, J. and Ginsburg, G. P. (1974) Emergent norms and choice shifts involving risk. *Sociometry*, 37, 205–18.

Blumberg, H., Hare, P., Kent, V. and Davies, M. (1983) *Small groups and social interaction*. New York: Wiley.

Bochner, S. and Ohsako, T. (1977) Ethnic role salience in racially homogeneous and heterogeneous societies. *Journal of Cross-Cultural Psychology*, 8, 477–92.

Bochner, S. and Perks, R. W. (1971) National role evocation as a function of cross-national interaction. *Journal of Cross-Cultural Psychology*, 2, 157–64.

Bonner, H. (1959) *Group dynamics: Principles and applications.* New York: Ronald Press.

Bornstein, G., Crum, L., Wittenbraker, J., Harring, K., Insko, C. A. and Thibaut, J. (1983a) On the measurement of social orientations in the minimal group paradigm. *European Journal of Social Psychology*, 13, 321–50.

Bornstein, G., Crum, L., Wittenbraker, J., Harring, K., Insko, C. A. and Thibaut, J. (1983b) Reply to Turner's comments. *European Journal of Social Psychology*, 13, 369–82.

Bovard, E. W. (1951) Group structure and perception. *Journal of Abnormal and Social Psychology*, 46, 398–405.

Boyanowsky, E. O. and Allen, V. L. (1973) Ingroup norms and self-identity as determinants of discriminatory behaviour. *Journal of Personality and Social Psychology*, 25, 408–18.

Branthwaite, A., Doyle, S. and Lightbown, N. (1979) The balance between fairness and discrimination. *European Journal of Social Psychology*, 9, 149–63.

Brewer, M. B. (1979) Ingroup bias in the minimal intergroup situation: a cognitive-motivational analysis. *Psychological Bulletin*, 86, 307–24.

Brewer, M. B. and Kramer, R. M. (1985) The psychology of intergroup attitudes and behaviour. *Annual Review of Psychology*, 36, 219–43.

Brewer, M. B. and Silver, M. (1978) Ingroup bias as a function of task characteristics. *European Journal of Social Psychology*, 8, 393–400.

Brown, R. (1965) *Social psychology.* New York: The Free Press.

Brown, R. J. (1984) Intergroup processes. *British Journal of Social Psychology*, 23, whole issue.

Brown, R. J. and Turner, J. C. (1979) The criss-cross categorization effect in intergroup discrimination. *British Journal of Social and Clinical Psychology*, 18, 371–83.

Brown, R. J. and Turner, J. C. (1981) Interpersonal and intergroup behaviour. In J. C. Turner and H. Giles (eds), *Intergroup behaviour.* Oxford: Basil Blackwell and Chicago: University of Chicago Press.

Bruner, J. S. (1957) On perceptual readiness. *Psychological Review*, 64, 123–51.

Bruner, J. S. and Perlmutter, H. V. (1957) Compatriot and foreigner: A study of impression formation in three countries. *Journal of Abnormal and Social Psychology*, 55, 353–60.

Burnstein, E. (1982) Persuasion as argument processing. In H. Brandstatter, J. H. Davis and G. Stocker-Kreichgauer (eds), *Group decision-making*. London: Academic Press.

Burnstein, E. and McRae, A. V. (1962) Some effects of shared threat and perjudice in racially mixed groups. *Journal of Abnormal and Social Psychology*, 64, 257–63.

Burnstein, E. and Vinokur, A. (1973) Testing two classes of theories about group induced shifts in individual choices. *Journal of Personality and Social Psychology*, 9, 123–37.

Burnstein, E. and Vinokur, A. (1975) What a person thinks upon learning he has chosen differently from others: Nice evidence for the persuasive-arguments explanation of choice shifts. *Journal of Experimental Social Psychology*, 11, 412–26.

Burnstein, E. and Vinokur, A. (1977) Persuasive argumentation and social comparison as determinants of attitude polarization. *Journal of Experimental Social Psychology*, 13, 315–32.

Buss, A. H. and Portnoy, N. W. (1967) Pain tolerance and group identification. *Journal of Personality and Social Psychology*, 6, 106–8.

Buss, A. R. (1978) Causes and reasons in attribution theory: A conceptual critique. *Journal of Personality and Social Psychology*, 36, 1311–21.

Byrne, D. (1971) *The attraction paradigm*. New York: Academic Press.

Byrne, D and Wong, T. J. (1962) Racial prejudice, interpersonal attraction and assumed dissimilarity of studies. *Journal of Abnormal and Social Psychology*, 65, 246–52.

Campbell, D. T. (1958) Common fate, similarity and other indices of the status of aggregates of persons as social entities. *Behavioural Science*, 3, 14–25.

Cannavale, F. J., Scarr, H. A. and Pepitone, A. (1970) De-individuation in the small group: Some further evidence. *Journal of Personality and Social Psychology*. 16, 141–47.

Cartwright, D. (1968) The nature of group cohesiveness. In D. Cartwright and A. Zander (eds), *Group dynamics*. London: Tavistock, 3rd edn.

Cartwright, D. (1971) Risk-taking by individuals and groups: An assessment of research employing choice-dilemmas. *Journal of Personality and Social Psychology*, 20, 361–78.

Cartwright, D. (1973) Determinants of scientific progress: The case of research on the risky-shift. *American Psychologist*, 28, 222–31.

Cartwright, D. (1979) Contemporary social psychology in historical perspective. *Social Psychology Quarterly*, 42, 82–93.

Cartwright, D. and Zander, A. (1968) *Group dynamics*. London: Tavistock, 3rd edn.

Cecil, E. A., Chertkoff, J. M. and Cummins, L. A. (1970) Risk-taking in groups as a function of group pressure. *Journal of Social Psychology*, 81, 273–4.

Charters, W. W. and Newcomb, T. M. (1952) Some attitudinal effects of experimentally increased salience of a membership group. In G. E. Swanson et al. (eds), *Readings in social psychology*. New York: Holt, Rinehart & Winston.

Chevalier, L. (1973) *Labouring classes and dangerous classes*. London: Routledge & Kegan Paul.

Clark, R. D. III and Crockett, W. H. (1971) Subjects' initial positions, exposure to varying opinions and the risky-shift. *Psychonomic Science*, 23, 277–9.

Codol, J.-P. (1975) On the so-called 'superior conformity of the self' behaviour: Twenty experimental investigations. *European Journal of Social Psychology*, 5, 457–501.

Cohen, A. I. (1981) Group cohesion and communal living. In H. Kellerman (ed.), *Group cohesion: Theoretical and clinical perspectives*. New York: Grune & Stratton.

Cohen, C. E. (1981) Goals and schemas in person perception: Making sense out of the stream of behaviour. In N. Cantor and J. Kihlstrom (eds), *Personality, cognition and social behaviour*. Hillsdale NJ: Erlbaum.

Colman, A. M. (1982) Experimental games. In A.M. Colman (ed.), *Co-operation and competition in humans and animals*. Wokingham, Berkshire, England: Van Nostrand Reinhold.

Cotton, J. L. and Baron, R. S. (1980) Anonymity, persuasive arguments and choice shifts. *Social Psychology Quarterly*, 43, 391–404.

Davis, J. H., Laughlin, P. R. and Komorita, S. S. (1976) The social psychology of small groups: Co-operative and mixed-motive interaction. *Annual Review of Psychology*, 27, 501–42.

Davis, N. Z. (1978) The rites of violence: Religious riot in sixteenth century France. *Past and Present*, 59, 51–91.

Dawes, R. M. (1980) Social dilemmas. *Annual Review of Psychology*, 31, 169–93.

Deutsch, M. (1949a) A theory of co-operation and competition. *Human Relations*, 2, 129–52.

Deutsch, M. (1949b) An experimental study of the effects of

co-operation and competition upon group process. *Human Relations*, 2, 199–232.

Deutsch, M. (1973) *The resolution of conflict*. New Haven, Conn.: Yale University Press.

Deutsch, M. and Gerard, H. B. (1955) A study of normative and informational social influences upon individual judgement. *Journal of Abnormal and Social Psychology*, 51, 629–36.

Diener, E. (1980) De-individuation: The absence of self-awareness and self-regulation in group members. In P. Paulus (ed.), *The psychology of group influence*. Hillsdale, New Jersey: Erlbaum.

Dion, K. L. (1973) Cohesiveness as a determinant of ingroup-outgroup bias. *Journal of Personality and Social Psychology*, 28, 163–171.

Dion, K. L. (1979) Intergroup conflict and intra-group cohesiveness. In W. G. Austin and S. Worchel (eds), *The social psychology of intergroup relations*. Monterey, Calif.: Brooks/Cole.

Dion, K. L., Earn, B. N. and Yee, P. H. N. (1978) The experience of being a victim of prejudice: An experimental approach. *International Journal of Psychology*, 13, 197–294.

Doise, W. (1969) Intergroup relations and polarization of individual and collective judgements. *Journal of Personality and Social Psychology*, 12, 136–43.

Doise, W. (1971a) Die experimentalle Untersuchung von Beziehungen zwischen Gruppen. *Zeitschrift Experimentalle-Angewandte Psychologie*, 18, 151–89.

Doise, W. (1971b) An apparent exception to the extremitization of collective judgements. *European Journal of Social Psychology*, 1, 511–18.

Doise, W. (1978) *Groups and individuals: Explanation in social psychology*. Cambridge: Cambridge University Press.

Doise, W., Csepeli, G., Dann, H. D., Gouge, C., Larsen, K. and Ostell, A. (1972) An experimental investigation into the formation of intergroup representations. *European Journal of Social Psychology*, 2, 202–4.

Doise, W., Deschamps, J.-C. and Meyer, G. (1978) The accentuation of intra-category similarities. In H. Tajfel (ed.), *Differentiation between social groups*. London: Academic Press.

Doise, W. and Sinclair, A. (1973) The categorization process in intergroup relations. *European Journal of Social Psychology*, 3, 145–57.

Doise, W. and Weinberger, M. (1973) Représentations masculines dans différentes situations de rencontres mixtes. *Bulletin de Psychologie*, 26, 649–57.

Douvan, E. and Adelson, J. (1966) *The adolescent experience*, New York: Wiley.

Downing, J. (1958) Cohesiveness, perception and values. *Human Relations*, 11, 157–66.

Dustin, D. S. and Davis, H. P. (1970) Evaluative bias in group and individual competition. *Journal of Social Psychology*, 80, 103–8.

Ebbesen, E. B. and Bowers, J. J. (1974) Proportion of risky to conservative arguments in a group discussion and choice shift. *Journal of Personality and Social Psychology*, 29, 316–27.

Ehrlich, H. J. (1973) *The social psychology of prejudice*. New York: Wiley.

Eiser, J. R. (1978) Co-operation and competition between individuals. In H. Tajfel and C. Fraser (eds), *Introducing social psychology*. Harmondsworth, Middlesex: Penguin.

Eiser, J. R. (1980) *Cognitive social psychology*. London: McGraw-Hill.

Eiser, J. R. (1983) Attribution theory and social cognition. In J. Jaspars, F. Fincham and M. Hewstone (eds), *Attribution theory: Essays and experiments*. London: Academic Press.

Eiser, J. R. and Stroebe, W. (1972) *Categorization and social judgement*. London: Academic Press.

Eisman, B. (1959) Some operational measures of cohesiveness and their interrelations. *Human Relations*, 12, 183–9.

Espinoza, J. A. and Garza, R. T. (1985) Social group salience and interethnic co-operation. *Journal of Experimental Social Psychology*, 21, 380–92.

Etzkowitz, M. (1971) The male sister: Sexual separation of labour in society. *Journal of Marriage and the Family*, 33, 431–4.

Exline, R. V. (1957) Group climate as a factor in the relevance and accuracy of social perception. *Journal of Abnormal and Social Psychology*, 55, 382–8.

Farr, R. M. and Moscovici, S. (1984) *Social représentations*. Cambridge: Cambridge University Press and Paris: Editions de la Maison des Sciences de l'Homme.

Feagin, J. R. and Hahn, M. (1973) *Ghetto revolts*. New York: Macmillan.

Feshbach, S. and Singer, R. (1957) The effects of personal and shared threats upon social prejudice. *Journal of Abnormal and Social Psychology*, 54, 411–16.

Festinger, L. (1947) The role of group belongingness in a voting situation. *Human Relations*, 1, 154–80.

Festinger, L. (1950) Informal social communication. *Psychological Review*, 57, 271–82.

Festinger, L. (1953) Group attraction and membership. In D. Cartwright and A. Zander (eds), *Group dynamics: Research and theory*. Evanston, I11.: Row Peterson.

Festinger, L. (1954) A theory of social comparison processes. *Human Relations*, 7, 117–40.

Festinger, L. (1980) Looking backwards. In L. Festinger (ed.), *Retrospections on social psychology*. New York: Oxford University Press.

Festinger, L., Pepitone, A. and Newcomb, T. (1952) Some consequences of de-individuation in a group. *Journal of Abnormal and Social Psychology*, 47, 382–9.

Festinger, L., Schachter, S. and Back, K. (1950) *Socal pressures in informal groups*. New York: Harper & Row.

Fiedler, F. E. (1967) The effect of intergroup competition on group member adjustment. *Personal Psychology*, 20, 33–44.

Fogelson, R. M. (1971) *Violence in protest*. New York: Doubleday.

Forgas, J. P. (1977) Polarization and moderation of person perception judgements as a function of group interaction style. *European Journal of Social Psychology*, 7, 175–87.

Fraser, C. (1971) Group risk-taking and group polarization. *European Journal of Social Psychology*, 1, 493–510.

Fraser, C., Gouge, C. and Billig, M. (1971) Risky shifts, cautious shifts and group polarization. *European Journal of Social Psychology*, 1, 7–29.

French, J. R. P. (1941) The disruption and cohesion of groups. *Journal of Abnormal and Social Psychology*, 36, 361–77.

Freud, S. (1921) *Group psychology and the analysis of the ego*. London: Hogarth Press.

Gerard, H. B. and Hoyt, M. F. (1974) Distinctiveness of social categorization and attitude toward ingroup members. *Journal of Personality and Social Psychology*, 29, 836–42.

Gergen, K. J. (1971) *The concept of self*. New York: Holt, Rinehart & Winston.

Gergen, K. J. and Gergen, M. M. (1981) *Social psychology*. New York: Harcourt Brace Jovanovich.

Giles, H. (1984) The dynamics of speech accommodation. *International Journal of the Sociology of Language*, 46, whole issue.

Goethals, G. R. and Darley, J. M. (1977) Social comparison theory: An attributional approach. In J. M. Suls and R. L. Miller (eds), *Social comparison processes*. Washington DC: Hemisphere.

Golembiewski, R. T. (1962) *The small group*. Chicago: University of Chicago Press.

Goodacre, D. M. (1951) The use of a sociometric test as a predictor of combat unit effectiveness. *Sociometry*, 14, 148–52.

Gross, E. (1954) Primary functions of the small group. *American Journal of Sociology*, 60, 24–30.

Gross, N. and Martin, W. E. (1952) On group cohesiveness. *American Journal of Sociology*, 57, 546–64.

Grundlach, R. H. (1956) Effects of on-the-job experiences with Negroes upon racial attitudes of white workers in union shops. *Psychological Reports*, 2, 67–77.

Hagstrom, W. O. and Selvin, H. C. (1965) The dimension of cohesiveness in small groups. *Sociometry*, 28, 30–43.

Hamilton, D. L. (1979) A cognitive-attributional analysis of stereotyping. In L. Berkowitz (ed.), *Advances in Experimental Social Psychology*. New York: Academic Press, vol. 12.

Hare, A. P. (1962) *Handbook of small group research*. New York: The Free Press.

Hartley, E. (1951) Psychological problems of multiple group membership. In J. H. Rohrer and M. Sherif (eds), *Social psychology at the crossroads*. New York: Harper.

Harvey, J. H., Ickes, W. J. and Kidd, R. F. (1976) *New directions in attribution research*. Hillsdale, NJ: Erlbaum, vol. 1.

Heider, F. (1958) *The psychology of interpersonal relations*. New York: Wiley.

Heider, F. (1983) *The life of a psychologist: An autobiography*. Lawrence Kans.: University Press of Kansas.

Heine, P. (1971) *Personality in social theory*. Chicago: Aldine.

Hensley, V. and Duval, S. (1976) Some perceptual determinants of perceived similarity, liking and correctness. *Journal of Personality and Social Psychology*, 34, 159–68.

Herman, S. and Schild, E. (1960) Ethnic role conflict in a cross-cultural situation. *Human Relations*, 13, 215–28.

Hewstone, M. (1983) *Attribution theory: Social and functional extensions*. Oxford: Basil Blackwell.

Hewstone, M., Jaspars, J. and Lalljee, M. (1982) Social representations, social attribution and social identity: The intergroup images of 'public' and 'comprehensive' schoolboys. *European Journal of Social Psychology*, 12, 241–69.

Higgins, E. T. and King, G. (1980) Accessibility of social constructs: Information processing consequences of individual and contextual variability. In N. Cantor and J. Kihlstrom (eds), *Personality, cognition and social behaviour*. Hillsdale, NJ: Erlabaum.

Higgins, E. T., Rholes, W. S. and Jones, C. R. (1977) Category accessibility and impression formation. *Journal of Experimental Social Psychology*, 13, 141–54.

Hogg, M. A. (1985a) Group cohesiveness (Cohesion de grupo). In C. Huici (dir.), *Estructura y procesos de grupo*, Tomo 1. Madrid: Universidad Nacional de Educacion a Distancia (English translation).

Hogg M. A. (1985b) Masculine and feminine speech in dyads and groups: A study of speech style and gender salience. *Journal of Language and Social Psychology, 4, 99–111.*

Hogg, M. A. and Abrams, D. (in press) *Social identifications: A social psychology of intergroup relations and group processes.* London: Methuen.

Hogg, M. A. and Turner, J. C. (1985a) Interpersonal attraction, social identification and psychological group formation. *European Journal of Social Psychology, 15, 51–66.*

Hogg, M. A. and Turner, J. C. (1985b) When liking begets solidarity: An experiment on the role of interpersonal attraction in psychological group formation. *British Journal of Social Psychology, 24, 267–81.*

Hogg, M. A. and Turner, J. C. (1987) *Intergroup behaviour, self-stereotyping and the salience of social categories. British Journal of Social Psychology, 26, 325–40.*

Homans, G. C. (1961) *Social behaviour: Its elementary forms.* New York: Harcourt Brace Jovanovitch.

Hornstein, H. A. (1972) Promotive tension: The basis of prosocial behaviour from a Lewinian perspective. *Journal of Social Issues, 28, 191–218.*

Horwitz, M. and Rabbie, J. M. (1982) Individuality and membership in the intergroup system. In H. Tajfel (ed.), *Social identity and intergroup relations.* Cambridge: Cambridge University Press and Paris: Editions de la Maison des Sciences de l'Homme.

Howard, J. and Rothbart, M. (1978) Social categorization and memory for ingroup and outgroup behaviour. *Journal of Personality and Social Psychology, 38, 301–10.*

Jackson, J. M. (1959) Reference group processes in a formal organization. *Sociometry, 22, 307–27.*

Jellison, J. and Arkin, R. (1977) A self-presentation approach to decision-making in groups. In J. M. Suls and R. L. Miller (eds), *Social comparison processes.* Washington DC: Hemisphere.

Jones, E. E. and Davis, K. E. (1965) From acts to dispositions: The attribution process in person perception. In L. Berkowitz (ed.), *Advances in Experimental Social Psychology.* New York: Academic Press, vol. 2.

Jones, E. E. and Gerard, H. B. (1967) *Foundations of social psychology.* New York: Wiley.

Jones, E. E. and McGillis, D. (1976) Correspondent inferences and the attribution cube: A comparative reappraisal. In J. H. Harvey, W. J. Ickes and R. F. Kidd (eds), *New directions in attribution research.* Hillsdale, NJ: Erlbaum, vol. 1.

Kalin, R. and Marlowe, D. (1968) The effects of intergroup competition, personal drinking habits and frustration in intragroup co-operation. *Proceedings of 76th Annual Convention A. P. A.*, 3, 405–6.

Kandel, D. B. (1978) Similarity in real-life adolescent friendship pairs. *Journal of Personality and Social Psychology*, 36, 306–12.

Kassin, S. M. (1979) Consensus information, prediction and causal attribution: A review of the literature and issues. *Journal of Personality and Social Psychology*, 37, 1966–81.

Kellerman, H. (1981) *Group cohesion: Theoretical and clinical perspectives.* New York: Grune & Stratton.

Kelley, H. H. (1955) Salience of membership and resistance to change of group-anchored attitudes. *Human Relations*, 8, 275–89.

Kelley, H. H. (1967) Attribution theory in social psychology. In D. Levine (ed.), *Nebraska Symposium on Motivation.* Lincoln, Neb.: University of Nebraska Press, vol. 15, 192–238.

Kelley, H. H. and Michela, J. L. (1980) Attribution theory and research. *Annual Review of Psychology*, 31, 457–503.

Kelley, H. H. and Thibaut, J. (1978) *Interpersonal relations: A theory of interdependence.* New York: Wiley.

Kiesler, C. A. and Kiesler, S. B. (1969) *Conformity.* Reading, Mass.: Addison-Wesley.

Kinney, E. E. (1953) A study of peer group social acceptability at the fifth-grade level at a public school. *Journal of Educational Research.* 47, 57–64.

Knowles, E. S. (1982) From individuals to group members. A dialectic for the social sciences. In W. Ickes and E. S. Knowles (eds), *Personality, roles and social behaviour.* New York: Springer.

Knowles, E. S. and Brickner, M. A. (1981) Social cohesion effects on spatial cohesion. *Personality and Social Psychology Bulletin*, 7, 309–13.

Kogan, N. and Carlson, J. (1969) Group risk-taking under competitive and non-competitive conditions in adults and children. *Journal of Educational Psychology*, 60, 158–67.

Kogan, N. and Wallach, M. A. (1964) *Risk taking: A study in cognition and personality.* New York: Holt, Rinehart & Winston.

Kramer, R. M. and Brewer, M. B. (1984) Effects of group identity on resource use in a simulated commons dilemma. *Journal of Personality and Social Psychology*, 46, 1044–57.

Kramerae, C. (1981) *Women and men speaking: A framework for analysis*. Rowley, Mass.: Newbury House.

Lalljee, M. (1981) Attribution theory and the analysis of explanations. In C. Antaki (ed.), *The psychology of ordinary explanations of social behaviour*. London: Academic Press.

Lalljee, M., Brown, L. B. and Ginsburg, G. P. (1984) Attitudes: Disposition, behaviour or evaluation. *British Journal of Social Psychology*, 23, 233–44.

Lambert, W. E., Libman, E. and Poser, E. G. (1960) The effect of increased salience of a membership group on pain tolerance. *Journal of Personality*, 28, 351–7.

Lamm, H. and Myers, D. G. (1978) Group-induced polarization of attitudes and behaviour. In L. Berkowitz (ed.), *Advances in Experimental Social Psychology*. New York: Academic Press, vol. 11.

Lamm, H. Schaude, E. and Trommsdorff, G. (1971) Risky-shift as a function of group members' value of risk and need for approval. *Journal of Personality and Social Psychology*, 20, 430–5.

Latané, B. (1981) The psychology of social impact. *American Psychologist*, 36, 343–56.

Latané, B. and Nida, S. (1080) Social impact theory and group influence: A social engineering perspective. In P. B. Paulus (ed.), *The psychology of group influence*. Hillsdale, NJ: Erlbaum.

LeBon, G. (1895, translated 1947) *The crowd: A study of the popular mind*. London: Ernest Benn (also London: Unwin, 1896).

Lemyre, L. and Smith, P. M. (1985) Intergroup discrimination and self-esteem in the minimal group paradigm. *Journal of Personality and Social Psychology*, 49, 660–70.

Leonard, D. (1980) *Sex and generation: A study of courtship and weddings*. London: Tavistock.

Levinger, G. and Schneider, D. J. (1969) Test of the 'risk is a value' hypothesis. *Journal of Personality and Social Psychology*, 11, 165–70.

Lewin, K. (1935) Psycho-social problems of a minority group. *Character and Personality*, 3, 175–87.

Lewin, K. (1936) *Principles of topological psychology*. New York: McGraw-Hill.

Lewin, K. (1939) Field theory and experiment in social psychology. *American Journal of Sociology*, 44, 868–97.

Lewin, K. (1948) *Resolving social conflicts*. New York: Harper.

Lewin, K. (1952) *Field theory in social science*. London: Tavistock.

Locksley, A., Ortiz, V. and Hepburn, C. (1980) Social categorization and discriminatory behaviour: Extinguishing the minimal intergroup discrimination effect. *Journal of Personality and Social Psychology*, 39, 773–83.

Lott, A. J. and Lott, B. E. (1961) Group cohesiveness, communication level and conformity. *Journal of Abnormal and Social Psychology*, 62, 408–12.

Lott, A. J. and Lott, B. E. (1965) Group cohesiveness as interpersonal attraction: A review of relationships with antecedent and consequent variables. *Psychological Bulletin*, 64, 259–309.

Lott, B. E. (1961) Group cohesiveness: A learning phenomenon. *Journal of Social Psychology*, 55, 275–86.

McArthur, L. Z. (1972) The how and what of why: Some determinants and consequences of causal attributions. *Journal of Personality and Social Psychology*, 22, 171–93.

McCallum, D. M., Harring, K., Gilmore, R., Drenan, S., Chase, J. P., Insko, C. A. and Thibaut, J. (1985) Competition and co-operation between groups and individuals. *Journal of Experimental Social Psychology*, 21, 301–20.

McDougall, W. (1921) *The group mind*. Cambridge: Cambridge University Press.

McGrath, J. E. and Kravitz, D. A. (1982) Group research. *Annual Review of Psychology*, 33, 195–230.

McGuire, W. J. (1985) Attitudes and attitude change. In G. Lindzey and E. Aronson (eds), *The handbook of social psychology*. New York: Random House, 3rd edn, vol. 2.

McGuire, W. J., McGuire, C. V., Child P. and Fujioka, T. (1978) Salience of ethnicity in the spontaneous self-concept as a function of one's ethnic distinctiveness in the social environment. *Journal of Personality and Social Psychology*, 36, 511–20.

McGuire, W. J., McGuire, C. V. and Winton, W. (1979) Effects of household sex composition on the salience of one's gender in the spontaneous self-concept. *Journal of Experimental Social Psychology*, 15, 77–90.

Mackie. D. (1986) Social identification effects in group polarization. *Journal of Personality and Social Psychology*, 50, 720–8.

Mackie, D. and Cooper, J. (1984) Attitude polarization: The effects of group membership. *Journal of Personality and Social Psychology*, 46, 575–85.

McKillip, J., DiMiceli, A. J. and Leubke, J. (1977) Group salience and stereotyping. *Social Behaviour and Personality*, 5, 81–5.

McLachlan, A. (1985) *Identity and group polarization*. Unpublished paper, Glasgow Institute of Technology.

McLachlan, A. (1986) The effects of two forms of decision reappraisal on the perception of pertinent arguments. *British Journal of Social Psychology*. 25, 129–38.

Marrow, A. J. (1969) *The practical theorist: The life and work of Kurt Lewin*. New York: Basic Books.

Mead, G. H. (1934) *Mind, self and society*. Chicago: University of Chicago Press.

Milgram, S. and Toch, H. (1969) Collective behaviour: crowds and social movements. In G. Lindzey and E. Aronson (eds), *The handbook of social pscholgy*. Reading, Mass.: Addison-Wesley, 2nd edn, vol. 4.

Miller, J. G. (1984) Culture and the development of everyday social explanation. *Journal of Personality and Social Psychology*, 46, 961–78.

Minard, R. D. (1952) Race relations in the Pocahontas Field. *Journal of Social Issues*, 8, 29–44.

Moreland, R. L. (1985) Social categorization and the assimilation of 'new' group members. *Journal of Personality and Social Psychology*, 48, 1173–90.

Moreno, J. L. (1934) *Who shall survive?* Washington, DC: Nervous and Mental Diseases Publishing Co..

Moscovici, S. (1972) Society and theory in social psychology. In J. Israel and H. Tajfel (eds), *The context of social psychology*. London: Academic Press.

Moscovici, S. (1976) *Social influence and social change*. London: Academic Press.

Moscovici, S. and Lecuyer, R. (1972) Studies in group decisions I: Social space, patterns of communication and group consensus. *European Journal of Social Psychology*, 2, 221–44.

Moscovici, S. and Paicheler, G. (1978) Social comparison and social recognition: Two complementary processes of identification. In H. Tajfel (ed.), *Differentiation between social groups*. London: Academic Press.

Moscovici, S. and Zavalloni, M. (1969) The group as a polarizer of attitudes. *Journal of Personality and Social Psychology*, 12, 125–35.

Mugny, G. (1982) *The power of minorities*. London: Academic Press.

Myers, A. (1962) Team competition, success, and the adjustment of group members. *Journal of Abnormal and Social Psychology*, 65, 325–32.

Myers, D. G., Bruggink, J. B., Kersting, R. C. and Schlosser, B. A. (1980) Does learning others' opinions change one's opinions? *Personality and Social Psychology Bulletin*, 6, 253–60.

Myers, D. G. and Kaplan, M. F. (1976) Group-induced polarization in simulated juries. *Personality and Social Psychology Bulletin*, 2, 63–6.

Myers, D. G. and Lamm, H. (1976) The group polarization phenomenon. *Psychological Bulletin*, 83, 602–27.

Newcomb, T. M. (1951) Social psychological theory: Integrating individual and social approaches. In J. H. Rohrer and M. Sherif (eds), *Social psychology at the crossroads*. New York: Harper.

Newcomb, T. M. (1953) An approach to the study of communicative acts. *Psychological Review*, 60, 393–404.

Newcomb, T. M. (1968) Interpersonal balance. In R. Abelson, E. Aronson, W. McGuire, T. M. Newcomb, M. Rosenberg and P. Tannenbaum (eds), *Theories of cognitive consistency: A sourcebook*. Chicago: Rand McNally.

Nisbett, R. E. and Borgida, E. (1975) Attribution and the psychology of prediction. *Journal of Personality and Social Psychology*, 32, 932–43.

Nisbett, R. E., Borgida, E., Crandall, R. and Reed, H. (1976) Popular induction: Information is not necessarily informative. In J. S. Carroll and J. W. Payne (eds), *Cognition and social behaviour*. Hillsdale, NJ: Erlbaum.

Nixon, H. L. (1976) Team orientations, interpersonal relations and team success. *Research Quarterly*, 47, 429–33.

Oakes, P. J. (1983) *Factors determining the salience of group membership in social perception*. Unpublished Ph.D thesis, University of Bristol.

Oakes, P. J. and Davidson, B. (1986) *Self-perception and the salience of social categories*. Unpublished paper, Macquarie University, Sydney.

Oakes, P. J. and Turner, J. C. (1980) Social categorization and intergroup behaviour: Does minimal intergroup discrimination make social identity more positive? *European Journal of Social Psychology*, 10, 295–301.

Oakes, P. J. and Turner, J. C. (1987) *Perceiving people as group members: A functional approach*. Unpublished paper, Macquarie University, Sydney.

Oakes, P. J. and Turner, J. C. (1986) Distinctiveness and the salience of social category membership: Is there an automatic perceptual bias towards novelty? *European Journal of Social Psychology*, 16, 325–44.

Oskamp, S. (1971) The effects of programmed strategies on co-operation in the Prisoner's Dilemma and other mixed-motive games. *Journal of Conflict Resolution*, 15, 225–59.

Pepitone, A. (1981) Lessons from the history of social psychology. *American Psychologist*, 36, 972–85.

Pepitone, A. and Reichling, G. (1955) Group cohesiveness and the expression of hostility. *Human Relations*, 8, 327–37.

Porter, L. W. and Lawler, E. E. (1968) *Managerial attitudes and performance*. Homewood, I11.: Richard D. Irwin.

Pruitt, D. G. (1971) Choice shifts in group discussion: An introductory review. *Journal of Personality and Social Psychology*, 20, 339–60.

Pruitt, D. G. and Kimmel, M. J. (1977) Twenty years of experimental gaming: critique, synthesis and suggestions for the future. *Annual Review of Psychology*, 28, 363–92.

Rabbie, J. M. and Wilkins, G, (1971) Intergroup competition and its effects on intragroup and intergroup relations. *European Journal of Social Psychology*, 1, 215–34.

Ramuz-Nienhuis, W. and Van Bergen, A. (1960) Relations between some components of attraction-to-group: A replication. *Human Relations*, 13, 271–7.

Rapoport, A. and Chammah, A. M. (1965) *Prisoner's Dilemma: A study in conflict and co-operation*. Ann Arbor, Mich.: University of Michigan Press.

Raven, B. H. and Rubin, J. Z. (1983) *Social psychology*. New York: Wiley.

Reddy, W. M. (1977) The textile trade and the language of the crowd at Rouen, 1752–1871. *Past and Present*, 74, 62–89.

Reicher, S. D. (1982) The determination of collective behaviour. In H. Tajfel (ed.), *Social identity and intergroup relations*. Cambridge: Cambridge University Press and Paris: Editions de la Maison des Sciences de l'Homme, 41–84.

Reicher, S. D. (1984a) The St Pauls riot: An explanation of the limits of crowd action in terms of a social identity model. *European Journal of Social Psychology*, 14, 1–21.

Reicher, S D. (1984b) Social influence in the crowd: attitudinal and behavioural effects of de-individuation in conditions of high and low group salience. *British Journal of Social Psychology*, 23, 341–50.

Reid, F. J. M. and Sumiga, L. (1984) Attitudinal politics in intergroup behaviour: Interpersonal and intergroup determinants of attitude change. *British Journal of Social Psychology*, 23, 335–40.

Roberts, J. C. and Castore, C. H. (1972) The effect of conformity, information and confidence upon subjects' willingness to take risks following a group discussion. *Organizational Behaviour and Human Performance*. 8, 384–94.

Rosch, E. (1978) Principles of categorization. In E. Rosch and B. B.

Lloyd (eds), *Cognition and categorization*. Hillsdale, NJ: Erlbaum, 27–48.

Ryen, A. H. and Kahn, A. (1975) The effects of intergroup orientation on group attitudes and proxemic behaviour: A test of two models. *Journal of Personality and Social Psychology*, 31, 302–10.

Sachdev, I. and Bourhis, R. (1984) Minimal majorities and minorities. *European Journal of Social Psychology*, 14, 35–52.

St Claire, L. and Turner, J. C. (1982) The role of demand characteristics in the social categorization paradigm. *European Journal of Social Psychology*, 12, 307–14.

St Jean, R. and Percival, E. (1974) The role of argumentation and comparison processes in choice shifts: Another assessment. *Canadian Journal of Behavioural Science*, 6, 297–308.

Sampson, E. E. (1977) Psychology and the American ideal. *Journal of Personality and Social Psychology*, 35, 767–82.

Sampson, E. E. (1981) Cognitive psychology as ideology. *American Psychologist*, 36, 730–43.

Sanders, G. S. and Baron, R. S. (1977) Is social comparison irrelevant for producing choice shifts? *Journal of Experimental Social Psychology*, 13, 303–14.

Schachter, S. (1959) *The psychology of affiliation*. Stanford, Calif.: Stanford University Press.

Schachter, S., Ellertson, N., McBride, D. and Gregory, D. (1951) An experimental study of cohesiveness and productivity. *Human Relations*, 4, 229–38.

Schellenberg, J. A. (1978) *Masters of social psychology*. New York: Oxford University Press.

Schlenker, B. R. (1974) Social psychology and science. *Journal of Personality and Social Psychology*, 29, 1–15.

Scott, W. A. (1965) *Values and organizations*. Chicago: Rand McNally.

Secord, P. F. and Backman, C. W. (1964) *Social psychology*. New York: McGraw-Hill.

Shaw, M. E. (1976) *Group dynamics: The psychology of small group behaviour*. New Delhi: Tata McGraw-Hill (revised edn, New York: McGraw-Hill, 1981).

Sherif, M. (1936) *The psychology of social norms*. New York: Harper (Harper Torchbook edn, 1966).

Sherif, M. (1951) Introduction. In J. H. Rohrer and M. Sherif (eds), *Social psychology at the crossroads*. New York: Harper.

Sherif, M. (1967) *Group conflict and co-operation: Their social psychology*. London: Routledge & Kegan Paul.

Sherif, M. and Sherif, C. W. (1969) *Social psychology.* New York: Harper & Row.

Singleton, R. Jr (1979) Another look at the conformity explanation of group-induced shifts in choice. *Human Relations,* 32, 37–56.

Skinner, M. and Stephenson, G. M. (1981) The effects of intergroup comparison on the polarization of opinions. *Current Psychological Research,* 1, 49–61.

Smith, D. (1980) Tonypandy 1910: Definitions of community. *Past and Present,* 87, 158–84.

Smith, K. K. and White, G. L. (1983) Some alternatives to traditional social psychology of groups. *Personality and Social Psychology Bulletin,* 9, 65–73.

Sole, K., Marton, J. and Hornstein, H. A. (1975) Opinion similarity and helping: Three field experiments investigating the bases of promotive tension. *Journal of Experimental Social Psychology,* 11, 1–13.

Steiner, I. (1974) Whatever happened to the group in social psychology? *Journal of Experimental Social Psychology,* 10, 94–108.

Steiner, I. (1983) Whatever happened to the touted revival of the group? In H. Blumberg, P. Hare, V. Kent and M. Davies (eds), *Small groups and social interaction.* New York: Wiley, vol. 2.

Stephenson, G. M. (1981) Intergroup bargaining and negotiation. In J. C. Turner and H. Giles (eds), *Intergroup behaviour.* Oxford: Basil Blackwell and Chicago: University of Chicago Press.

Stoner, J. A. F. (1961) *A comparison of individual and group dimensions involving risk.* Unpublished Master's thesis, School of Industrial Management, Massachusetts Institute of Technology.

Suls, J. M. and Miller, R. L. (1977) *Social comparison processes.* Washington, DC: Hemisphere.

Tajfel, H. (1959) Quantitative judgement in social perception. *British Journal of Psychology.* 50, 16–29.

Tajfel, H. (1969a) Social and cultural factors in perception. In G. Lindzey and E. Aronson (eds), *Handbook of social psychology.* Cambridge, Mass.: Addison-Wesley, vol. 3.

Tajfel, H. (1969b) Cognitive aspects of prejudice. *Journal of Social Issues,* 25, 79–97.

Tajfel, H. (1970) Experiments in intergroup discrimination. *Scientific American,* 223, 96–102.

Tajfel, H. (1972a) La catégorisation sociale. In S. Moscovici (ed.), *Introduction à la psychologie sociale.* Paris: Larousse, 272–302.

Tajfel, H. (1972b) Experiments in a vacuum. In J. Israel and H. Tajfel (eds), *The context of social psychology*. London: Academic Press.

Tajfel, H. (1974) *Intergroup behaviour, social comparison and social change*. Unpublished Katz-Newcomb lectures. University of Michigan, Ann Arbor.

Tajfel, H. (1978) *Differentiation between social groups: Studies in the social psychology of intergroup relations*. London: Academic Press.

Tajfel, H. (1980) The 'New Look' and social differentiations: A semi-Brunerian perspective. In D. Olson (ed.), *The social foundations of language and thought: Essays in honour of J. S. Bruner*. New York: Norton.

Tajfel, H. (1981a) *Human groups and social categories*. Cambridge: Cambridge University Press.

Tajfel, H. (1981b) Social stereotypes and social groups. In J. C. Turner and H. Giles (eds), *Intergroup behaviour*. Oxford: Basil Blackwell and Chicago: University of Chicago Press.

Tajfel, H. (1982a) *Social identity and intergroup relations*. Cambridge: Cambridge University Press and Paris: Editions de la Maison des Sciences de l'Homme.

Tajfel, H. (1982b) The social psychology of intergroup relations. *Annual Review of Psychology*, 33, 1–39.

Tajfel, H. (1984) *The social dimension: European developments in social psychology*. Cambridge: Cambridge University Press and Paris: Editions de la Maison des Sciences de l'Homme, vols. 1 and 2.

Tajfel, H., Flament, C., Billig, M.G. and Bundy, R. F. (1971) Social categorization and intergroup behaviour. *European Journal of Social Psychology*. 1, 149–77.

Tajfel, H. and Turner, J. C. (1979) An integrative theory of intergroup conflict. In W. G. Austin and S. Worchel (eds), *The social psychology of intergroup relations*. Monterey, Calif.: Brooks/Cole.

Tajfel, H. and Turner, J. C. (1986) The social identity theory of intergroup behaviour. In S. Worchel and W. G. Austin (eds), *Psychology of intergroup relations*. Chicago: Nelson-Hall, 7–24.

Tajfel, H. and Wilkes, A. L. (1963) Classification and quantitative judgement. *British Journal of Psychology*. 54, 101–14.

Tajfel, H. and Wilkes, A. L. (1964) Salience of attributes and commitment to extreme judgements in the perception of people. *British Journal of Social and Clinical Psychology*, 3, 40–9.

Tarde, G. (1901) *L'opinion et la foule*. Paris: Felix Alcan.

Taylor, S. E. (1981) A categorization approach to stereotyping. In D. L. Hamilton (ed.), *Cognitive processes in stereotyping and intergroup behaviour*. Hillsdale, NJ: Erlbaum.

Taylor, S. E. and Fiske, S. T. (1978) Salience, attention and attribution: Top-of-the-head phenomena. In L. Berkowitz (ed.), *Advances in Experimental Social Psychology*. New York: Academic Press, vol. 11.

Taylor, S. E., Fiske, S. T., Etcoff, N. and Ruderman, A. (1978) The categorical and contextual bases of person memory and stereotyping. *Journal of Personality and Social Psychology*. 36, 778–93.

Teger, A. I. and Pruitt, D. G. (1967) Components of risk-taking. *Journal of Experimental Social Psychology*, 3, 189–205.

Thibaut, J. W. and Kelley, H. H. (1959) *The social psychology of groups*. New York: Wiley.

Thibaut, J. W. and Strickland, L. H. (1956) Psychological set and social conformity. *Journal of Personality*. 25, 115–29.

Thompson, E. P. (1971) The moral economy of the English crowd in the eighteenth century. *Past and Present*, 50, 76–136.

Tilly, C., Tilly, L. and Tilly, R. (1975) *The rebellious century: 1830–1930*. London: Dent.

Triandis, H. (1977) *Interpersonal behaviour*. Monterey, Calif.: Brooks/Cole.

Trotsky, L. (1977) *A history of the Russian revolution*. London: Pluto.

Turner, J. C. (1975) Social comparison and social identity: some prospects for intergroup behaviour. *European Journal of Social Psychology*, 5, 5–34.

Turner, J. C. (1978) Social categorization and social discrimination in the minimal group paradigm. In H. Tajfel (ed.), *Differentiation between social groups*. London: Academic Press.

Turner, J. C. (1980) Fairness or discrimination in intergroup behaviour? A reply to Branthwaite, Doyle and Lightbown. *European Journal of Social Psychology*, 10, 131–47.

Turner, J. C. (1981a) Some considerations in generalizing experimental social psychology. In G. M. Stephenson and J. H. Davis (eds), *Progress in Applied Social Psychology*. Chichester: Wiley.

Turner, J. C. (1981b) The experimental social psychology of intergroup behaviour. In J. C. Turner and H. Giles (eds), *Intergroup behaviour*. Oxford: Basil Blackwell and Chicago: University of Chicago Press.

Turner, J. C. (1982) Towards a cognitive redefinition of the social group. In H. Tajfel (ed.), *Social identity and intergroup relations*. Cambridge: Cambridge University Press and Paris: Editions de la Maison des Sciences de l'Homme, 15–40. Reprinted in *Cahiers de Psychologie Cognitive*, 1981, 1, 93–118, and V. Ugazio (ed.) (in press), *Social cognition*. Franco Angeli Libri.

Turner, J. C. (1983a) Some comments on . . . 'the measurement of social orientations in the minimal group paradigm'. *European Journal of Social Psychology*, 13, 351–67.

Turner, J. C. (1983b) A second reply to Bornstein, Crum, Wittenbraker, Harring, Insko and Thibaut on the measurement of social orientations. *European Journal of Social Psychology*, 13, 383–7.

Turner, J. C. (1984) Social identification and psychological group formation. In H. Tajfel (ed.), *The social dimension: European developments in social psychology*. Cambridge: Cambridge University Press and Paris: Editons de la Maison des Sciences de l'Homme, vol. 2.

Turner, J. C. (1985) Social categorization and the self-concept: A social cognitive theory of group behaviour. In E. J. Lawler (ed.), *Advances in Group Processes*. Greenwich, Conn.: JAI Press, vol. 2, 77–122.

Turner, J. C., Brown, R. J. and Tajfel, H. (1979) Social comparison and group interest in ingroup favouritism. *European Journal of Social Psychology*, 9, 187–204.

Turner, J. C. and Giles, H. (1981a) Introduction: The social psychology of intergroup behaviour. In J. C. Turner and H. Giles (eds), *Intergroup behaviour*. Oxford: Basil Blackwell and Chicago: University of Chicago Press.

Turner, J. C. and Giles, H. (1981b) *Intergroup behaviour*. Oxford: Basil Blackwell and Chicago: University of Chicago Press.

Turner, J. C., Hogg, M. A., Oakes, P. J. and Smith, P. M. (1984) Failure and defeat as determinants of group cohesiveness. *British Journal of Social Psychology*, 23, 97–111.

Turner, J. C. and Oakes, P. J. (1986) The significance of the social identity concept for social psychology with reference to individualism, interactionism and social influence. *British Journal of Social Psychology*, 25, 237–52.

Turner, J. C., Sachdev, I. and Hogg, M. A. (1983) Social categorization interpersonal attraction and group formation. *British Journal of Social Psychology*, 22, 227–39.

Turner, R. H. and Killian, L. (1972) *Collective behaviour*. Englewood Cliffs, NJ: Prentice-Hall.

Tversky, A. (1977) Features of similarity. *Psychological Review*, 84, 327–52.

Tversky, A. and Gati, I. (1978) Studies of similarity. In E. Rosch and B. B. Lloyd (eds), *Cognition and categorization*, Hillsdale, NJ: Erlbaum.

Van Knippenberg, A., Pruyn, A. and Wilke, H. (1982) Intergroup perception in individual and collective encounters. *European Journal of Social Psychology*, 12, 187–93.

Vidmar, N. (1974) Effects of group discussion on category width judgements. *Journal of Personality and Social Pyschology*, 29, 187–95.

Vinacke, W. E. (1957) Stereotypes as social concepts. *Journal of Social Psychology*, 46, 229–43.

Vinokur, A. (1971) Review and theoretical analysis of the effects of group processes upon individual and group dimensions involving risk. *Psychological Bulletin*, 76, 231–50.

Vinokur, A. and Burnstein, E. (1974) The effects of partially shared persuasive arguments on group-induced shifts: A problem solving approach. *Journal of Personality and Social Psychology*, 29, 305–15.

Vinokur, A. and Burnstein, E. (1978a) Novel argumentation and attitude change: The case of polarization following group discussion. *European Journal of Social Psychology*, 8, 335–48.

Vinokur, A. and Burnstein, E. (1978b) Depolarization of attitudes in groups. *Journal of Personality and Social Psychology*, 36, 872–85.

Vinokur, A., Trope, Y. and Burnstein, E. (1975) A decision making analysis of persuasive argumentation and the choice shift effect. *Journal of Experimental Social Psychology*, 11, 127–48.

Waddell, N. and Cairns, E. (1986) Situational perspectives on social identity in Northern Ireland. *British Journal of Social Psychology*, 25, 25–32.

Wagner, U., Lampen, L. and Syllwasschy, J. (1986) Ingroup inferiority, social identity and outgroup devaluation in a modified minimal group study. *British Journal of Social Psychology*, 25, 15–24.

Watson, G. and Johnson, D. (1972) *Social psychology: Issues and insights*. Philadelphia, Pa: Lippincott.

Wetherell, M. S. (1982) Cross-cultural studies of minimal groups: Implications for the social identity theory of intergroup relations. In H. Tajfel (ed.), *Social identity and intergroup relations*. Cambridge: Cambridge University Press and Paris: Editions de la Maison des Sciences de l'Homme.

Wetherell, M. S. (1983) *Social identification, social influence and group polarization*. Unpublished Ph.D thesis, University of Bristol.

Wetherell, M. S. and Turner, J. C. (in preparation a) *Group polarization and the salience of subgroups*. University of St Andrews.

Wetherell, M. S. and Turner, J. C. (in preparation b) *Group polarization and the accuracy frame of reference hypothesis*. University of St Andrews.

Wetherell, M. S., Turner, J. C. and Hogg, M. A. (1985) *A referent informational influence explanation of group polarization*.

Unpublished paper, University of St Andrews and Macquarie University.

Wilder, D. A. (1978) Reduction of intergroup discrimination through individuation of the outgroup. *Journal of Personality and Social Psychology*, 36, 1361–74.

Wilder, D. A. (1981) Perceiving persons as a group: Categorization and intergroup relations. In D. L. Hamilton (ed.), *Cognitive processes in stereotyping and intergroup behaviour*. Hillsdale, NJ: Erbaum.

Wilder, D. A. (1984) Predictions of belief homogeneity and similarity following social categorization. *British Journal of Social Psychology*, 23, 323–3.

Wilder, D. A. and Cooper, W. (1981) Categorization into groups: Consequences for social perception and attribution. In J. H. Harvey, W. J. Ickes and R. F. Kidd (eds), *New directions in attribution research*. Hillsdale, NJ: Erlbaum, vol. 3.

Wilder, D. A. and Shapiro, P. N. (1984) Role of outgroup cues in determining social identity. *Journal of Personality and Social Psychology*, 47, 342–8.

Wilder, D. A. and Thompson, J. (1980) Intergroup contact with independent manipulation of ingroup and outgroup interaction. *Journal of Personality and Social Psychology*, 38, 589–603.

Wilson, W. (1971) Reciprocation and other techniques for inducing co-operation in the Prisoner's Dilemma Game. *Journal of Conflict Resolution*, 15, 167–95.

Wilson, W., Chun, N. and Kayatani, M. (1965) Projection, attraction and strategy choices in intergroup competition. *Journal of Personality and Social Psychology*, 2, 432–5.

Wilson, W. and Kayatani, M. (1968) Intergroup attitudes and stategies in games between oponents of the same or of a different race. *Journal of Personality and Social Psychology*, 9, 24–30.

Wolf, S. (1979) Behavioural style and group cohesiveness as sources of minority influence. *European Journal of Social Psychology*, 9, 381–95.

Worchel, S. (1979) Co-operation and the reduction of intergroup conflict: Some determining factors. In W. G. Austin and S. Worchel (eds), *The social psychology of intergroup relations*. Monterey, Calif.: Brooks/Cole.

Worchel, S. (1985) The role of co-operation in reducing intergroup conflict. In S. Worchel and W. G. Austin (eds), *Psychology of intergroup relations*. Chicago: Nelson-Hall, pp. 288–304.

Worchel, S., Andreoli, V. A. and Folger, R. (1977) Intergroup co-operation and intergroup attraction: The effect of previous interaction and outcome of combined effort. *Journal of Experimental Social Psychology*, 13, 131–40.

Worchel, S., Axsom, D., Ferris, F., Samaha, C. and Schweitzer, S. (1978) Factors determining the effect of intergroup co-operation on intergroup attraction. *Journal of Conflict Resolution*, 22, 429–39.

Wyer, R. S. and Srull, T. K. (1980) Category accessibility: Some theoretical and empirical issues concerning the processing of social stimulus information. In E. T. Higgins, C. P. Herman and M. P. Zanna (eds), *Social cognition: The Ontario symposium on personality and social psychology*. Hillsdale, NJ: Erlbaum.

Zaleska, M. (1978) *Climat des relations interpersonelles et polarization des attitudes dans les groupes*. Unpublished paper, Laboratoire de Psychologie Sociale de l'Université, Paris VII.

Zander, A. (1979) The psychology of group processes. *Annual Review of Psychology*, 30, 417–51.

Zavalloni, M. N. and Louis-Guerin, C. (1979) Social psychology at the crossroads: The encounter with cognitive and ecological psychology and the interactive perspective. *European Journal of Social Psychology*, 9, 307–21.

Zimbardo, P. G. (1969) The human choice: individuation, reason and order versus de-individuation, impulse and chaos. In W. J. Arnold and D. Levine (eds), *Nebraska Symposium on Motivation*. Lincoln, Neb.: University of Nebraska Press, vol. 17.

Index

Index by Fiona F. Barr